Corpus Approaches
to the Language of Sports

Corpus and Discourse

Series editors: Wolfgang Teubert, University of Birmingham, and Michaela Mahlberg, University of Nottingham

Editorial Board: Paul Baker (Lancaster), Frantisek Čermák (Prague), Susan Conrad (Portland), Geoffrey Leech (Lancaster), Dominique Maingueneau (Paris XII), Christian Mair (Freiburg), Alan Partington (Bologna), Elena Tognini-Bonelli (Siena and TWC), Ruth Wodak (Lancaster), Feng Zhiwei (Beijing).

Corpus linguistics provides the methodology to extract meaning from texts. Taking as its starting point the fact that language is not a mirror of reality but lets us share what we know, believe and think about reality, it focuses on language as a social phenomenon, and makes visible the attitudes and beliefs expressed by the members of a discourse community.

Consisting of both spoken and written language, discourse always has historical, social, functional and regional dimensions. Discourse can be monolingual or multilingual, interconnected by translations. Discourse is where language and social studies meet.

The *Corpus and Discourse* series consists of two strands. The first, *Research in Corpus and Discourse*, features innovative contributions to various aspects of corpus linguistics and a wide range of applications, from language technology via the teaching of a second language to a history of mentalities. The second strand, *Studies in Corpus and Discourse*, comprises key texts bridging the gap between social studies and linguistics. Although equally academically rigorous, this strand will be aimed at a wider audience of academics and postgraduate students working in both disciplines.

Research in Corpus and Discourse
Conversation in Context
Christoph Rühlemann

Corpus-Based Approaches to English Language Teaching
Edited by Mari Carmen Campoy, Begona Bellés-Fortuno and Maria Lluïsa Gea-Valor

Corpus Linguistics and World Englishes
Vivian de Klerk

Corpus Linguistics and 17th-Century Prostitution
Anthony McEnery and Helen Baker

Corpus Stylistics in Heart of Darkness and Its Italian Translations
Lorenzo Mastropierro

Evaluation and Stance in War News
Edited by Louann Haarman and Linda Lombardo

Evaluation in Media Discourse
Monika Bednarek

Historical Corpus Stylistics
Patrick Studer

Idioms and Collocations
Edited by Christiane Fellbaum

Investigating Adolescent Health Communication
Kevin Harvey

Keywords in the Press
Lesley Jeffries and Brian Walker

Learner Corpus Research
Vaclav Brezina and Lynne Flowerdew

Meaningful Texts
Edited by Geoff Barnbrook, Pernilla Danielsson and Michaela Mahlberg

Multimodality and Active Listenership
Dawn Knight

New Trends in Corpora and Language Learning
Edited by Ana Frankenberg-Garcia, Lynne Flowerdew and Guy Aston

The Prosody of Formulaic Sequences
Phoebe Lin

Representation of the British Suffrage Movement
Kat Gupta

Rethinking Idiomaticity
Stefanie Wulff

Sadness Expressions in English and Chinese
Ruihua Zhang

Working with Spanish Corpora
Edited by Giovanni Parodi

Studies in Corpus and Discourse

Corpus Linguistics in Literary Analysis
Bettina Fischer-Starcke

English Collocation Studies
John Sinclair, Susan Jones and Robert Daley. Edited by Ramesh Krishnamurthy

Text, Discourse, and Corpora. Theory and Analysis
Michael Hoey, Michaela Mahlberg, Michael Stubbs and Wolfgang Teubert

Web as Corpus
Maristella Gatto

Corpus Approaches to the Language of Sports

Texts, Media, Modalities

Edited by
Marcus Callies and Magnus Levin

BLOOMSBURY ACADEMIC
LONDON • NEW YORK • OXFORD • NEW DELHI • SYDNEY

BLOOMSBURY ACADEMIC
Bloomsbury Publishing Plc
50 Bedford Square, London, WC1B 3DP, UK
1385 Broadway, New York, NY 10018, USA
29 Earlsfort Terrace, Dublin 2, Ireland

BLOOMSBURY, BLOOMSBURY ACADEMIC and the Diana logo are
trademarks of Bloomsbury Publishing Plc

First published in Great Britain 2019
This paperback edition published in 2021

Copyright © Marcus Callies and Magnus Levin, 2019

Marcus Callies and Magnus Levin have asserted their right under the Copyright,
Designs and Patents Act, 1988, to be identified as Editors of this work.

Photograph © Getty Images / Brian T. Evans

All rights reserved. No part of this publication may be reproduced or transmitted
in any form or by any means, electronic or mechanical, including photocopying,
recording, or any information storage or retrieval system, without prior permission in
writing from the publishers.

Bloomsbury Publishing Plc does not have any control over, or responsibility for,
any third-party websites referred to or in this book. All internet addresses given in this
book were correct at the time of going to press. The author and publisher regret any
inconvenience caused if addresses have changed or sites have ceased to exist, but
can accept no responsibility for any such changes.

A catalogue record for this book is available from the British Library.

A catalog record for this book is available from the Library of Congress.

ISBN: HB: 978-1-3500-8820-7
       PB: 978-1-3502-5004-8
       ePDF: 978-1-3500-8821-4
       eBook: 978-1-3500-8822-1

Series: Corpus and Discourse

Typeset by Integra Software Services Pvt. Ltd.

To find out more about our authors and books visit www.bloomsbury.com
and sign up for our newsletters.

Contents

List of Illustrations ix
Notes on Contributors xiii

1 Introduction. Corpus Approaches to the Language of Sports: Texts, Media, Modalities *Marcus Callies and Magnus Levin* 1

Part I Texts. Contrastive and Comparative Aspects of the Phraseology of Football Match Reports

2 Formulaic Language and Text Routines in Football Live Text Commentaries and Match Reports – A Cross- and Corpus-linguistic Approach *Simon Meier* 13
3 The Language of Football Match Reports in a Contrastive Perspective *Signe Oksefjell Ebeling* 37
4 Lexical Features of Football Reports: Computer- vs. Human-mediated Language *Rita Juknevičienė and Paulius Viluckas* 63

Part II Media. Expanding the Scope of Research to New Contexts of Use

5 *Such a Nice Guy Who Loved Racing His Bike*: Framing in Media Accounts of Fatal Crashes Involving Competitive Cyclists *Turo Hiltunen* 87
6 *When Did I Do Dangerous Driving Then?*: Structures and Functions of Formula One Race Radio Messages *Jukka Tyrkkö and Hanna Limatius* 111
7 The Emotional Content of English Swearwords in Football Chatspeak: *WTF* and Other Pragmatic Devices *Isabel Balteiro* 139
8 Fighting for Integrity against a Corrupting Disease: The Legal Metaphors of Sports Fraud *Miguel Ángel Campos-Pardillos* 161

Part III Modalities. Multimodal Studies

9 A Multimodal Analysis of Football Live Text Commentary
   Valentin Werner 183
10 'Fear and Disgust' – A Corpus Study of Sentiment towards
   Sporting Events as Expressed Multimodally on 4chan's/sp/board
   Peter Crosthwaite and Joyce Cheung 219
11 A Comparative Multimodal Corpus Study of Dislocation
   Structures in Live Football Commentary *Marcus Callies
   and Magnus Levin* 253

Index 270

List of Illustrations

Figures

4.1	Distribution of lexical bundles across structural types	75
4.2	Distribution of lexical bundles across functional types	78
5.1	Topic framework of crash report	96
5.2	Main functional categories across texts in the *Crash report corpus*	98
6.1	Distribution heatmap of turn and word length in teams' messages by part-of-race and driver tier	120
6.2	Distribution heatmap of turn and word length in drivers' messages by part-of-race and driver tier	121
6.3	Decision tree for turn length	122
6.4	Decision tree for sentence length	123
6.5	Box plot of select drivers' and their race engineers' turn and sentence lengths	125
6.6	Decision tree for word length	126
6.7	Box plot of binned word lengths (%) by part-of-race and driver tier	126
6.8	Decision tree for proportion of interrogative sentences	127
6.9	Hierarchical cluster dendrogram of part-of-speech distributions by part of race and message direction	128
9.1	Screenshot from GUAR. Source: https://www.theguardian.com/football/live/2018/jan/30/huddersfield-town-v-liverpool-premier-league-live	191
9.2	Screenshot from SPON. Source: http://www.spiegel.de/sport/fussball/bundesliga-live-ticker-tabelle-ergebnisse-spielplan-statistik-a-842988.html#contest=bl1&matchday=17	192
9.3	SPON – alternative display (SPON L) of zone 3. Source: http://www.spiegel.de/sport/fussball/bundesliga-live-ticker-tabelle-ergebnisse-spielplan-statistik-a-842988.html#contest=bl1&matchday=17	194
9.4	SPON – alternative display (SPIX) of zone 4. Source: http://www.spiegel.de/sport/fussball/bundesliga-live-ticker-tabelle-ergebnisse-spielplan-statistik-a-842988.html#contest=bl1&matchday=17	196
9.5	The potentials of sports reporting (Caple 2017: 213)	197

9.6	Frequencies of occurrence of additional material in FLT (normalized per 1,000 words of commentary)	204
9.7	GUAR – post with photorealistic image. Source: https://www.theguardian.com/football/live/2018/jan/30/huddersfield-town-v-liverpool-premier-league-live	205
9.8	SPON H – abstract image with statistical information and comment. Source: http://www.spiegel.de/sport/fussball/bundesliga-live-ticker-tabelle-ergebnisse-spielplan-statistik-a-842988.html#contest=bl1&matchday=16	206
9.9	SPON H – tweet with statistics from external source. Source: https://twitter.com/OptaFranz/status/967773893300715521	207
9.10	SPON H – audience poll during live match coverage. Source: http://www.spiegel.de/sport/fussball/bundesliga-live-ticker-tabelle-ergebnisse-spielplan-statistik-a-842988.html#contest=bl1&matchday=19	209
10.1	Hyperlinked response to a specific poster	222
10.2	Hyperlinked text discussion of Ronda Rousey	227
10.3	4chan posters predicting the night's winners	228
10.4	Component score comparison across 4chan and CROWN corpora	229
10.5	Image meme used to express negative sentiment	232
10.6	Green text as internal thought processes	233
10.7	Dominick Cruz photoshop meme	235
10.8	UFC president Dana White photoshop meme	235
10.9	Wojak/Feels Guy meme as representative of 4chan posters' identity	236
10.10	Manipulation of Wojak/Feels Guy	236
10.11	Pepe the Frog expressing positive sentiment	237
10.12	Pepe used to express racist sentiment	237
10.13	Pepe used to express misogynistic sentiment	238
10.14	Feels guy recontextualized as Pepe the Fong	238
10.15	Pepe the Frog recontextualized as Feels Guy	238
10.16	Negative reaction image post	239
10.17	Positive reaction image post	239
10.18	Request image	240
10.19	Feels Guy as sentiment of frustration	242
10.20	Pepe as sentiment of anger	242
10.21	Human image as sentiment of anxiety	242

10.22	Orson Welles as sentiment of humiliation	243
10.23	Carlos Condit as sentiment of power	243
10.24 and 10.25	White male fighters as powerful figures	245
10.26, 10.27 and 10.28	Black fighter as sentiment of derision	246
10.29	Black starving child manipulated for intended racist comic effect	246
10.30 and 10.31	Images of female fighters used to expresses sexist/misogynistic sentiment	247

Tables

2.1	Corpora	16
2.2	Key lemmas	17
2.3	Most frequent adpositional phrases of the type *aus* _ADJA _NN (Kicker corpus)	18
2.4	Most frequent adpositional phrases of the type *from (a)* _JJ _NN (Sportsmole Corpus)	22
2.5	Before _VVG	24
2.6	Statistically significant word pairs	27
3.1	Overview of the highest ranked nouns (highlighted) in the ENMaRC	43
3.2	Top 20 3-4-Grams in the English and Norwegian Match Reports	44
3.3	Most prominent personal pronouns/possessive determiners among the keywords	49
A	Overview of premiership teams, URLs and tokens in the individual corpus files	55
B	Overview of *Eliteserie* teams, URLs and tokens in the individual corpus files	56
C	Win keywords in the English and Norwegian match reports (shaded cells contain proper nouns)	57
D	Loss keywords in the English and Norwegian match reports (shaded cells contain proper nouns)	60
4.1	Keywords in Corpus$_{FM}$ and Corpus$_{BBC}$	69
4.2	Twenty most frequent lexical bundles in the corpora with normalized frequency per 10,000 words	72
4.3	Shared lexical bundles and their normalized frequencies per 10,000 words	73
5.1	Most 'newsworthy' crashes included in the corpus	93

5.2	Examples of functional categories	94
5.3	Some examples of text structure	99
5.4	Nouns used in describing crashes	100
5.5	Verbs in material clauses describing crashes	101
6.1	Messages during different parts of the race	118
6.2	Basic descriptive statistics	121
6.3	Predictor variables and levels in the decision tree partitioning	122
1	Drivers, nationalities, team, assigned tiers and counts of messages	137
8.1	Metaphorical domains in corpus	165
9.1	Corpus frequency information	188
9.2	Content word categories from the top 100 *AntConc* wordlists	199
9.3	Five most frequent 4-Grams	199
10.1	Corpus thread, word and image counts	223
10.2	Fear and disgust sentiment in 4chan Text Posts	231
10.3	Negative adjectives used in 4chan text posts	233
10.4	Structure of images and memes	234
10.5	Sentiment of image posts	241
10.6	Object of human image posts	244
11.1	Overview of corpus material analysed	256
11.2	Frequencies of occurrence of left and right dislocation in the corpus material	257
11.3	Frequencies of occurrence of left and right dislocation in spontaneous, unplanned speech in previous corpus studies	257
11.4	Frequencies of occurrence of right dislocation by individual speaker	258
11.5	Breakdown of all instances of right dislocation by discourse function	265

Notes on Contributors

Isabel Balteiro is senior lecturer in English Linguistics at the University of Alicante, Spain. Her main research interests are in the fields of Lexicology and English for Specific Purposes, with special focus on word-formation mechanisms and lexical creativity in both general English and ESP. Within the latter, she primarily deals with the language of fashion and sports in general and in computer-/digital-mediated communication, but she has also touched upon other specialized fields such as videogames.

Marcus Callies obtained his Dr. phil. in English linguistics from the University of Marburg, Germany, in 2006. Since 2014 he is full professor and chair of English Linguistics at the University of Bremen, Germany. His main research interests are Learner Corpus Research with a focus on lexico-grammatical variation, English for Academic Purposes, teacher education, conceptual metaphor and the language of sports.

Miguel Ángel Campos-Pardillos obtained his PhD in English Linguistics from the University of Alicante, Spain, in 1994, and since 1997 he has been senior lecturer at the University of Alicante in a number of subjects involving specialized languages and translation. He has published extensively in various areas of English for Specific Purposes (including Anglicisms in the language of sports), legal language and translation. His most recent work concerns metaphor in various areas of law and law enforcement.

Joyce Cheung is a research fellow in the Division of Graduate Studies at Lingnan University, Hong Kong China. She holds a Masters degree in English Language Studies and Bachelor degree in Communication. Her research interest is the application of corpus linguistics to a variety of discourse and multimodal contexts.

Peter Crosthwaite received his PhD in English and Applied Linguistics from Cambridge University, UK, in 2014. Since 2014 he was assistant professor of Applied Linguistics at the University of Hong Kong, and is currently lecturer in Applied Linguistics at the University of Queensland, Australia. His research interests include second-language acquisition, learner corpus linguistics, English for Academic and Specific Purposes and corpus-based, data-driven learning.

Signe Oksefjell Ebeling received her PhD in English linguistics from the University of Oslo, Norway, in 2003. Since 2014 she is professor of English linguistics at the University of Oslo, Norway. Her research interests include corpus-based contrastive analysis on topics such as verb semantics, phraseology and idiomaticity.

Turo Hiltunen obtained his PhD in English from the University of Helsinki, Finland, in 2010. Currently he works as senior lecturer in English at the same university. His main scholarly interests include phraseology and grammar, English for Academic Purposes, the language of science and medicine from the early modern period to the present day and the language of Wikipedia.

Rita Juknevičienė received her PhD in linguistics from Vilnius University, Lithuania, in 2011. Since 2017 she is associate professor at the Faculty of Philology, Vilnius University. Her research interests include phraseology, learner corpus research, language testing and assessment and translation.

Hanna Limatius is a doctoral candidate of English at Tampere University, Finland. Her PhD thesis explores aspects of community, identity and empowerment through interaction in plus-size fashion blogs. Her research interests include computer-mediated discourse, online communities (of practice), blogging, social media and fashion discourse. Her focus is on discourse analysis, and she has an interest in corpus-linguistic methods.

Magnus Levin received his PhD in English linguistics from Lund University, Sweden, in 2001. Since 2012 he is associate professor of English linguistics at Linnaeus University, Sweden. His research interests include change and variation in English, phraseology, global Englishes, translation studies and the language of sports.

Simon Meier received his PhD in German linguistics from Bern University, Switzerland, in 2012. He has been a research assistant of general linguistics at Berlin Institute of Technology, Germany, since 2013. Currently, he is acting professor at the Technical University at Dresden, Germany. His research interests include corpus linguistics, media linguistics, phraseology and the language of sports.

Jukka Tyrkkö is full professor of English at Linnaeus University and visiting professor of Digital Humanities at the University of Turku (2018–2019). He has published extensively on a variety of topics including corpus-linguistic methods, historical lexis and phraseology, computer-mediated communication, political language use and book history.

Paulius Viluckas received his BA in English Philology from Vilnius University, Lithuania, in 2017. He is currently a reporter and translator at the news agency Baltic News Service. His research interests include translation, sports discourse and corpus-driven phraseology.

Valentin Werner obtained his PhD in English linguistics from the University of Bamberg, Germany, where he has worked as assistant professor since 2014. His main research areas are applied linguistics (esp. Learner Englishes/Second Language Acquisition), variational linguistics (esp. World Englishes), linguistics and culture (esp. the language of pop culture), computer-mediated communication and stylistics.

1

Introduction. Corpus Approaches to the Language of Sports: Texts, Media, Modalities

Marcus Callies and Magnus Levin

In recent decades, the world of sports has witnessed fundamental change and transformation in terms of a diversification of types of sports and sports events, an increasing commercialization and globalization of major spectator sports such as football or basketball, accompanied by an ever-growing popularity and intensive coverage in various kinds of media and modalities. Despite this increasing popularization and public attention, research on the language and discourse of sports is still comparatively heterogeneous in nature and scattered across different academic disciplines. Publications can be found in a diversity of outlets with only few thematically focused collections existing to date (see e.g. Adelmann et al. 2003; Settekorn 2007; Lavric et al. 2008; Burkhardt and Schlobinski 2009; Taborek et al. 2012; Caldwell et al. 2017). To date, there is no single, specialized journal in the field of (applied) linguistics that serves as a research outlet, although several journals in the larger field of social studies engage with the language and discourse of sports to varying degrees: *Soccer & Society, Sport in Society: Cultures, Commerce, Media, Politics* (published since 2004, formerly known as *Culture, Sport, Society* published from 1998 to 2003) and *Communication and Sport*.

   At the same time, the emergence of new genres of sports reporting in the age of online computer-mediated communication has opened up many new and innovative ways of studying sports discourse, e.g. by means of large electronic corpus resources. The compilation and accessibility of a broad range of computer corpora and software tools for linguistic analysis has revolutionized (applied) linguistics in the last few decades, and the study of language and discourse has greatly benefitted from corpus-based and corpus-driven investigations of real-world language as it is actually used by speakers and writers in different contexts and for different purposes. This timely volume brings together innovative empirical studies that adopt a usage-based perspective and make use of (multimodal) corpus data and corpus-linguistic methods to examine language and communication occurring in different types of sports in a variety of genres and contexts of use. The contributions add to current efforts to extend the scope of (applied) linguistic research on sports beyond football/soccer which has been very much at the centre of attention. Moreover, the book aims to advance the scope of corpus-linguistic research more generally in that it highlights the potential and the necessity of studying the language of sports in association with its accompanying audio-visual modes of communication from a multimodal perspective. As of yet, the compilation and analysis of corpora has mostly been limited to a monomodal, i.e. the textual level. Multimodal corpus approaches, employing digitized collections of language and communication-related material that draw on more than one modality (e.g. text, image, audio and video), should be put more explicitly on the agenda of corpus linguistics to fully describe and understand the complexities of human communication through various channels (Adolphs and Carter 2013). This introductory chapter first briefly reviews previous linguistic work on the language of sports with a view to main research topics and recent trends. We also highlight some new research initiatives and resources and then introduce and contextualize the chapters of this volume.

When considering the research that has accumulated over the past few decades, football/soccer has largely dominated the research agenda with studies on other types of sports such as tennis (e.g. Mikos and Shea 1976; Schiffer 1992; Swerts and van Wijk 2010; Caballero 2012), horse racing (Kuiper and Austin 1990) or ice hockey (Kuiper and Haggo 1985; Arthurs 1988) being few and far between. Most football-related research has focused on structural-linguistic aspects in various types of sports reporting such as post-match reports and live commentary on radio and TV, in particular with a view to phraseology, including specialized terminology and jargon (see e.g. Liu and Farha 1996; Levin 2008; Berg and Ohlander 2012; Wyatt and Hadikin 2015; Chovanec 2017). This line of research is receiving new fuel by the increasing availability of large new corpus resources that allow a broader and comparative, but also more fine-grained, examination of the characteristics of sports reporting that occurs in online genres such as live-text or play-by-play commentary (see e.g. Pérez-Sabater et al. 2008; Jucker 2010; Werner 2016; Chovanec 2018). Linguistic borrowing, in particular the impact of the English language on football lexis in European languages, has also been studied extensively (see most recently Bergh and Ohlander 2017), while much fewer studies on sports reporting have examined its grammar and syntax (e.g. Ferguson 1983; Krone 2005; Müller 2007). Recently, we have also seen diachronic studies that trace the history of reporting genres, e.g. the emergence of match reports (Chovanec 2014). Similar to phraseology, the field of conceptual metaphor and metaphorical expressions has been a central topic in studies of the language of sports (e.g. Callies 2011; Thalhammer 2015). By contrast, features of spoken language such as prosody have only rarely been addressed (see e.g. Bonnett 1980; Kern 2010).

Outside of sports reporting, several studies have analysed the (socio-) linguistic aspects and significance of football chants (e.g. Clark 2006; Luhrs 2008; Hoffmann 2015). With the language of football in particular having made inroads into mainstream, general language use, it is not surprising that the occurrence of sports-related metaphorical expression and idioms in particular has also been examined in other domains of use such as law and politics (e.g. Seagrave 1994; Semino and Masci 1996; Archer and Cohen 1997). Generally speaking, it appears that research has become more diverse and interdisciplinary in the last fifteen years or so with an increasing number of studies approaching sports language from the perspective of discourse analysis (e.g. Bishop and Jaworski 2003; Gerhardt 2014; Wilton 2017), gender studies (e.g. Adams et al. 2010; Aull and West Brown 2013) and culture (Meân and Halone 2010). The relevance of sports, in particular football, for (foreign language) teaching and its application to the classroom has also been discussed in several publications (see e.g. Thaler 2006a, b; Kern and Siehr 2016).

Several useful resources and initiatives are worth mentioning in this overview. The *Innsbruck Football Research Group* (https://www.uibk.ac.at/romanistik/personal/lavric/sprache_fussball) brought together researchers interested in football language for a workshop prior to the 2008 European Championships hosted in Austria and Switzerland, an effort which resulted in the first comprehensive collection of studies on the linguistics of football (Lavric et al. 2008). This research group also published the *Football and Language Bibliography Online* (Lavric and Giorgianni 2013), a very comprehensive, multilingual and extremely useful reference source for published interdisciplinary research on football. Another highly useful resource is Simon Meier's collection of electronic corpora of football reporting in German, Dutch, English and Russian (Meier 2017).

Several researchers have recently initiated the introduction of a new Research Network 'Applied Linguistics in Sport' within the *International Association of*

Applied Linguistics ('Association Internationale de Linguistique Appliquée', AILA; see Gurzynski-Weiss 2018) that is intended to foster interdisciplinary collaboration and to provide a platform for information, support and scholarship for researchers and students with an interest in the application of linguistics to sports. The network includes researchers who apply a broad range of linguistic methods, theories and research paradigms (e.g. sociolinguistics, corpus linguistics or discourse analysis) and who promote and establish inter- and cross-disciplinary research, e.g. with researchers from the fields of sociology, psychology or sports science.

The present volume adds to and expands on previous research in that it offers innovative empirical studies that use new corpus resources to showcase the structural-linguistic and discourse aspects of a range of sports (e.g. football, cycling, motor racing and mixed martial arts), genres (chatspeak and message boards, post-match reports, live commentary on TV and online, race radio messaging and legal texts) and contexts of use (sports media, in-team communication, fan talk and chat in social media, and sports-related professional discourse).

The studies in the first part of this volume, 'Texts. Contrastive and Comparative Aspects of the Phraseology of Football Match Reports', adopt a comparative or contrastive linguistic approach by analysing the phraseology of football reporting across different text types and languages. **Simon Meier** examines writers' strategies when producing live text commentary and online match reports under high time pressure. He argues that in order to stage the match as emotional, writers have to avoid the impression of being routinized. Based on new corpora of German and English live text commentaries and online match reports Meier applies data-driven methods and identifies formulaic syntactic patterns that serve as templates for describing recurrent events (enriched by a large set of mostly expressive lexical items) which are rather similar in the two languages. **Signe Oksefjell Ebeling** introduces a new comparable corpus of online post-match reports from the English Premier League and the Norwegian 'Eliteserie'. She also applies corpus-driven extraction methods in the form of (key)word lists and n-grams and finds that the post-match reports in the two languages under study are similar to other text types in the use of time and space expressions, at the same time uncovering cross-linguistic differences when reporting on victories and defeats. In the third paper in this section, **Rita Juknevičienė and Paulius Viluckas** compare computer-generated post-match reports in the computer game *Football Manager 2017* and reports by professional writers published on a news website. A corpus-driven analysis of keywords and lexical bundles reveals a number of differences between the two genres, e.g. with a view to the frequency of use of certain word lemmas and recurrent lexical sequences.

Part two, 'Media. Expanding the Scope of Research to New Contexts of Use', features four studies that extend the existing research to new media and also add to the small body of research on sports discourse outside of football. **Turo Hiltunen** explores the concept of framing in news reports on the death of competitive cyclists who died either during training or in a race. He identifies and describes the main textual functions and lexico-grammatical patterns in these reports on the basis of an 80,000-word corpus of 230 English-language reports collected from the internet. Hiltunen's findings suggest that the cyclists are identified and described in detail in the data, while drivers of motor vehicles are usually represented through impersonalization. **Jukka Tyrkkö and Hanna Limatius** explore the genre of race radio in Formula One in which drivers and their race engineers communicate by radio during a Grand Prix, exchanging information about race strategy, the performance of the car and events on the track. Assuming that cumulative stress affects both the drivers' and the race engineers' linguistic performance, the authors test two hypotheses: first, the physical and mental demands of the race will result in a significant reduction of complexity, and second, a driver's level of experience may serve to curb these effects. They do find effects of stress in some variables but not in others, and also significant differences between individual drivers and race engineers during a race. **Isabel Balteiro** examines the use of English expletives such as *WTF, fucking*, and *fuck* by Spanish football followers in spontaneous synchronic comments in online chats. She discusses these code-switching practices and compares their distribution and semantico-pragmatic functions in English and Spanish. The main interest of the study lies on the functions of these expletives as pragmatic markers and their interactional significance, position, and distribution in discourse. They have an intense emotional load which conveys different highly context-dependent pragmatic meanings such as anger, frustration, disbelief, shock, surprise or dismissal. In the fourth chapter in this section, **Miguel Ángel Campos-Pardillos** analyses sports-related legal discourse based on data from specialized journal papers and book chapters dealing with various practices of sports fraud (e.g. match-fixing, bribing, doping or misuse of inside information). He focuses on how scholars in the field of law use metaphorical language in order to justify the fight against these practices, and how this metaphorical discourse is influenced by its identification with other criminal activities.

In the final part, 'Modalities. Multimodal Studies', three chapters provide analyses of sports language and discourse from a multimodal perspective which has only rarely been applied to the language of sports. Chovanec (2017) is a recent exception who examines wordplay in headlines and the creative use of verbal and visual means on the front pages of British daily newspapers, arguing that the creation of humour in this genre involves instances of verbal and multimodal play. First, **Valentin Werner** explores how the genre of live-text commentary has developed in view of technological advances reflected both in the overall layout and in the style of reporting. Accounting for the combined linear and non-linear nature of live text commentaries his findings indicate that the genre increasingly taps into elements from various external sources (e.g. information from a commercial statistics provider and images) that also enable audience participation, e.g. by means of tweets, thus merging as a hybrid and complex multimodal ensemble characterized by media convergence. **Peter Crosthwaite and Joyce Cheung** examine multimodal discourse practices in a less-studied section of the internet, i.e. *4chan*, an anonymous online community where users post images and text on a wide variety of topics. The authors carry out a sentiment analysis on a multimodal corpus of 4chan's sports board's user coverage of a mixed martial arts event, examining how posters juxtapose text, image and videos while communicating their reactions to the event itself and to other posters as the fights during the event unfold. Their results contribute to a greater understanding of online sports discourse as mediated by thousands of users in (semi) real-time. Finally, **Marcus Callies and Magnus Levin** present a comparative study of dislocation in live TV football commentary, zooming in on the (con-)textual functions of dislocation in relation to the live action visible on the screen. Their findings show that right dislocation is a functionally motivated, register-specific feature of live TV football commentary, being ten times more frequent in this genre. Their study also highlights the necessity of examining language use in association with accompanying modes of communication and visualization in terms of a multimodal corpus approach.

References

Adams, A., E. Anderson and M. McCormack (2010), 'Establishing and Challenging Masculinity: The Influence of Gendered Discourses in Organized Sport', *Journal of Language and Social Psychology*, 29 (3): 278–300.

Adelmann, R., R. Parr and T. Schwarz, eds (2003), *Querpässe – Beiträge zur Literatur, Kultur- und Mediengeschichte des Fußballs*, Heidelberg: Synchron Publishers.

Adolphs, S. and R. Carter (2013), *Spoken Corpus Linguistics. From Monomodal to Multimodal*, London and New York: Routledge.

Archer, M. and R. Cohen (1997), 'Leaving Women Out in Left Field: Sports Metaphors, Women, and Legal Discourse', *Women and Language*, 20: 2–6.

Arthurs, J. (1988), 'Terminology vs Jargon: Canadian Hockey Talk', in A. R. Thomas and M. J. Ball (eds), *Methods in Dialectology*, 155–163, Clevedon: Multilingual Matters.

Aull, L. L. and D. West Brown (2013), 'Fighting Words: A Corpus Analysis of Gender Representations in Sports Reportage', *Corpora*, 8 (1): 27–52.

Bergh, G. and S. Ohlander (2012), '*Free Kicks, Dribblers* and *WAGs*. Exploring the Language of "the People's Game"', *Moderna Språk*, 106 (1): 11–46.

Bergh, G. and S. Ohlander (2017), 'Loan Translations Versus Direct Loans: The Impact of English on European Football Lexis', *Nordic Journal of Linguistics*, 40 (1): 5–35.

Bishop, H. and A. Jaworski (2003), ' "We Beat 'em": Nationalism and the Hegemony of Homogeneity in the British Press Reportage of Germany versus England during Euro 2000', *Discourse and Society*, 14: 243–271.

Bonnet, G. (1980), 'A Study of Intonation in the Soccer Results. Wolverhampton Wanderers 2 Nottingham Forest ?' *Journal of Phonetics*, 8 (1): 21–38.

Burkhardt, A. and P. Schlobinski, eds (2009), *Flickflack, Foul und Tsukuhara. Der Sport und seine Sprache*, Mannheim: Dudenverlag.

Caballero, R. (2012), 'The Role of Metaphor in Tennis Reports and Forums', *Text & Talk*, 32 (6): 703–726.

Caldwell, D., J. Walsh, E. W. Vine and J. Jureid, eds (2017), *The Discourse of Sport. Analyses from Social Linguistics*, London and New York: Routledge.

Callies, M. (2011), 'Widening the Goalposts of Cognitive Metaphor Research', in M. Callies, W. R. Keller and A. Lohöfer (eds), *Bi-Directionality in the Cognitive Sciences*, 57–81, Amsterdam: Benjamins.

Chovanec, J. (2014), ' " … but there were no broken legs". The Emerging Genre of Football Match Reports in *The Times* in the 1860s', *Journal of Historical Pragmatics*, 15 (2): 228–254.

Chovanec, J. (2017), 'Wordplay and Football: Humour in the Discourse of Written Sports Reporting', in W. Chlopicki and D. Brzozowska (eds), *Humorous Discourse*, 131–154, Berlin: de Gruyter.

Chovanec, J. (2018), *The Discourse of Online Sportscasting. Constructing Meaning and Interaction in Live Text Commentary*, Amsterdam: Benjamins.

Clark, T. (2006), ' "I'm Scunthorpe 'til I die": Constructing and (Re)negotiating Identity through the Terrace Chant', *Soccer & Society*, 7 (4): 494–507.

Ferguson, C. A. (1983), 'Sports Announcer Talk. Syntactic Aspects of Register Variation', *Language in Society*, 12: 153–172.

Gerhardt, C. (2014), *Appropriating Live Televised Football through Talk*, Leiden: Brill.

Gurzynski-Weiss, L. (2018), 'AILA Matters', *International Journal of Applied Linguistics*, 28 (1): 196–218.

Hoffmann, T. (2015), 'Cognitive Sociolinguistic Aspects of Football Chants: The Role of Social and Physical Context in Usage-based Construction Grammar', *Zeitschrift für Anglistik und Amerikanistik*, 63 (3): 273–294.

Jucker, A. (2010), ' "Audacious, Brilliant!! What a Strike!": Live Text Commentaries on the Internet as Real-time Narratives', in C. R. Hoffmann (ed.), *Narrative Revisited: Telling a Story in the Age of New Media*, 57–77, Amsterdam: Benjamins.

Kern, F. (2010), 'Speaking Dramatically: The Prosody of Live Radio Commentary of Football Matches', in D. Barth-Weingarten, E. Reber and M. Selting (eds), *Prosody in Interaction*, 217–238, Amsterdam: Benjamins.

Kern F. and K.-H. Siehr, eds (2016), *Sport als Thema im Deutschunterricht*, Potsdam: Universitätsverlag Potsdam.

Krone, M. (2005), *The Language of Football. A Contrastive Study of Syntactic and Semantic Specifics of Verb Usage in English and German Match Commentaries*, Stuttgart: Ibid.

Kuiper, K. and J. P. M. Austin (1990), 'They're Off and Racing Now: The Speech of the New Zealand Race Caller', in A. Bell and J. Holmes (eds), *New Zealand Ways of Speaking English*, 195–220, Bristol: Multilingual Matters.

Kuiper, K. and D. Haggo (1985), 'On the Nature of Ice Hockey Commentaries', in R. Berry and J. Acheson (eds), *Regionalism and National Identity: Multidisciplinary Essays on Canada, Australia and New Zealand*, 167–175, Christchurch: Association for Canadian Studies in Australia and New Zealand.

Lavric, E. and E. Giorgianni (2013), *Football and Language Bibliography Online*, https://www.uibk.ac.at/romanistik/personal/lavric/sprache_fussball/bibliography.

Lavric, E., G. Pisek, A. Skinner and W. Stadler, eds (2008), *The Linguistics of Football*, Tübingen: Narr.

Levin, M. (2008), '"Hitting the Back of the Net Just before the Final Whistle": High-frequency Phrases in Football Reporting', in E. Lavric, G. Pisek, A. Skinner and W. Stadler (eds), *The Linguistics of Football*, 143–155, Tübingen: Narr.

Liu, D. and B. Farha (1996), 'Three Strikes and You're Out. A Study of the Use of Football and Baseball Jargon in Present-day American English', *English Today*, 12: 36–40.

Luhrs, J. (2008), 'Football Chants and 'Blason Populaire': The Construction of Local and Regional Stereotypes', in E. Lavric, G. Pisek, A. Skinner and W. Stadler (eds), *The Linguistics of Football*, 233–244, Tübingen: Narr.

Meân, L. and K. Halone, eds (2010), 'Sport, Language, and Culture: Issues and Intersections', Special issue of *Journal of Language and Social Psychology*, 29 (3): 253–396.

Meier, S. (2017), 'Korpora zur Fußballlinguistik – eine mehrsprachige Forschungsressource zur Sprache der Fußballberichterstattung', *Zeitschrift für germanistische Linguistik*, 45 (2): 345–349.

Mikos, M. J. and L. R. Shea (1976), 'Tennis Slang', *American Speech*, 51 (3–4): 292–295.

Müller, T. (2007), *Football, Language and Linguistics. Time-critical Utterances in Unplanned Spoken Language, Their Structures and Their Relation to Non-linguistic Situations and Events*, Tübingen: Narr.

Pérez-Sabater, C., G. Pena-Martinz, E. Turney and B. Montero-Fleta (2008), 'A Spoken Genre Gets Written: Online Football Commentaries in English, French, and Spanish', *Written Communication*, 25: 235–261.

Schiffer, P. (1992), 'Metaphern in der englischen und deutschen Tennisberichterstattung', *Lebende Sprachen*, 37 (2): 60–66.

Seagrave, J. O. (1994), 'The Perfect 10: "Sportspeak" in the Language of Sexual Relations', *Sociology of Sport Journal*, 11 (2): 95–113.

Semino, E. and M. Masci (1996), 'Politics Is Football: Metaphor in the Discourse of Silvio Berlusconi in Italy', *Discourse and Society*, 7 (2): 243–269.

Settekorn, W., ed (2007), *Fußball – Medien/Medien – Fußball. Zur Medienkultur eines weltweit populären Sports* (Hamburger Hefte zur Medienkultur 7), Hamburg: Institut für Medien und Kommunikation des Departments SLM I der Universität Hamburg (IMK).

Swerts, M. and C. van Wijk (2010), ' "New balls, please!" – The Prosody of Tennis Scores', *Discourse Processes*, 47 (1): 55–76.

Taborek, J., A. Tworek and L. Zieliński, eds (2012), *Sprache und Fußball im Blickpunkt linguistischer Forschung*, Hamburg: Verlag Dr. Kovač.

Thaler, E. ed (2006a), *Fußball – Fremdsprachen – Forschung*, Aachen: Shaker.

Thaler, E., ed. (2006b), 'Football', Special thematic issue of *Der fremdsprachliche Unterricht Englisch* 40/79.

Thalhammer, E. J. (2015), 'They Have to Die for the Goals. WAR Metaphors in English and German Football Radio Commentary', in J. B. Herrmann and T. Berber Sardinha (eds), *Metaphor in Specialist Discourse*, 101–130, Amsterdam: Benjamins.

Werner, V. (2016), 'Real-time Online Text Commentaries: A Cross-cultural Perspective', in C. Schubert and C. Sanchez-Stockhammer (eds), *Variational Text Linguistics: Revisiting Register in English*, 271–305, Berlin: Mouton de Gruyter.

Wilton, A. (2017), 'The Interactional Construction of Evaluation in Post-match Football Interviews', in D. Caldwell, J. Walsh, E. W. Vine and J. Jureidini (eds), *The Discourse of Sport. Analyses from Social Linguistics*, 92–112, London: Routledge.

Wyatt, M. and G. Hadikin (2015), ' "They Parked Two Buses": A Corpus Study of a Football Expression', *English Today*, 31: 34–41.

Part One

Texts. Contrastive and Comparative Aspects of the Phraseology of Football Match Reports

2

Formulaic Language and Text Routines in Football Live Text Commentaries and Match Reports – A Cross- and Corpus-linguistic Approach

Simon Meier

1. Introduction

Authors of football live text commentaries and online match reports must, first and foremost, be quick. In live text commentaries, the entries need to be published 'minute by minute', and even match reports must go online shortly after or even at the final whistle. As the text producers have to describe these open-ended games under high time pressure, they have to make extensive use of sequences of formulaic language that may be activated as prefabricated patterns (Wray and Perkins 2000: 1) and thus relieve them of encoding efforts. However, they also need to display emotional involvement in order to deliver appealing and entertaining narratives and to create suspense (Kern 2014), and must therefore avoid the impression of acting merely on a routine basis.

In this chapter, I will make use of data-driven, corpus-linguistic methods to investigate the writers' strategies to meet this challenge of reconciling linguistic routines on the one hand and the task of emotionalization on the other. Based on large corpora of German and English data (approx. 13 mio. tokens) I will focus on two types of formulaicity. First, I will show how writers make use of recurrent schematic constructions (Croft 2001: 25) that are filled with an extraordinarily rich set of mostly expressive synonyms of, say, motion verbs. Second, I will discuss the role of idioms that allow for a routinized, yet vivid and community-building, narration of sports events. The results of my corpus analyses will give evidence to what Sinclair (1991: 109ff.) has pointed to as the complementarity of the open-choice principle on the one hand and the idiom principle on the other (Erman and Warren 2009). The production of texts oscillates between word-for-word combinations and preconstructed patterns, yet in a register-specific way that is tied to the communicative and social needs in the domain of sports coverage.

2. Sports coverage between emotion and routine

Linguistic research on sports coverage and football coverage in particular has shown that it is hardly ever limited to objective reports on the course of the games and the results. Even match reports have to be designed as exciting stories that allow the readers to re-experience the games, and especially live commentary is characterized by a high number of dramatic enrichments (Bryant et al. 1977) by lexical and prosodic means (Kern 2010). Since the target audience of football coverage is the fans who have an emotional connection to 'their' team or to football in general,[1] the games have to be staged as highly emotional and emotionalizing spectacles that convey the experience of 'being there' even to a non-present audience (Kirschner and Wetzels 2017: 261ff.). In the history of sports coverage, a typical register with a high degree of expressivity has emerged in order to meet these specific needs of its customers.

The language of football is also known for its high degree of formulaicity (Pfeiffer 2014: 491ff.). Numerous popular publications have diagnosed a certain clichedness of football coverage, where seemingly pointless set phrases, platitudes and stereotyped metaphors are pervasive (e.g. Raack 2015; Telegraph Sport 2016). Even dialogic genres like post-match interviews seem to be predictable and lacking in content just because of the much-used formulaic language (Wilton 2017: 92). Linguistic research has also variously focused on the role of idioms (Matulina and Ćoralić 2008), metaphors (Nordin 2008) and highly recurrent constructions (Levin 2008) in football genres like match reports and live commentary, showing that the language of football has a rich vocabulary of typical terms and multi-word expressions on the one hand and makes frequent use of (metaphorical) phrasemes from other domains like military (Bergh 2011) on the other.

While popular accounts usually emphasize the apparent pointlessness of the so-called clichés like 'You couldn't write a script like this!' or 'This is a must-win game', linguistic approaches seek to reveal the functionality of formulaic language in terms of language production as well as social functions. As linguistic manifestations of cognitive and pragmatic routines they serve as readymade solutions for recurrent communicative tasks that – due to their prepatterning – help the speakers to cope with the time constraints under which they are produced (Chovanec 2015: 79) and limit the interpretative possibilities on the recipients' side (Günthner 2007: 129). Moreover, formulaic sequences serve as markers of the register of football coverage itself (Ferguson 1983: 167; Levin 2008: 150). They are expected parts of football reports and thus build up contextualization cues (Gumperz 1982: 131) by indicating the context of sports coverage where, for example, military terms like *marching orders* are not to be taken literally. Finally, by their register-marking functions, formulaic sequences may serve as a *shibboleth* for asserting and reaffirming group identity (Wray and Perkins 2000: 14), which in the context of this chapter is the collective identity of the football fans. Formulaic sequences are expected by the followers of football and thus 'both serve to include those who are familiar with the phraseology and to exclude those who are not' (Levin 2008: 146).

Popular accounts on formulaic language in football coverage usually focus on set phrases, idiomatic expressions and lexicalized metaphors. From a linguistic perspective, however, less salient routines like recurrent syntactic patterns are of interest too. Following Feilke (2010), I call them 'text routines' and they can be defined as domain and register-specific procedures of writing. They can take the shape of (more or less lexicalized) grammatical constructions or of recurring means of structuring texts.[2] Like formulaic sequences in the narrower sense, text routines also serve as convenient and register-marking solutions for the task of writing under time pressure. Moreover, as they normally have empty slots that can be flexibly filled with expressive lexical or phraseological items (Erman and Warren 2009: 34; Croft 2001: 25), they can counterbalance the stereotypicality and conciliate it with the task of staging the football game as a uniquely emotional and emotionalizing event. Only on the basis of routines, the 'dramatic embellishment' (Bryant et al. 1977: 140) of the commentator's narrative can be achieved, and 'the background of habitualized activity opens up a foreground for deliberation and innovation' (Berger and Luckmann 1966: 71). As I will show below, corpus-linguistic methods are particularly suitable to demonstrate how this conciliation works within the register of online football coverage.

3. Data and methods

The present analysis is based on a large corpus of texts from two online genres: a) football live text commentaries (LTC), that is, 'written accounts of sports events that are produced and published incrementally on the Internet while the event is unfolding' (Jucker 2010: 58; for an overview on linguistic research on LTC cf. Werner 2016); and b) football match reports (MR). The texts are taken from one German (www.kicker.de) and one English (www.sportsmole.co.uk) media outlet. The corpus is part of the public *Corpora for Football Linguistics* (www.fussballlinguistik.de/korpora, cf. Meier 2017). The German *Kicker* corpus contains all LTCs and the respective MRs of all Bundesliga matches of ten Bundesliga seasons from 2006 to 2016. The English *Sportsmole* corpus contains the LTCs and MRs of every match of five Premier League seasons from 2012 to 2017 (see Table 2.1 for details). The data was extracted from the HTML source code and transformed to XML.[3] Every text was linguistically annotated with the *TreeTagger* (Schmid 1994)[4] and then uploaded to the web-based tool CQPweb (Hardie 2012), which allows flexible queries of the annotated data and various statistical analyses. Every text is enriched with metadata, including a URL link to the original text in its multimodal appearance.[5]

As reference corpora, I am using random sets of 100,000 sentences each from English and German online news of 2015 taken from the *Leipzig Corpora Collection* (Goldhahn et al. 2012). By contrasting the football data with these thematically non-specific corpora, i.e. by key word analysis (Bondi 2010),[7] I will determine some lexical items as a starting point for further analyses, including n-gram analysis and collocation analysis, in order to detect (partly) schematic constructions which are lexically not fully specified, and their highly variable filler items (chapter 4.1). Furthermore, I will make use of the *Ngram Statistics Package* (Banerjee and Pedersen 2003) that allows users to detect statistically significant n-grams in a corpus without any lexical specification based on association measures alone. This method will help to find idiomatic expressions and to show their pervasiveness in the corpus (Section 5).

Table 2.1 Corpora[6]

	No. of texts	No. of tokens
Kicker LTC (2006–2016)	3,058	4,055,353
Kicker MR (2006–2016)	3,057	2,145,189
Sportsmole LTC (2012–2017)	1,530	5,810,800
Sportsmole MR (2012–2017)	1,727	719,155
Total	**9,327**	**12,730,497**

4. Results I: Syntactic patterns and text routines

Compared to the reference corpora of the respective languages, the lexemes shown in Table 2.2 turn out to be significant for LTCs and MRs (based on lemmata, using log-likelihood statistic with a minimum frequency 3 in list #1 and #2, showing the first fifteen positions without proper names and punctuation marks; overlap between the German and English data is indicated by underlines).

4.1. German *Kicker* corpus

The key lemma lists of the German subcorpora suggest that LTCs tend to describe every single 'scene' (Schmidt 2009: 120) by specifying its spatial parameters, whereas in MRs more comprehensive descriptions of the game in its temporal dimension can be found as well. With 49,503 matches (7,983 pmw), the spatial preposition *aus*, which can be translated with *out (of the)* and *from*, is highly frequent in LTCs. A frequency breakdown of the part-of-speech annotations shows that the most frequent trigrams with *aus* include distance specifications (*aus _CARD Metern [from _CARD meters*, 12,839 hits) and directionals (*aus dem/r _NN [from the _NN]*, 6,483 hits) where only the specific distances and positions (e.g. *aus dem Mittelfeld [from the midfield]*) have to be inserted (Kuiper 1996: 96). Moreover, adpositional phrases of the type *aus _ADJA _NN* (4,553 hits) seem particularly suitable, as they allow to characterize a player's move vividly without having to give exact details (1–3).

Table 2.2 Key lemmas[8]

Subcorpus	Key lemma
Kicker: LTC	**Ball** [ball], **Spielerwechsel** [substitution], **links** [left], **gelb** [yellow], **Meter** [meter], **Karte** [card], **Tor** [goal], **Strafraum** [box], **Halbzeit** [half], **Ecke** [corner], **rechts** [right], **Freistoß** [free kick], **aus** [from/out], **vorbei** [past], **aber** [but]
Kicker: MR	**nach** [after], **Minute** [minute], **Ball** [ball], **Tor** [goal], **gegen** [against], **Meter** [meter], **Partie** [match], **Strafraum** [box], **links** [left], **Gast** [guest], **Chance**, **Führung** [lead], **erst** [first], **Spiel** [game], **rechts** [right]
Sportsmole: LTC	**ball, goal**, League, **but**, side, chance, match, minute, game, Premier, **box, half, corner**, win, shot, season
Sportsmole: MR	**minute, goal, ball**, League, Premier, the, half, side, effort, wide, corner, shot, **chance**, when, **box**

(1) Mkhitaryan schießt **aus spitzem Winkel** von rechts – in die Arme von Tyton. (k_BL1516_lt_3025)[9]
Mkhitaryan shoots **from a tight angle** from the right side – into the arms of Tyton.
(2) Zimling hämmert einen Freistoß **aus aussichtsreicher Position** in die Stuttgarter Mauer. (k_BL1213_lt_2134)
Zimling hammers a free kick **from a promising position** into the Stuttgart wall.
(3) Johnson flankt **aus vollem Lauf** in die Mitte. (k_BL1516_lt_2979)
Johnson crosses **at full speed** to the centre.

Many of these adpositional phrases turn out to be set expressions that deliver most succinct accounts of the scenes and are also suitable for MRs. Table 2.3 shows the frequencies of the most common instantiations in both subcorpora.

While in LTCs the time display of every entry is delivered as a meta datum (e.g. in a separate column or highlighted in bold and colour), in MRs the time specifications have to be verbalized. Aside from constructions with the key lemma *Minute* like *in der x.ten Minute [in the xth minute]* (3,117 hits, cf. Levin 2008 for English), constructions with the temporal preposition *nach [after]*, which is the most significant key lemma, are also highly frequent. On the one hand, they are used to indicate time periods relative to the basic time structure of football games (e.g. *nach der Pause [after the break]*). On the other hand, adpositional phrases of the type *nach (_ART) _ADJA _NN* (3,451 hits) allow for very condensed, but vivid, descriptions of what happened right before a player's move (4–5).

Table 2.3 Most frequent adpositional phrases of the type *aus _ADJA _NN* (Kicker corpus)

	No. of texts (LTC/MR)	Absolute and relative (pmw) no. of tokens (LTC/MR)
aus linker/rechter/ … Position [from the left/right/ … side]	1015/539	1488/656 (366.9/305.8)
aus spitzem Winkel [from a tight angle]	1120/490	1464/545 (361.0/254.1)
aus kurzer/langer/ … Distanz [from close/long/ … range]	866/835	1057/989 (260.6/461.0)
aus vollem Lauf [at full speed]	192/45	202/45 (50.6/21.0)

(4) **Nach schöner Vorarbeit** von Matmour traf Neuville erneut nur den Pfosten. (k_BL0809_spb_652)
After a beautiful assist of Matmour, Neuville, again, only hit the post.

(5) Rudnevs kam nach Jansens Flanke knapp zu spät (9.), Skjelbred traf den Ball **nach toller Kombination** im Zentrum nicht voll (11.). (k_BL1213_spb_1952)
Rudnevs was a little late after Jansen's cross (9.), Skjelbred didn't quite hit the ball **after a great combination** in the centre (11.).

With constructions of this type a whole series of preparatory moves (among the most frequent nouns we find *Vorarbeit* [assist], *Zuspiel* [pass], *Kombination* [combination] and *Solo* [solo run]) can be expressed in just three words. Beyond a merely temporal determination, the preposition is given a causal reading according to the implicature-based principle *post hoc, ergo propter hoc* (Pinto 1995) and is therefore particularly suitable for giving an account of the emergence *(Entstehung)* of a shot or the like. Moreover, the adjective slot allows for an evaluative description of the scene. The most frequent adjectives with primarily evaluative meaning are the following:

gut [good], *schön* [beautiful], **toll** [great], *fein* [fine], **stark** [strong], **gelungen** [successful], **schwach** [weak], **sehenswert** [worth seeing], **klasse** [great], **glänzend** [brilliant], **schlimm** [bad], **klug** [clever], **katastrophal** [disastrous], **perfekt** [perfect], **präzise** [precise]

In the noun slot, we can often find compounds with proper names of players or teams as in (6), making the description even more concise.

(6) Diouf lief **nach feinem Pinto-Pass** alleine auf das Tor zu, wurde dann aber noch von Russ eingeholt, der klären konnte (58.). (k_BL1112_spb_1796)
After a fine Pinto pass, Diouf ran towards the goal alone, but Russ caught up and was able to clear (58.).

Thus, the syntactic pattern *nach _ADJA _NN* provides a useful and flexible template for MRs that helps the writers to re-narrate and evaluate the temporal unfolding of the game and at the same time to provide causal explanations of what was going on.

The prevalence of evaluative means, as was shown for the pattern *nach _ADJA _NN*, also proves for the descriptions of shots with the noun *Ball*, which is the most significant key lemma for the LTC subcorpus. In this subcorpus, the most frequent POS-trigram is *VVFIN ART Ball* (8,843 hits); adding vernacular synonyms for *Ball* to the query, even 16,050 hits are returned.[10] In most cases the trigram is extended to the right by an adpositional phrase like *ins Netz* [into the net] (8,082 hits) to indicate the path of the ball or by an adverbial adjective (2,179 hits).[11] A count of the verbs used to instantiate this pattern shows up many expressive jargon words. Some of them specify the manner of shooting, e.g. by describing the shooting technique (*löffeln* [to spoon], *spitzeln* [to poke], *zirkeln* [to curl]). But especially for powerful shots there seems to be a rich variety of synonyms (in descending frequency):

> *treiben, jagen, hämmern, dreschen, knallen, hauen, nageln, donnern, feuern, zimmern, schweißen, bolzen, kloppen, ballern, prügeln, semmeln*

Since the core meaning of all these verbs is something like 'to shoot powerfully', differences of their denotational semantics can hardly be determined. Some of them seem to be metaphorical loans from the source domain of craft (*hämmern* [to hammer], *nageln* [to nail], *dreschen* [to thresh], *schweißen* [to weld], etc.), but the very specifics of these actions are not projected on the target domain of shooting except the feature of powerfulness. The main function of this richness of synonyms is likely to be the diversification of descriptions of the ever-repeating act of shooting to keep them vivid and suspenseful.[12] This may be further intensified by adverbial adjectives. Some of them characterize the manner of shooting with respect to its motion-related aspects like *flach [flat]* or *quer [across]*, but the majority are more expressive than descriptive (in descending frequency):

> **stark** [strongly], **perfekt** [perfectly], **sehenswert** [worth seeing], **schön** [beautifully], **gefühlvoll** [with feeling], **elegant** [elegantly], **souverän** [confidently], **humorlos** [humourlessly], **wunderbar** [wonderfully], **mühelos** [effortlessly], **trocken** [dryly], **artistisch** [artistically]

Rather than specifying, for example, the path of the ball these adjectives express the writer's emotional attitude towards the effort in the first place. Again, the pattern _VVFIN den Ball _ADJD _APPR provides a useful and flexible template for describing the repetitive event of shooting in ever new and appealing ways.

Lastly, the adversative conjunction *aber [but]* (30,984 hits) is a highly significant key lemma for the LTC subcorpus. Adversative constructions with *aber* or other conjunctions like *doch* are used recurrently to describe wasted chances or other misses, and since in football failed shots are much more frequent than successful ones, many fixed phrases, some of them with metaphorical meanings, have emerged. They can be detected by a collocation analysis (with a collocation window of 7 to the right). In the following examples

(7–9) the significant collocates are italicized, while all of the adversative phrases are typical, but rather flexible, instantiations:

(7) Der Flügelangreifer feuert das Leder scharf nach innen, **findet aber keinen** *Abnehmer*. (k_BL1516_lt_2921)
The winger fires a sharp cross into the centre, **but does not find any** *buyers*.
(8) Der Bremer Angriffs-Allrounder *bleibt* **aber an der Berliner Abwehr** *hängen*. (k_BL1516_lt_2919)
But the Bremen allrounder *gets stuck* **in Berlin's defence**.
(9) Den Abpraller krallt sich Holtby, **wird aber wegen Abseits** *zurückgepfiffen*. (k_BL1415_lt_2500)
Holtby grabs the rebound, **but he is** *whistled back* **for offside**.

Of course, the miss can be framed as an intervention from the defender's perspective (10–11).
(10) Gute Flanke von Chandler, **aber Tah** *klärt*. (k_BL1516_lt_3015)
Good cross by Chandler, **but Tah** *clears*.
(11) Dost kommt im Strafraum an den Ball, **aber Wiedwald hat gut** *aufgepasst*. (k_BL1516_lt_3017)
Dost gets to the ball in the penalty area, **but Wiedwald has been very** *attentive*.

To sum up so far, the described sets of more or less fixed syntactic patterns already provide the basic means to describe a prototypical scene of a football game. In combination, they form a three-step text routine available to the writers of both LTCs and MRs containing (1) the description of some preparatory steps, e.g. a one-on-one or an assist; (2) the effort or shot itself and 3) the miss or the intervention. Most schematically, this routine can be represented as follows:

[*nach* ...]$_{\text{PREPARATION/ASSIST}}$ [...]$_{\text{EFFORT}}$ *aber/doch* [...]$_{\text{MISS/INTERVENTION}}$

(12–13) are two examples from the corpus which put the players' effort into words in exactly the way described above, that is, with an adjective and an adpositional phrase indicating the path of the ball[13]:

(12) [Nach einem Eckball von der linken Seite]$_{\text{ASSIST}}$ [verlängert Bender den Ball am kurzen Pfosten geschickt mit dem Kopf aufs Tor]$_{\text{EFFORT}}$ doch [Zieler passt auf und hält knapp vor der Torlinie]$_{\text{INTERVENTION}}$ (k_BL1415_lt_2701)
[After a corner from the left]$_{\text{ASSIST}}$ [Bender skillfully extends the ball towards the goal at the near post with his head]$_{\text{EFFORT}}$ but [Zieler is attentive and saves just in front of the goal line]$_{\text{INTERVENTION}}$

(13) [Erst nach einer Eckballhereingabe von Hajnal]$_{ASSIST}$ [köpfte Eggimann gefährlich aufs Tor]$_{EFFORT}$ aber [Ulreich klärte mit den Fingerspitzen (15.)]$_{INTERVENTION}$ (k_BL0708_spb_489)
[Only after a corner kick from Hajnal]$_{ASSIST}$ [Eggimann headed dangerously on goal]$_{EFFORT}$ but [Ulreich cleared with his fingertips]$_{INTERVENTION}$

This schema builds up the basic linguistic structure of a most common and register-typical text routine. As a rather abstract schema it can be adapted easily and variably enriched with a notably large set of expressive and vivid filler items. Although the single instantiations seem to be unique descriptions of unique scenes, a corpus-linguistic analysis shows their extremely schematic nature, 'an underlying rigidity of phraseology, despite a rich superficial variation' (Sinclair 1991: 121). This very interaction of idiomaticity and open-choice is constitutive for the register of football coverage.

4.2. English *Sportsmole* corpus

Many of the findings presented above also hold for the English data. For example, spatial descriptions with the preposition *from* (like *from (about/around) CD yards* (2,904 hits) or *from the edge of the area/box* (1,706 hits) can be found frequently. Again, the pattern *from (a) _JJ _NN* is suitable for both genres, even if the frequency Table 2.4 shows a clear dominance in the MRs, where exact details can be omitted.

In the LTC subcorpus, a highly frequent part-of-speech trigram with the key lemma *ball* is *VVZ DT ball* (5,276 hits). It is mostly followed by a preposition (2,551 hits) (14) or an adverb (1,335 hits) (15), both of which are mainly used to specify the path of the ball.

Table 2.4 Most frequent adpositional phrases of the type *from (a) _JJ _NN* (Sportsmole Corpus)

	No. of texts (LTC/MR)	Absolute and relative (pmw) no. of tokens (LTC/MR)
from close/long/point-blank range	636/536	974/662 (167.6/920.52)
from a tight/narrow/acute angle	384/156	460/162 (79.2/225.3)
from a good/wide/central position	118/48	126/49 (21.7/68.1)

(14) Gerrard moves forward and **whips the ball into the box**. (spm_PL1415_lt_978)

(15) Welbeck breaks away down the left and **pulls the ball back** for Bellerin. (spm_PL1516_lt_1282)

As in the German data, a count of the filler items for the verb slot shows up a rich variety of synonyms. The most frequent agentive verbs within this pattern *gives, plays* and *sends (the ball)* are rather neutral and unspecific, but there are many others which characterize the manner of shooting like *heads, lifts, pokes, curls (the ball)*. And again, for denoting powerful shots the range of available verbs seems to be particularly wide:

flicks, whips, knocks, fires, smashes, lashes, strikes, punches, blasts, hammers, fizzes, slams, blazes, flashes, powers, pumps, whacks, cannons, smacks, thunders

In the LTC corpus, the adversative conjunction *but* is also a highly significant key lemma (53,448 hits, 9,198 pmw). Applying the same method as above, that is a collocation analysis with a window of 7 to the right, the following examples (16–19) are typical ways of describing misses or, from the defender's perspective, interventions (significant collocates, which all rank among the first twenty positions in the collocation list, are italicized):

(16) West Ham continue to threaten as Payet delivers a brilliant free kick onto the head of Collins, **but his *effort* is wide of the post**. (spm_PL1617_lt_1418)

(17) Almost a chance for Liverpool from a corner as Mane finds a bit of space, **but *can't get enough* on his header at the front post**. (spm_PL1617_lt_1502)

(18) Janmaat clips the ball into the box, **but it is far *too* close to Cech** and he is able to collect. (spm_PL1617_lt_1525)

(19) De Bruyne and Sterling link up before the England international delivers in a cross, **but Watford *clear* the danger**. (spm_PL1617_lt_1479)

Counterparts of the patterns with *nach* can also be found in the English data. A query for the pattern *after _DT _JJ _NN* returns 956 (LTC) and 254 (MR) hits, and again it is used to indicate the overall time structure of the game (*after the half-hour mark*), but also the preparatory steps of specific scenes (*after a great/clever/fabulous run/pass/cross*).

In the English data the temporal subordinating conjunction *before* is frequent, too (see 20–23). Like *after*, it links two different moves into one scene, but focuses more strongly on the preceding event, while the subsequent event is – grammatically spoken – subordinated. In most cases it is combined with a gerund. This pattern is distributed as shown in Table 2.5.

As was shown for the pattern *nach _ADJA _NN* in the German data, the pattern *before _VVG* can be combined to a three-step account of a scene, which turns out to be a widely used text routine in LTCs (20–21).[14]

(20) [Ibrahimovic collects a long pass]$_{ASSIST}$ before [cutting inside and shooting]$_{EFFORT}$ but [Dann makes the block]$_{INTERVENTION}$ (spm_PL1617_lt_1480)

(21) [Sigurdsson gets the ball on the edge of the box]$_{ASSIST}$ before [trying to swerve it past Schmeichel]$_{EFFORT}$ but [the Leicester keeper makes a stop]$_{INTERVENTION}$ (spm_PL1617_lt_1394)

This pattern can also frequently be found in MRs (22).

(22) [The midfielder played a one-two with Lukaku]$_{PREPARATION}$ before [thumping a shot at goal]$_{SHOT}$ but [it nestled into the side-netting]$_{MISS}$ (spm_PL1516_spb_1351)

But in MRs it is often additionally introduced by a temporal specification with regard to the overall structure of the game (23).

(23) [On the stroke of half time]$_{TIME}$ [Villa skipper Fabian Delph worked some space from the left of the area]$_{PREPARATION}$ before [curling a strike towards goal]$_{SHOT}$ [but it cannoned off the base of the post]$_{MISS}$ (spm_PL1415_spb_997)

Moreover, in MRs constructions with the adverb *when* (which proves to be a key lemma for the MR subcorpus) are also frequent. A collocation analysis of the 4,935 hits in the MR subcorpus shows that in 1,596 cases (32%) it is preceded by an exact time specification with the lemma *minute*. This time specification is usually combined with an indication of the state of the match or, more precisely, a change of this state. To give some examples from the corpus:

(24) [Reading regained the lead]$_{STATE\ OF\ MATCH}$ [on 62 minutes]$_{TIME}$ when [Noel Hunt headed home]$_{GOAL}$ [from McAnuff's swinging cross]$_{ASSIST}$ (spm_PL1213_spb_24)

Table 2.5 Before_VVG

	No. of texts	No. of tokens
LTC	1,327	5,280 (908.7 pmw)
MR	747	1,091 (1517.1 pmw)

(25) [Lambert made the breakthrough]$_{\text{STATE OF MATCH}}$ [after 32 minutes]$_{\text{TIME}}$ when [he reacted quickest to a deflected Lallana free kick]$_{\text{PREPARATION}}$ [to poke home from close range]$_{\text{GOAL}}$ (spm_PL1213_spb_105)

(26) [Steve Clarke's side did equalize]$_{\text{STATE OF MATCH}}$ [in the 43rd minute]$_{\text{TIME}}$ when [another Brunt corner was met by Jonas Olsson and Bunn could only tip onto the bar]$_{\text{ASSIST}}$ [with Gera following up to score West Brom's first goal in four games]$_{\text{GOAL}}$ (spm_PL1213_spb_144)

With this text routine, the task of reporting on both the overall game and its decisive scenes can be fulfilled in a most economical way. As already noted for the German data, the text routine leaves some open choices and is flexible enough to insert most varied and often very expressive descriptions of the players' moves, but still it provides a useful template to combine these components in proven manner. Thus, not only the lexical items themselves, but also their embedding in approved syntactic patterns, are constitutive and indicative for the register of football coverage.

5. Results II: Idioms

In Section 4, I analysed recurrent syntactic patterns with little or no lexical specifications that constitute the formulaicity of LTCs and MRs in a rather abstract manner. In this section, I turn to the opposite pole of the continuum of formulaicity (Wray and Perkins 2000: 5) and focus on idiomatic expressions, i.e. nearly immutable and mostly semantically opaque sequences of words.

It has often been noted that sports coverage in the (online) press is characterized by a particularly high density of idiomatic expressions. Although the majority of the studies are based on rather intuitive assessments, recent work has provided quantitative analyses of the high degree of phraseological fixedness of sports coverage in comparison to other fields like politics or arts (Pfeiffer 2014). However, the database used by Pfeiffer is rather small and the analysis is based on a manual count of qualitative categorizations.

In addition to this interpretative procedure, I follow a data-driven approach of detecting idioms based on statistical n-gram analysis. In contrast to the type of n-gram analysis applied in Section 4, which looked for fixed patterns with one or more specified items (at least on the part-of-speech level), statistical n-gram analysis works without any previous specification but calculates the statistical association score for every n-gram in a corpus (Evert 2009). I am using the open source *Ngram Statistics Package* (Banerjee and Pedersen 2003). In a first step, the software counts all occurrences of all n-grams (here: bigrams or word pairs) in the corpus within a window of up to five words. Then, the statistical association is calculated for every word pair type by comparing its observed frequency with its expected frequency based on the assumption of a random distribution. The results are ranked by their association scores (i.e. significance) according to a chi-square test. That way, the software detects word pairs that may occur relatively rarely (a minimum frequency of 5 is set as standard), but if they occur at all, they do so in this very combination (co-occurrence). In other words, the software detects fixed word pairs.

As the software works on the basis of bare counting of word forms without any linguistic (morpho-syntactic or lexical) information, it does not differentiate between the various classes of phrasemes as defined in the literature (e.g. idioms vs. structural phrasemes like *with regard to*). Moreover, proper names like *Garry Monk* are typically ranked very high for they best meet the requirement of co-occurrence of their components. But after taking out proper names (of persons, clubs and stadiums), the remaining word pairs are components of mostly idiomatic expressions. Table 2.6 presents the first fifteen word pairs ranked by their association score and its absolute frequency in the subcorpora (every word pair was checked in the corpus to determine the shape it usually takes in the texts; the main components according to the software output are highlighted in bold).

As the table shows, the software is able to detect word pairs that can easily be completed to meaningful and conventional formulaic expressions by any human reader. Most of them are semantically opaque idioms (*to be at sixes and sevens*), often with figurative meanings (*to put the icing on the cake*), but routine formulae (*Ladies and Gentlemen*) are also detected. In some cases, the idiomaticity derives from metaphoric transfer from another domain (*one-way traffic; mit angezogener Handbremse* [*with the hand brake applied*]). Some word pairs, especially in the Sportsmole MR subcorpus, are technical terms (*free kick, relegation zone, five-at-the-back system*).[16] However, it is striking that (at least through the lens of the applied methods of automatized n-gram detection) the majority of the detected formulaic expressions in both languages are not sport-specific idioms but are borrowed from other domains, including (but not limited to) the well-known domain of warfare (Bergh 2011). A great number of the used idioms thus link football coverage to everyday language. They may sound 'sporty', especially to sports followers that do know that they are frequently used in sports, but a specific trait of the language of sports coverage seems to be not only its technical

Table 2.6 Statistically significant word pairs

Sportsmole LTC	Sportsmole MR
to claim **bragging rights** (56)	to claim **bragging rights** (10)
to **whet** the **appetite** (25)	to be given one's **marching orders** (26)
huff(ing) and **puff(ing)** (37)	**south coast** (16)
to be at **sixes** and **sevens** (10)	to add/put the **icing** on the **cake** (14)
to get into the **nitty gritty** (7)	**one-way traffic** (15)
to be **surplus** to **requirements** (5)	**free kick** (854)
a **collector's item** (5)	**relegation zone** (166)
to be **licking** one's **lips** (23	for a second **bookable offence** (16)
doom and **gloom** (38)	from a **tight angle** (112)
alarm bells ringing (12)	**this afternoon** (744)
to throw the **kitchen sink** (25)	for **large parts** (22)
last-chance saloon (7)	to/a **share** (of) the **spoils** (64)
the **grand scheme** of things (14)	to keep one's **clean sheet** (intact) (62)
ladies and **gentlemen** (28)	**five-at-the-back system** (6)
one-way traffic (84)	**exchanged passes** (39)

Kicker LTC[15]	Kicker MR
Herzlich Willkommen [welcome] (32)	*ad acta legen* [to shelve sth.] (8)
Lucky Punch [i.e. decisive (last-minute) goal] (60)	*weder Fisch noch Fleisch* [neither fish nor fowl] (8)
auf Messers Schneide [on a knife edge] (9)	*unter Dach und Fach* [approx. wrapped up] (56)
never change a winning team (5)	*never change a winning team* (6)
Wechselkontingent ausgeschöpft [out of substitutions] (43)	*auf Messers Schneide* [on a knife edge] (19)
Standing Ovations (8)	*in trockene Tücher packen* [approx. to make sth. being home and dry] (13)
der Drops ist gelutscht [approx. it's done and dusted] (7)	*wie das Kaninchen vor der Schlange* [approx. like a rabbit caught in the headlights] (10)
Freund und Feind [friend and foe] (245)	*oberstes Gebot* [top priority] (5)
weder Fisch noch Fleisch [neither fish nor fowl] (16)	*freies Schussfeld* [free field of fire] (6)
Dreh- und Angelpunkt [pivotal point] (5)	*im wahrsten Sinne des Wortes* [in the truest sense of the word] (9)
in höchster Not [in the nick of time] (299)	*Freund und Feind* [friend and foe] (35)

Sportsmole LTC	Sportsmole MR
rote **Hosen** und blaue **Stutzen** [red shorts and blue socks] (132)	im **Großen** und **Ganzen** [approx. generally speaking] (28)
Hin und **Her** [back and forth] (8)	mit **Zähnen** und **Klauen** [tooth and nail] (8)
Big Point (7)	sich die **Butter** vom **Brot** nehmen lassen [to let sb. take the bread out of one's mouth] (6)
mit **vereinten Kräften** [with united forces] (81)	mit **angezogener Handbremse** [with the handbrake applied] (18)
das **rettende Ufer** [approx. dry land] (28)	**Wechselbad** der **Gefühle** [approx. roller-coaster of emotions] (13)

terminology but rather its integration of idiomatic patterns that are used in other domains too.[17] It is rather the frequency and the combination of idioms than the idioms themselves that constitute the register specifics of football coverage and that will be recognized and appreciated by those who are familiar with it.

While the syntactic patterns described in Section 4 serve as templates that still need to be filled individually, idioms can be described rather as prefabricated building blocks that can be used as they are. Also, their functional range differs: Whereas the syntactic patterns are used for the description of single game scenes, the idioms mostly serve to give more general assessments of a game. Since both the writers of LTCs and MRs have to give summarizing and evaluative accounts of the game events, the mostly figurative idioms are functional and, in terms of language production, an economical choice. As well-established means of description, they can provide vivid and intuitively accessible accounts without the need of giving further details.

Although idioms usually are lexically fixed and lose their idiomaticity after changing one of their components, they still show a certain degree of variability on the text level (Levin 2008: 145). For reasons of textual cohesion and coherence, but also for demonstrating creativity as a journalist, even idioms with non-exchangeable parts can be modified to some degree, as long as its default form is still recognizable. In (27), the idiom *to throw the kitchen sink at sb.*, which can be paraphrased as a team's 'trying to break down the other side with everything they have got', is intensified by insertion of new elements (Jaki 2014: 24).

(27) Now, will Fulham **throw the kitchen sink, the microwave and the utensils** at Chelsea? (spm_PL1314_lt_537)

Cases of clipping (Jaki 2014: 25) can be found, too (28–29):

(28) It's **kitchen sink time** for Liverpool. (spm_PL1516_lt_1218)
(29) It's well and truly **kitchen sink stuff** here but West Ham holding so, so strong. (spm_PL1516_lt_1084)

These formulations might be described as elliptic forms of *time to throw the kitchen sink* or the like, but as parallel forms to set exclamations like *it's party time!* they also gain new pragmatic functions.

In the German data, the idiomatic expression *mit angezogener Handbremse* [*with the handbrake applied*], which approx. means 'decelerated', is used in that exact form in 29 out of 36 cases. However, the idiom can be syntactically adjusted as in (30).

(30) Mit zunehmender Spieldauer **zog** der FC **die Handbremse immer weiter an** und achtete nun stärker auf die Defensive. (k_BL1415_spb_2696)
As the game progressed, the club applied the handbrake more and more and paid more attention to its defence.

Arguably, the supplement *immer weiter* [*more and more*] would not make sense for real hand brakes, yet it shows that its figurative meaning of 'decelerating' remains activated. In other cases, the corresponding verb is reversed (31).

(31) Nach dem Seitenwechsel **löste** der FSV **die Handbremse und legte den Vorwärtsgang ein**. (k_BL1314_spb_2443)
After changing sides, the FSV **released the handbrake and engaged forward gear**.

In this new variant, the idiom can be combined with another one from the same domain of car driving (*Vorwärtsgang einlegen* [*to engage forward gear*]), thus providing a figurative means of establishing textual coherence. In (32), the idiom is strongly truncated:

(32) Das Passspiel ist gewohnt sicher, **nach Handbremse sieht es nicht wirklich aus**. (k_BL1415_lt_2582)
Passing is safe as usual, **it doesn't really look like handbrake**.

Here, the (syntactically non-embedded) lexical item *Handbremse* still invokes the overall judgement usually passed by the whole idiom, while this very judgement is rejected with regard to the actual impression of the game (*sieht nicht nach x aus* [*doesn't look like x*]). Thus, this example shows a creative and allusive use of idioms that fulfils community-building functions (Wray and Perkins 2000: 14). Although the idiom is used in other domains, too, this truncated formulation will be fully understandable only for those who are familiar with the register of football coverage.

6. Conclusion

In this study, I have used data-driven, corpus-linguistic methods to investigate two types of formulaic sequences within German and English football live text commentaries and match reports. First, syntactic patterns that serve as templates for describing recurring events like efforts, misses or goals were described. As rather schematic patterns, they can be flexibly adjusted and filled with a large set of mostly expressive and vivid lexical items to render them unique and emotionalizing despite their schematic nature. In combination, these patterns serve as text routines that are available to the writers and serve as register-marking devices. Second, methods for automatized detection of idioms were applied. It was shown that besides special phrasemes idioms from other domains are also frequently used for giving summarizing and evaluating accounts of the games. Although these idioms link football coverage to everyday language, their density and combination serve as a register-marking device. Moreover, variations and modifications of these idioms can be found, which, by alluding to register typical ways of writing, have community-building functions. To take up Sinclair (1991: 109ff.) again, the corpus analytic results have shown that writers rely on a broad range of prestructured patterns, which still leave enough open choices to demonstrate creativity and deliver appealing narratives of the games. These corpus-linguistic findings largely confirm those of previous work on the topic, but due to the quantity of data and the applied methods a more comprehensive inventory of formulaic language use could be established. Moreover, the study has shown the common features of live text commentaries and match reports with regard to formulaicity.

This study focused on German and English data and showed that apart from minor differences in the syntactic details many types of formulaic sequences can be found in both languages. Exploratory analyses based on random samples already suggest that many of the findings hold for other languages, too, and indicate that football coverage can be seen as cross-cultural registers (Werner 2016: 298ff.). For example, the three-step text routine described, that links the description of an assist, an effort and an interception, can also be found in French (33), Spanish (34) and Italian (35) live text commentaries.

(33) **Après une frappe lointaine d'Iloki** déviée en corner, **le centre de Thomasson** est repris par Sigthorsson, **mais** Barrada dégage le ballon de la tête sur sa ligne. (med_L1_15_lt_404)[18]
After a long-range shot by Iloki deflected to the corner, **Thomasson's centre** is taken up by Sigthorsson, **but** Barrada clears the ball with his head on the line.

(34) Se dedicó el turco a regatear hasta a dos rivales dentro del área **antes de sacar un centro** entre dos jugadores béticos al límite del área pequeña, **pero** lo rechazó bien el Betis. (as_PD1314_lt_287)[19]
The turk dribbles towards two opponents in the box **before crossing** from between two Betis players at the edge of the penalty area, **but** it is well denied by Betis.

(35) **Dopo una bella serpentina** De Paul la **mette in mezzo** dalla destra **ma** Badu non inquadra la porta di testa. (git_SA1617_lt_61)[20]
After a beautiful serpentine [slalom], De Paul **puts it into the center** from the right, **but** Badu can't head the ball into the goal.

Just as football is a transcultural practice, so are at least some of the formulaic patterns of writing about it. Future research might consider in more detail if this transculturality also affects other linguistic and textual levels like the use of metaphors, ways of staging orality and emotional involvement. Also, recent developments in automatized text generation and translation which are supposed to homogenize football coverage will raise new issues regarding formulaicity and transculturality.

Notes

1 Following Giulianotti's (2002) taxonomy of spectator identities in football, the term 'fans' refers to persons with a 'hot', that is, affective, relationship to a team, a player or the like. But as opposed to the 'supporters', whose emotional investment typically resists the commodification of sports (Merkel 2012), the fans' 'identification with the club and its players is [...] authenticated most readily through the consumption of related products' (Giulianotti 2002: 36) like fan articles and the whole variety of media services.

2 Good examples include patterns used in weather reports like *with occasional* $X_{TIME\_OF\_DAY}$ $Y_{WEATHER\_PHENOMENON}$ or text structuring devices in scientific writing like *first... thereafter... finally*.

3 Some Perl scripts for automatized data extraction and transformation are available on GitHub (https://github.com/fussballlinguist/livetext).

4 Legends for part-of-speech tags set by the Treetagger can be found under http://www.cis.uni-muenchen.de/~schmid/tools/TreeTagger/. Note that the German and English tagsets differ.

5 In this chapter, I will not go into the topic of multimodality any further. See Werner (this volume).

6 The quantity of the texts does not match the exact number of games, because some links on both websites are misdirected. Also note that on sportsmole.co.uk reports

on selected FA cup and Champions League games with the participation of Premier League clubs are tagged as 'Premier League', too. However, the vast majority of the texts are about Premier League games.

7   'In a quantitative perspective, keywords are those whose frequency (or infrequency) in a text or a corpus is statistically significant, when compared to the standards set by a reference corpus' (Bondi 2010: 3).

8   Note that live text commentaries include automated entries (or parts of them) indicating the beginnings and ends of the games, substitutions, yellow/red cards, etc. – even more so in the German data than in the English ones.

9   The sigles of the corpus documents are structured as follows: {source}_ {competition+season}_{texttype}_{ID}. My translations are rather literal and seek to cover most of the German syntax-semantics knowing that they sometimes are at odds with a canonical English translation.

10 In German, a rich variety of (metaphorical and metonymical) synonyms are used to denote the ball (in descending frequency): *Leder* [leather], *Kugel* [bullet], *Spielgerät* [game equipment], *Rund* [round], *Sportgerät* [sports equipment], *Pille* [pill], *Kirsche* [cherry], *Ei* [egg], *Murmel* [marble].

11 In German, adjectives that are used as adverbs are not marked by a suffix as in English *-ly* and therefore not formally distinguishable from predicate adjectives. For this reason, the German equivalents to, for example, *strongly* are classified and tagged as 'adverbial adjectives' (_ADJD) rather than just adverbs.

12 If at all, a distributional semantic specification of these verbs based on combinatorial preferences seems feasible (Dalmas et al. 2015). As a tendency, vernacular terms for the ball go together with metaphorical verbs (e.g. *drischt das Leder* [thrashes the leather]), whereas the unmarked Term *Ball* is combined with neutral verbs like *schießen* [to shoot] or non-agentive verbs like *landen* [to land]).

13 More examples can be found with the following query: 'nach'%c [pos='ART']? [pos='ADJA']? [pos='NN'] [pos!='\$.*']* ',' 'aber|.*doch'.

14 More examples can be found with the query: 'before' [pos='VVG'] [pos!='SENT']* 'but'.

15 I am excluding word pairs that are caused by automatized LTC entries like **Gelbe Karte** *[yellow card]* or **Anpfiff** *1./2.* **Halbzeit** *[kickoff 1st/2nd half]*.

16 Due to morphological reasons, in German such technical terms are realized as compounds (*Freistoß* [free kick], *Abstiegszone* [relegation zone]).

17 The pervasiveness of the detected expressions beyond sports can be checked by querying them in the British National Corpus or the *Deutsches Referenzkorpus*.

18 http://www.matchendirect.fr/foot-score/2046024-nantes-marseille.html.

19 https://resultados.as.com/resultados/futbol/primera/2013_2014/directo/regular_a_29_2673.

20 http://www.goal.com/it/match/udinese-vs-lazio/2305821/live-commentary.

References

Banerjee, S. and T. Pedersen (2003), 'The Design, Implementation, and Use of the Ngram Statistics Package', *Proceedings of the 4th International Conference on Computational Linguistics and Intelligent Text Processing*, 370–381, Berlin, Heidelberg: Springer-Verlag.

Berger, P. L. and Th. Luckmann (1966), *The Social Construction of Reality: A Treatise in the Sociology of Knowledge*, Garden City: Anchor Books.

Bergh, G. (2011), 'Football Is War. A Case Study of Minute by Minute Football Commentary', *Veredas*, 15 (2): 83–93.

Bondi, M. (2010), 'Perspectives on Keywords and Keyness: An Introduction', in M. Bondi and M. Scott (eds), *Studies in Corpus Linguistics*, 1–18, Amsterdam: Benjamins.

Bryant, J., P. Comisky and D. Zillmann (1977), 'Drama in Sports Commentary', *Journal of Communication*, 27 (3): 140–149.

Chovanec, J. (2015), 'Participant Roles and Embedded Interactions in Online Sports Broadcasts', in M. Dynel and J. Chovanec (eds), *Participation in Public and Social Media Interactions*, vol. 256, 67–95, Amsterdam: John Benjamins Publishing Company.

Croft, W. (2001), *Radical Construction Grammar: Syntactic Theory in Typological Perspective*, Oxford, New York: Oxford University Press.

Dalmas, M., D. Dobrovol'skij, D. Goldhahn and U. Quasthof (2015), 'Bewertung durch Adjektive. Ansätze einer Korpusgestützten Untersuchung zur Synonymie', *Zeitschrift für Literaturwissenschaft und Linguistik*, 45 (1): 12–29.

Erman, B. and B. Warren (2009), 'The Idiom Principle and the Open Choice Principle', *Text*, 20 (1): 29–62.

Evert, St. (2009), 'Corpora and Collocations', in A. Lüdeling (ed.), *Corpus Linguistics. An International Handbook*, 1212–1248, Berlin/Boston: De Gruyter Mouton.

Feilke, H. (2010), '„Aller Guten Dinge sind Drei" – Überlegungen zu Textroutinen & Literalen Prozeduren', in I. Bons, Th. Gloning and D. Kaltwasser (eds), *Fest-Platte für Gerd Fritz*. Available online: http://www.festschrift-gerd-fritz.de/files/feilke_2010_literale-prozeduren-und-textroutinen.pdf.

Ferguson, Ch.A. (1983), 'Sports Announcer Talk: Syntactic Aspects of Register Variation', *Language in Society*, 12 (2): 153–172.

Giulianotti, R. (2002), 'Supporters, Followers, Fans, and Flaneurs. A Taxonomy of Spectator Identities in Football', *Journal of Sport and Social Issues*, 26 (1): 25–46.

Goldhahn, D., Th. Eckart and U. Quasthoff (2012), 'Building Large Monolingual Dictionaries at the Leipzig Corpora Collection: From 100 to 200 Languages', *Proceedings of the 8th International Language Ressources and Evaluation (LREC'12)*, 759–765.

Gumperz, J. J. (1982), *Discourse Strategies*, Cambridge, New York: Cambridge University Press.
Günthner, S. (2007), 'Intercultural Communication and the Relevance of Cultural Specific Repertoires of Communicative Genres', in H. Kotthoff and H. Spencer-Oatey (eds), *Handbook of Intercultural Communication*, 127–152, Berlin, New York: Mouton de Gruyter.
Hardie, A. (2012), 'CQPweb – Combining Power, Flexibility and Usability in a Corpus Analysis Tool', *International Journal of Corpus Linguistics*, 17 (3): 380–409.
Jaki, S. (2014), *Phraseological Substitutions in Newspaper Headlines: 'More than Meats the Eye'*, Amsterdam/Philadelphia, PA: Benjamins.
Jucker, A. H. (2010), '"Audacious, Brilliant!! What a Strike!" Live Text Commentaries on the Internet as Real-time Narratives', in Ch. R. Hoffmann (ed.), *Narrative Revisited. Telling a Story in the Age of New Media*, 57–78, Amsterdam: Benjamins.
Kern, F. (2010), 'Speaking Dramatically: The Prosody of Live Radio Commentary of Football Matches', in D. Barth-Weingarten, E. Reber and M. Selting (eds), *Prosody in Interaction*, 217–238, Amsterdam: Benjamins.
Kern, F. (2014), '"und der schlägt soFORT nach VORne" – Zur Konstitution von Spannung und Raum in Fußball-Livereportagen im Radio', in P. Auer and P. Bergmann (eds), *Sprache im Gebrauch: Räumlich, Zeitlich, Interaktional. Festschrift für Peter Auer*, 327–342, Heidelberg: Universitätsverlag Winter.
Kirschner, H. and M. Wetzels (2017), '"We Sell Emotions". Die Kommunikative Konstruktion von Sportübertragungen am Beispiel Fußball und eSport', in J. Reichertz and R. Tuma (eds), *Der kommunikative Konstruktivismus bei der Arbeit*, 256–290, Weinheim, Basel: Beltz Juventa.
Kuiper, K. (1996), *Smooth Talkers: The Linguistic Performance of Auctioneers and Sportscasters*, Mahwah, NJ: L. Erlbaum Associates.
Levin, M. (2008), '"Hitting the Back of the Net Just Before the Final Whistle": High-frequency Phrases in Football Reporting', in E. Lavric, G. Pisek, A. Skinner and W. Stadler (eds), *The Linguistics of Football*, 143–155, Tübingen: Narr.
Matulina, Ž. and Z. Ćoralić (2008), 'Idioms in Football Reporting', in E. Lavric, G. Pisek, A. Skinner and W. Stadler (eds), *The Linguistics of Football*, 101–111, Tübingen: Narr.
Meier, S. (2017), 'Korpora zur Fußballlinguistik – eine Mehrsprachige Forschungsressource zur Sprache der Fußballberichterstattung', *Zeitschrift für Germanistische Linguistik*, 45 (2): 345–349.
Merkel, U. (2012), 'Football Fans and Clubs in Germany. Conflicts, Crises and Compromises', *Soccer & Society*, 13 (3): 359–376.
Nordin, H. (2008), 'The Use of Conceptual Metaphors by Swedish and German Football Commentators', in E. Lavric, G. Pisek, A. Skinner and W. Stadler (eds), *The Linguistics of Football*, 113–120, Tübingen: Narr.

Pfeiffer, Ch. (2014), 'Phraseologie in der Fußballberichterstattung der Printmedien. Eine Quantitative Analyse', in V. Jesensek and D. Dobrovol'skij (eds), *Phraseologie und Kultur*, 491–515, Maribor: Univerza v Mariboru.

Pinto, R. C. (1995), 'Post Hoc, Ergo Propter Hoc', in H. V. Hansen and R. C. Pinto (eds), *Fallacies. Classical and Contemporary Readings*, 302–311, University Park, PA: Pennsylvania State University Press.

Raack, A. (2015), *Den MUSS er machen! Phrasen, Posen, Plattitüden – die Wunderbare Welt der Fußball-Klischees*, Hamburg: Edel.

Schmid, H. (1994), 'Probabilistic Part-of-Speech Tagging Using Decision Trees', *Proceedings of International Conference on New Methods in Language Processing*, Manchester, UK.

Schmidt, Th. (2009), 'The Kicktionary – A Multilingual Lexical Resource of Football Language', in H. C. Boas (ed.), *Multilingual FrameNets in Computational Lexicography Methods and Applications*, 101–131, Berlin, Boston: De Gruyter Mouton.

Sinclair, J. (1991), *Corpus, Concordance, Collocation*, Oxford: Oxford University Press.

Telegraph Sport (2016), 'The Football Buzzwords, Clichés and Stock Phrases that Need to Die, Immediately', *The Telegraph*, March: 9.

Werner, V. (2016), 'Real-time Online Text Commentaries: A Cross-cultural Perspective', in Ch. Schubert and Ch. Sanchez-Stockhammer (eds), *Variational Text Linguistics. Revisiting Register in English*, 271–306, Berlin, Boston: De Gruyter.

Wilton, A. (2017), 'The Interactional Construction of Evaluation in Post-match Football Interviews', in D. Caldwell, J. Walsh, E. W. Vine and J. Jureidini (eds), *The Discourse of Sport: Analyses From Social Linguistics*, 92–112, New York, London: Routledge.

Wray, A. and M. R. Perkins (2000), 'The Functions of Formulaic Language. An Integrated Model', *Language & Communication*, 20 (1): 1–28.

3

The Language of Football Match Reports in a Contrastive Perspective

Signe Oksefjell Ebeling

1. Introduction and aims

Since the release of the English-Norwegian Parallel Corpus (ENPC) in the mid-1990s, a great number of contrastive studies between these two languages have been published.[1] Naturally, the focus has been on the text types contained in the ENPC, notably fiction and a very broad and heterogeneous non-fiction category. Thus, little has, to date, been done contrastively on the language of other, more specific and arguably more homogeneous non-fictional text types. The present study aims to contribute to filling this gap by exploring data from a specialized corpus of football match reports in the two languages: the English-Norwegian Match Report Corpus (ENMaRC).

The ENMaRC is a comparable corpus still in its infancy and contains one season of written match reports in each language. One reason for compiling such a corpus is my long-standing interest in (English) football in general, and the language associated with football in particular. With a corpus such as the ENMaRC we can investigate linguistic features that are characteristic of match reporting and how these deviate (or not) from the language of other text types. An additional factor, and the main focal point in the current context, is the contrastive aspect of match reporting. It should be stressed, though, that this study is exploratory in nature, and will offer some first and preliminary observations from a new comparable corpus still under development. The corpus is arguably too small at the moment to offer more in-depth studies of specific linguistic tendencies. The focus will be on lexico-grammatical features in the material that may lead to new insights regarding the extent to which Norwegian and English journalists resort to the same linguistic features in match reports, and the way in which wins vs. losses are typically reported in the two languages.

For the purpose of these first explorations of the material, corpus-driven extraction methods, such as word lists and n-gram lists, will be applied. In addition, a keyword list analysis of match reports describing victories vs. defeats will be performed in order to shed light on the language of winning and losing in the two languages. Although the focus will be on vocabulary, some thoughts on recurrent word-combinations will also be commented on.

This chapter has the following structure: Section 2 reports on previous research relevant to the current study, while Section 3 offers a detailed outline of the contrastive method and the corpus used. Section 4 gives an account of, and interprets, some of the main (cross-)linguistic tendencies observed in word frequency lists generated on the basis of the match reports, followed by a cross-linguistic comparison of the language of winning and losing. Finally, Section 5 offers some concluding remarks and food for thought.

2. Previous research

The language of football has received some attention by linguists over the years, notably so in the edited volume entitled *The Linguistics of Football* (Lavric et al. 2008) and in several publications by Bergh and Ohlander (e.g. 2012; 2016). A number of topics have been addressed from different angles and with different foci. Of particular relevance in the current context are the following two chapters from Lavric et al.: (1) Levin's chapter, in which he 'shows that the language of English football reporting largely consists of semi-fixed phrases with conventionalized functions to describe recurrent events in the game' (Lavric 2008: 6); and (2) Richard's chapter, in which he describes how 'non-victory' is represented in televised football commentaries. Although both Levin (2008) and Richard (2008) bear some resemblance to the present one, there are also several differences to note.

Levin's (2008) method of identifying his object of study is similar to the corpus linguistic extraction methods used here. However, while the current study is also interested in overall tendencies, Levin quickly shifts his focus to high-frequency phrases with *net, minute(s)* and *whistle* in order to study their use in context. Using material from the *British National Corpus* (newspaper section) and the *Independent* (on CD-ROM), Levin's study is monolingual,[2] and shows how semi-fixed phrases have gained conventionalized functions in newspaper match reports, e.g. hit *the ball in the net* = goal, whereas have *the ball in the net* = disallowed goal. Quoting Kuiper (1996: 22), who suggests 'that recurring events tend to be associated with formulaic language', Levin finds that this is indeed the case, as evidenced by frequent goal-scoring sequences with *net* and frequent time-specifying sequences with *nth minute*. In fact, Levin claims that newspaper match reports seem to have developed their own register-specific phraseology to specify time (Levin 2008: 151).

Richard (2008) is also a monolingual (French) study and has relevance in the current context because of its focus on the language of defeats. Apart from this point of overlap, Richard's analysis of the French live commentary of a game between a winning German and losing French side bears little resemblance to the present study. Drawing on Critical Discourse Analysis, Richard shows how defeat can be euphemized, through the reporters' 'account of non-victory [of the French team] (not: defeat!)' (Richard 2008: 194). Moreover, from the French commentators' perspective, there is sympathy for the defeated French team, while '[i]nstead of a positive comment on the [winning] German team or players, the commentators focus on a negative aspect to undermine them' (Richard 2008: 197). Richard moves on to say that, although the journalists are expected to give a neutral, informative commentary, 'the presence of a French team leads them to show some preference' (Richard 2008: 197). Similarly, in the match reports under study here – written and posted by the respective teams' journalists – it may be hypothesized that there is a certain bias in their reporting. In the light of Richard's observations, it will be interesting to learn how the English and Norwegian football clubs themselves represent defeats vs. victories through linguistic means.

To sum up, the previous studies mentioned serve as a relevant backdrop and source of inspiration in the contrastive analysis of a slightly different kind of match report than those mentioned above, in being online, in-house match reports rather than live commentary or (objective) newspaper/general website reports.

3. Method and material

Before I introduce the method and material used, it is important to note that the ENMaRC is not the first or only resource of its kind. Meier (2017), for example, outlines a multilingual research resource for the language of football, mainly in German and English. However, as will become clear, Meier's resource differs from ENMaRC as, according to Meier's website (http://fussballlinguistik.de/korpora/), the sources from which the data are culled include a variety of text types acquired from general websites on sports/football (e.g. kicker.de, weltfussball.de, sportsmole.co.uk).

3.1. The comparable contrastive method

Corpus-based, or indeed corpus-driven, contrastive analysis tends to rely on (at least) one of two main corpus types (see e.g. Aijmer 2008: 9):

- Comparable corpus (containing comparable original – i.e. non-translated – texts in two or more languages)
- Parallel corpus (containing original texts in one or more languages with their respective translations)

A parallel corpus containing originals and translations may be unidirectional (L1 → L2) or bidirectional (L1 ↔ L2), the latter being both comparable and parallel in nature.

In modern contrastive studies, the bidirectional model is often endorsed as translations (in such a corpus) function as a solid *tertium comparationis*, i.e. 'a background of sameness, a constant, on which similarities as well as differences between the languages will show' (Ebeling and Ebeling 2013: 17). However, given the fact that not all text types are translated between languages, a comparable corpus may sometimes be the only option, even if it may not be ideal for contrastive analysis (Aijmer 2008: 278). The reason for this is that the *tertium comparationis* may be seen to be weaker, in the sense that it is harder to objectively guarantee full comparability between items across languages in this way. We rely on the comparability of the texts through factors such as text type, date of publication, topic and ultimately the bi- or multilingual knowledge of the researcher.

In this study, a comparable corpus is the main source of contrastive data. As the corpus is highly specialized and also matched at many levels of comparability (text type = match reports; date of publication = from the same year/season; topic = football at the highest competitive level in two countries; situational context = written by in-house journalists primarily for fans of the respective clubs), it is likely that the cross-linguistic observations will be valid.

3.2. The corpus

The ENMaRC is currently under construction and so far contains written football match reports from one season: the 2016/2017 season in the case of the English Premier League and the 2017 season in the case of the Norwegian 'Eliteserie'.[3]

There are some differences between the two leagues that have a bearing on the make-up of the corpus. First, there are twenty teams in the Premier League (PL) and sixteen in the 'Eliteserie' (ES). Moreover, while all the twenty PL teams regularly publish their reports, only thirteen ES teams do the same. The length of the reports also varies and the Norwegian ones are generally much shorter than the English ones. The English match reports range from around 12,000 to 38,000 words, whereas the Norwegian ones range from around 5,000 to 17,000. Thus, the size of the two subcorpora in terms of running words is not balanced, with the PL match reports reaching more than 500,000 tokens and the ES match reports reaching roughly 155,000 tokens (see the overview in Tables A and B in the Appendix).

Being downloaded from the respective clubs' official websites, the reports represent the clubs' own account of the matches, i.e. they are written by staff/journalists employed by the clubs, published online right after the final whistle. It will thus be interesting to see to what extent the reports are objective in their account of wins vs. losses (see Section 4.3.1).

The reports, each representing one game, were saved as raw text files, each of which was given a minimal header containing some relevant metadata. An example is given in (1), where the line in bold explains each tab-separated piece of information in the header (surrounded by < ... >).

Some post-processing of the downloaded texts was required, and typically involved removing the following features: images/videos + captions, team line-ups, URLs, links to interviews, name of journalist (often missing anyway),[4] clubs' copyright statement, (most) statements/quotes from players and managers, lists of 'talking points' (bullet points) and (most) thanks to fans/spectators. Following this manual 'clean-up', the corpus analysis tool, AntConc (Anthony 2014), was

(1)	Team	Season	Round	Home/ Away	Opposition	Date	Score	Win/ Draw/ Loss	URL
	<Arsenal	16/17	3	A	Watford	27/8	1–3	W	URL>

used in a bottom-up approach to explore and extract data from the corpus. Of most relevance are the concordance tool, clusters/n-grams tool and the word list and keyword list tools available in AntConc. By 'bottom-up' is meant that the analysis is primarily driven by the output from different types of frequency lists (word, n-gram and keyword lists).[5]

4. English and Norwegian match reports: Cross-linguistic tendencies

This section offers the first explorations of the ENMaRC as outlined in the introduction above. Frequency lists identifying recurring words and patterns in the English and Norwegian match reports will be scrutinized in Sections 4.1 and 4.2. Following the overviews of word lists in Section 4.1 and n-gram lists in Section 4.2, Section 4.3 focuses on keyword lists, more specifically the keywords of winning and losing in the English vs. Norwegian match reports (Section 4.3.1).

4.1. Word lists

The natural starting point for a general overview of the language represented in a corpus is to generate a (word) frequency list, which, according to Gries (2009: 12), is 'the most basic corpus-linguistic tool'. The Word list tool in AntConc ranks types according to frequency (in terms of tokens), and, not surprisingly, the top end of the lists in both the English and Norwegian subcorpora is dominated by function words (*the, a, to* ... /*i* 'in', *og* 'and', *på* 'on', etc.). This is similar to lists generated on the basis of general corpora in both languages.[6] Differences do, however, emerge quite quickly, especially with regard to which pronouns and lexical words first appear on the lists.

The most frequent pronouns in the English match reports are *his* (rank 13), *he* (rank 27), *their* (rank 36) and *we* (rank 83). In Norwegian, *vi* 'we' is, relatively speaking, even more frequent, at rank 19, followed by *han* 'he' (rank 21), *seg* '-self' (rank 24), and *de* 'they/the (pl.)' (rank 27).[7] In lists generated on the basis of large monolingual corpora (see endnote 6), *I/jeg* and *she/hun* are frequent; these are, for obvious reasons, completely absent from the match report lists, while more prominence, rank-wise, is given to *his* and *their* in English and *vi* 'we' in Norwegian.[8] The former point is interesting from a text-type perspective, while the latter point is interesting in a cross-linguistic perspective, as possessives are only found much further down the list in Norwegian, with *sin* 'his/her/its' at rank 60 and *hans* 'his' at rank 275. Possessives in English and Norwegian have, in fact, received some attention cross-linguistically, e.g. as one of the stated topics within the project 'Language as product and process' where English and Scandinavian are said to have only partially overlapping (possessive) systems.[9] This may be worth exploring further with regard to this specific text-type once the corpus contains more material.

As far as lexical words are concerned, some of the most frequent ones in the ENMaRC lists are nouns that, as expected, are clearly related to the overarching topic of the corpus texts: football. In both languages *goal/mål* and *ball/ballen* 'the ball' are found among the top 30. Table 3.1 gives a snapshot of types ranked according to frequency, highlighting the nouns ranked between 15 and 38. The reason for pruning the word lists in this way and not starting from the top is that the first noun is found at rank 15 in Norwegian (*ballen* 'the ball') and at rank 18 in English (*minutes*). In addition to the obvious football-related nouns, we also find a couple of nouns to do with time: *minutes* and *minutter*, both ranked

Table 3.1 Overview of the highest ranked nouns (highlighted) in the ENMaRC

	English		Norwegian		
Rank	# occ.	Type	# occ.	type	gloss
...	...	...	...	...	
15	...	...	1512	ballen	the ball
16	3735	at	1424	et	a (neuter)
17	3594	it	1411	fra	from
18	3033	minutes	1275	minutter	minutes
19	3016	into	1133	vi	we
20	2900	by	1050	inn	in
21	2769	goal	1024	han	he
22	2735	after	1012	ikke	not
23	2561	ball	984	er	is/are
24	2558	half	973	seg	-self
...	...	...	...	...	
30	2184	when	830	mål	goal
31	2173	who	826	kampen	the match
...	...	...	...	...	
37	1908	time	625	kom	came
38	1862	side	616	omgang	half

at 18 and *time*, ranked 37 in English. This last observation is in line with Levin's (2008) finding that an important feature of match reports is to specify time.

The frequency lists clearly set the current material apart from language in general. In the more general and representative corpora of English and Norwegian referred to above, the highest ranked (clear-cut) lexical word is a reporting verb (*said* at rank 53 and *sa* 'said' at rank 44). The first nouns to appear are *time* (rank 69) and *people* (rank 83) in English and *år* 'year' (rank 63) and *dag* 'day' (rank 98) in Norwegian.

4.2. N-gram lists

Comparing sequences of words (n-grams, lexical bundles) across languages has been shown to be challenging (see e.g. Granger 2014; Ebeling and Ebeling 2017; Hasselgård 2017). To meet some of the challenges, the n was set at 3–4 in AntConc, as this was thought to yield the most interesting n-grams in both languages. Although 2-grams might work well for Norwegian, producing frequent sequences such as *minutter senere* 'minutes later', the most frequent 2-grams in English are generally combinations of function words, e.g. *of the, in the*. It is also interesting to observe in Table 3.2 that no Norwegian 4-grams are found among the top 20 3-4-grams, although a couple of them are glossed as sequences of four words. This serves to illustrate, and indeed underline, one of the challenges in comparing n-gram lists across languages. For example, the 3-gram *ballen i mål* 'the ball in goal' would not work as a 3-gram in English because of the different ways of encoding definiteness in English (preceding article) and Norwegian (suffix). Moreover, *mål* 'goal' is indefinite in the Norwegian 3-gram but would have to be definite in English, i.e. 'the ball in the goal'.

Table 3.2 Top 20 3–4-Grams in the English and Norwegian Match Reports

Rank	English top-20 3-4 grams	Norwegian top-20 3-4 grams	Gloss
1	the second half	i andre omgang	in second half
2	edge of the	ballen i mål	the ball in goal
3	the edge of	i det # minutt	in the # minute
4	the edge of the	inn i feltet	in into the area
5	the premier league	i første omgang	in first half
6	of the season	de første minuttene	the first minutes

Rank	English top-20 3–4 grams	Norwegian top-20 3–4 grams	Gloss
7	the other end	alene med keeper	alone with keeper
8	of the game	men det var	but it was
9	at the other	og det var	and it was
10	at the other end	minutter før slutt	minutes before end
11	the home side	nok en gang	once again
12	over the bar	det var en	it was a
13	the first half	eirik ulland andersen	[proper name]
14	into the box	i feltet og	in the field and
15	from close range	etter å ha	after to have
16	in the premier	minutter ut i	minutes out in
17	in the premier league	til tross for	in spite of
18	it was a	det lengste hjørnet	the farthest corner
19	the penalty area	minutter senere var	minutes later was
20	the th minute	og det er	and it is

To some extent, n-gram lists in the English and Norwegian parts of the ENMaRC also lend support to Levin's observation regarding the presence of time-references in match reports. There is great overlap of frequent time expressions in English and Norwegian, including (*in*) *the th minute/i det (#) minutt*, *the second half/i andre omgang* 'in second half', *the first half/i første omgang* 'in first half'; see Table 3.2. All three sequences have been used by all clubs in the English match reports, while between nine and eleven of the thirteen Norwegian clubs have used them. Thus, we can safely say that an important feature for both the English and Norwegian match reporters is to specify when the action takes place. In fact, this is a characteristic that is more prominent in the Norwegian data: of the top 3–4-grams being used by at least half of the clubs, seven out of the top 20 are time expressions in Norwegian, compared to three in English.[10]

Further, Table 3.2 shows that, among the top 20 3–4-grams in English, spatial sequences, including the words *edge, end, bar* and *box*, e.g. *edge of the box, the other end, over the bar*, seem to be more salient than the temporal ones, e.g. *minutes from time, before half time*. The only 3-gram bearing resemblance to any of the English spatial sequences in the top 20 Norwegian 3–4-grams is *inn i feltet* 'into the area'.

Thus, the English match reports seem to rely heavily on where on the pitch the action takes place and when it happened, e.g. the 3-gram *the edge of* and *the th minute*, as shown in examples (2) and (3), and similarly with n-grams denoting time in the Norwegian material, e.g. *de første minuttene* 'the first minutes' in example (4).

(2) Okazaki went for goal from *the edge of* the penalty area ... (MFC)
(3) Our reward came in *the 56th minute* when Alex Iwobi scored ... (AFC)
(4) *De første minuttene* av kampen eies av Odd ... (OBK)
Lit.: The first minutes of the game are owned by Odd

These observations are more or less in agreement with findings in previous cross-linguistic studies of fiction texts, where it has been shown that temporal expressions are more frequently used in Norwegian fiction than in English fiction (Ebeling et al. 2013; Hasselgård 2017), while spatial ones seem to be more frequently used in English when compared to Norwegian (Ebeling and Ebeling 2017), although morpho-syntactic differences may play a role here (Ebeling and Ebeling 2017: 25ff). The fact that these two text types (fiction and match reports) behave similarly in their use of temporal and spatial expressions may indicate some general trends in English vs. Norwegian.

A final tendency worth reporting from the n-gram lists, also noted by Levin (2008), is the fact that frequently occurring sequences in the two languages typically refer to goals (not) scored. The way in which this is commonly done includes n-grams featuring *net/nettet* 'the net' and *goal/mål*. Levin's (2008) point about semi-fixed phrases having gained conventionalized functions in newspaper match reports also seems to hold for online, in-house match reports, as in the case of <u>hit</u> *the ball in the net* = goal and <u>have</u> *the ball in the net* = disallowed goal (see Section 2). The ENMaRC material further suggests that, while a disallowed goal requires a form of the verb HAVE, as in example (5), most expressions containing the sequence V + NP *in(to) the net* reflect that a goal is scored, i.e. the verb HIT is not a requirement, as attested in (6).

(5) ... and when he did <u>have</u> *the ball in the back of the net* three minutes after the restart, the flag was up for offside. (MU)
(6) ... who <u>sent</u> *a beautiful half volley into the back of the net* for his maiden City goal (LC)

The n-gram lists suggest that English has a wider range of expressions available to refer to the goal-scoring part of the game, including recurrent word-combinations with (V +) *home (from close range)*, (V + *the ball*) *past* and (*into the side-*)*netting* where the former two typically refer to goals scored, and the latter to goals not scored. Examples (7)–(9) serve to illustrate these semi-fixed phraseologies.

(7) ... found its way to Calum Chambers who poked *home* from close range. (MC)
(8) ... when Theo Walcott rolled *the ball past* Willy Caballero. (AFC)
(9) ... who saw his effort smash *into the side-netting*. (AFCB)

Although similar expressions to those in (8) and (9) are also attested in the Norwegian material (e.g. V + *ballen bak* as in *heade ballen bak* 'head the ball behind' and V + *ballen i nettveggen* as in *satte ballen i nettveggen* 'put the ball in the net wall'), they do not match the English expressions in terms of frequency of recurrence. The most frequent phraseologies in Norwegian do not seem to recur as identical 3–4 grams; however, interrupted sequences such as V + *i mål* 'in goal' are highly recurrent with more than 200 hits, typically with a span of 1–5 words between the verb and *i mål*, an example of which is given in (10).

(10) ... og han *headet* ballen *i mål* fra to meter. (TIL)
Lit.: '... and he headed the ball in goal from two meters'

4.3. Keyword lists

4.3.1. The language of winning and losing

Although the focus and approach in the current chapter are very different from Richard's (2008) referred to above, some bias in the match reports may be expected with regard to the clubs' account of victory vs. defeat.

The first step in this part of the study was to split the English and Norwegian subcorpora into texts reporting on the individual teams' wins, draws and losses. The keyword list function in AntConc was used to compare the win files with the combined draw-and-loss files as a reference corpus, and similarly for the loss files with the combined draw-and-win files as a reference corpus. The default setting for generating keywords in AntConc is Log Likelihood (see Anthony 2014); this was thus the statistical measure applied in the current study to calculate the keyness of words in the win vs. loss files. More than 500 win keywords in both English (502) and Norwegian (537) were above the significance value of 3.84 (95th percentile; 5% level; $p < 0.05$). The cross-linguistic comparison will focus on the ones that are above the significance value of 10.83 (99.9th percentile; 0.1% level; $p < 0.001$), where English has ninety-three win keywords, while Norwegian has thirty-three. As far as the loss keywords are concerned, English has sixty-one above the 99th percentile threshold, while Norwegian has twenty-one. See Tables C and D in the Appendix for an overview of the win and loss keywords.

Although perhaps not (cross-)linguistically very interesting, quite a few proper nouns, mainly including references to players and teams, feature on both the winning and losing keyword lists in the two languages. Nevertheless, it is somewhat intriguing to note how the teams typically refer extensively to some of their own players rather than the oppositions'. One curious case in this respect is the keyword 'sanchez', ranked 2 in the English loss keywords. In most of these instances reference is made to Alexis Sanchéz by the opposing team. However, the keyword 'alexis' is found at rank 11 in the English win keywords mainly due to the frequent use of 'Alexis' by his own team's (Arsenal) reporters. Generally, reference to players is more prominent among the win keywords in the Premier League texts, whereas the opposite tendency is noted in the 'Eliteserie' texts. We can only speculate whether this reflects a tendency to name players in a positive context in English (giving credit for success) and in a negative context in Norwegian (blaming players for defeat). In order to establish this with any certainty, a more thorough investigation is called for.

Not unexpectedly, the win lists are dominated by clearly positive keywords, e.g. *win, victory, memorable, seier* 'win', *deilig* 'wonderful', *jubel* 'cheer'. Even some of the nouns that seem to be more general in nature turn out to be used in positive turns of phrase, as the case of *rad* 'row' in example (11), where it is understood that *5 på rad* '5 in a row' means 5 victories in a row.

(11)   … og dermed er 5 på <u>rad</u> er et faktum! (OBK)
Lit.:   and so is 5 in a row a fact

The one arguably negative keyword in the English win list – *nervy* – demonstrates the importance of a win in the closing minutes of a game, illustrated by a typical example in (12), thus revealing a phraseology of *nervy* (with a positive outcome) that may be unique to this material?

(12)   We looked to be in for a *nervy* last 10 minutes or so, but Alexis smashed home a crucial third goal on 83 minutes. (AFC)

A similar trend for the lists generated from the loss texts can be noted, i.e. they are dominated by negative keywords, e.g. *defeat, disappointing, beaten, tap* 'loss/ defeat', *tapte* 'lost', *verst* 'worse/worst'. Some of these items are worth commenting on, as both cross-linguistic similarities and differences emerge. First of all, the items with the highest keyness score in both languages – *defeat* and *tap* – speak for themselves, in the sense that reporters in both languages feel the need to hit home that they have witnessed their team lose, without hiding behind a euphemism.

On the other hand, a difference that can be observed is the preference in the English loss reports for a passive verb phrase with *beaten* (example 13), while the active *tapte* 'lost' (example 14) is the favoured verb of defeat in the Norwegian ones. This suggests that the reporters operate from opposite perspectives. In a sense the Norwegian reporters are more direct, blaming their own players for actively losing, while the English players are depicted as being less responsible for the defeat; they are the affected participant.

(13) The Tigers were *beaten* 1–0 by Middlesbrough at the Riverside Stadium on Monday night. (HC)[11]
(14) Godset *tapte* 3–0 borte mot Brann i den andre serierunden. (SIF)[12]
Lit.: Godset lost 3–0 away against Brann in the second round

An unexpected finding, and related to the observation about seemingly opposite perspectives, was that personal pronouns and possessive determiners feature in the keyword lists. The types of pronouns and determiners are found to differ between the two languages. This is seemingly one of the main points of contrast between the English and Norwegian match reports that can be deduced from all the lists generated in this study. However, the overwhelming keyness of *we, our* and *us* in the English win material in particular is not due to a general trend, but rather down to three teams' ways of reporting in particular – Arsenal, Chelsea and Tottenham. Nevertheless, Table 3.3 gives an overview of the items in question.

Quite clearly, the reporters from these three teams are typically identifying themselves as part of the team they are working for: the use of *we, our* and *us* in examples (15)–(17) all attest to this. The report is seen from the perspective of different categories of members of the club: players, fans or indeed reporters who are very often seen as the main protagonists in the action leading to victory.

(15) *We* started the game determined to stamp *our* authority … (AFC)
(16) The Belgian instigated *our* first clear chance, … (CFC)

Table 3.3 Most prominent personal pronouns/possessive determiners among the keywords

English win	Norwegian win	English loss	Norwegian loss
we	han 'he'	they	vi 'we'
our			
us			

(17) Kieran Trippier [...] combined twice with Kane to send *us* on *our* way ... (TH)

More interesting, perhaps, is the keyness of English *they* versus Norwegian *vi* 'we' in the loss reports, as these have a much better distribution across the reports. Although *they* may be used to refer to the opposition, it is also used to refer to 'us', i.e. the reporters use *they* to distance themselves from their own team, by using a third person pronoun, as in example (18), where the Sunderland reporter writes about Sunderland players' using *they*. The Norwegian in-house journalists, on the other hand, stand tall and report defeats from a *vi* perspective, as in example (19), even *vi tapte* 'we lost' is used in some cases, as shown in example (20).

(18) Moments later *they* were watching once more, and this time they were punished. (SAFC)
(19) Det ble kanskje ikke poeng i dag, men *vi* har i alle fall Norges beste supportere. (SIF)
Lit.: It may not have been any points today but we have at least Norway's best supporters
(20) ... *vi tapte* til slutt etter overtidsdrama. (TIL)
Lit.: We lost in the end after an injury time drama

A more thorough analysis of the uses of personal pronouns in the match reports is clearly called for as their keyness seems to point to some potentially interesting differences in their use across the two languages.

Regarding the use of euphemisms to report on defeats (see Richard 2008), this is not in evidence in the current material in either language. However, the Norwegian reporters seem to reveal a softer spot for their players through their use of the adjective *uheldig* 'unlucky', very often followed by the name of the unlucky player, as in example (21).

(21) Ballen spratt i stolpen, før en *uheldig Jakob Glesnes* satte ballen i eget nett. (SIF)
Lit.: The ball hit the post before an unlucky Jakob Glesnes put the ball in his own net

Finally, a similarity between the English and Norwegian reports on defeats is the presence of the keywords *hope(s)* and *håp* 'hope'. Although they, in some cases, reflect genuine hope for the future, this is very rarely the case. The only attested example in the loss files is (22) where *hope* functions as a verb. Generally, the context reveals that they are dashed hopes, as in (23) and (24). Thus, English and Norwegian seem to agree on a preference for hopes not being fulfilled.

(22) West Ham will *hope* to turn their fortunes around in the EFL Cup on Wednesday as they host Accrington Stanley. (WHU)
(23) However those *hopes* were dashed on 55 minutes when the Gunners added a second. (CPFC)
(24) Det tente et ørlite *håp* som ble knust desto mer brutalt fem minutter etter. (VFK)
Lit.: That lit a tiny hope that was dashed even more brutally five minutes later

5. Conclusion

The corpus linguistic methods used in this study have revealed some of the potential of a highly specialized comparable corpus for use in cross-linguistic studies. Admittedly, the study has but scratched the surface by scrutinizing different types of frequency lists from different angles, i.e. word lists, n-gram lists and keyword lists. Even if these have not been exploited to the full in this chapter, as only some of the most salient features emerging from the lists have been commented on, they have provided food for thought, pointing to several avenues for further research.

Moreover, the keyword lists generated for victory vs. defeat suggest that, from a cross-linguistic perspective, it would be particularly rewarding to look more deeply into the use of active vs. passive voice and the use of personal pronouns.

Although this study has mainly been word-based in its approach (Sections 4.1 and 4.3.1), some insights extending beyond the word have been provided, notably in the section on n-gram lists (4.2), but also in the previous section (4.3.1) where observations were made on the extended contexts for certain keywords. It was speculated that some of the observed phraseologies may prove to be typical of match reports in English and/or Norwegian, as in the case of *nervy* used in positive contexts in the English (win) match reports and in the case of *hope/håp* typically being used in contexts where hopes are dashed in the loss match reports. While awaiting further study, it is tempting to speculate that seemingly positive words (e.g. *hope/håp*) in the loss keyword lists and seemingly negative words (e.g. *nervy*) in the win keyword lists take on a semantic prosody that is the opposite of what might be the case in general language.[13] As suggested by these potentially football(/sports)-specific phraseologies, and, as pointed out by Bergh and Ohlander (2016: 36), 'football language is also special by virtue of certain syntactic and semantic features, [...] related to the situational context of football as well as to certain specific football-related genres, such as match reports and commentary'. At a more general level,

> all special subject areas tend to create their own contextual framework, involving a specific semantic-pragmatic sphere. This, in turn, paves the way for constructions and collocations that may deviate considerably – even spectacularly – from those applying in general language, thus helping to distinguish special languages from general language. Football language, it appears, is an obvious case in point. (ibid.: 37)

For future studies it is crucial that the ENMaRC continues to grow, so that a larger set of match reports is available in both languages. This is particularly important for more phraseologically geared investigations that can tell us more about the lexico-grammatical nature of this specialized text type across languages.

Acknowledgements

Credit is given to all the football clubs for making their match reports available online – see Tables A and B in the Appendix for pointers to the clubs' home pages (i.e. the sources of all the material included in the ENMaRC). I am grateful to two anonymous reviewers for their suggestions and feedback on a previous version of this chapter.

Notes

1   See Johansson (2007) and the ENPC bibliography at http://www.hf.uio.no/ilos/tjenester/kunnskap/sprak/omc/enpc_espc_publications_2014.pdf
2   Levin, in collaboration with Callies, has more recently studied features of football reporting in a contrastive perspective (Callies and Levin, this volume).
3   While the football season in England runs from August until May (hence 2016/2017), the Norwegian season runs from March until November (hence 2017).
4   The clubs who do name the journalist/reporter generally seem to have two or three different people as part of their match report staff.
5   See also Juknevičienė and Viluckas (this volume) who use similar methods in their study of computer- vs. human-mediated language in football reports.

6   Comparisons were made with lists generated on the basis of the British National Corpus (for English) (http://ucrel.lancs.ac.uk/bncfreq/lists/1_2_all_freq.txt – list generated by UCREL, Lancaster University) and on the basis of novels and newspapers (for Norwegian) (http://www.korrekturavdelingen.no/ord-uttrykk-frekvensordliste-500-vanligste-norsk.htm – list generated by the University of Bergen).
7   All these pronouns, with the exception of *vi* 'we', have been used by all the clubs. Not surprisingly, the only club that has not used *vi* is Sogndal, and the reason for this is the fact that their match reports are written in the *nynorsk* standard, where the first-person plural pronoun is *me* 'we'. The remaining match reports are written in the *bokmål* standard, where the first-person plural pronoun is *vi* 'we'.
8   *It* and *det* 'it', at rank 17 and 4 respectively, are perhaps less interesting, as they are ranked 7 and 3 in the general corpora.
9   http://www.hf.uio.no/ilos/english/research/projects/language-as-product-and-process/index.html. See also Behrens (2017).
10 In addition to the three already mentioned, Norwegian also has the following among the top 20: *de første minuttene* 'the first minutes', *minutter før slutt* 'minutes before end', *minutter ut i* 'minutes into', *minutter senere var* 'minutes later was'.
11 The Tigers is the nickname for Hull City (HC).
12 Godset 'the Estate' is the nickname for Strømsgodset (SIF).
13 Semantic prosody refers to the communicative function of extended units of meaning (Sinclair 1996; Stubbs 2013), i.e. 'the semantic prosody of an item is the reason why it is chosen, over and above the semantic preferences that also characterise it' (Sinclair 1998: 20).
14 FC in the abbreviations stands for 'Football Club', while AFC stands for 'Association Football Club', with the exception of Arsenal Football Club (AFC).
15 The three Norwegian clubs that do not publish match reports online are Brann, Haugesund and Molde.
16 FK in the abbreviations stands for *fotballklubb* 'football club', BK stands for *ballklubb* 'ball club', IF and IL stand for *idrettsforening/idrettslag* 'sports club', and F stands for *fotball* 'football'.
17 *Pris* as in *sette pris på* 'set price on' = 'appreciate'.

References

Aijmer, K. (2008), 'Parallel Corpora and Comparable Corpora', in A. Lüdeling and M. Kytö (eds), *Corpus Linguistics. An International Handbook, Vol. 1*, 275–292, Berlin/New York: Walter de Gruyter.

Anthony, L. (2014), *AntConc (Version 3.4.2)* [Computer Software], Tokyo, Japan: Waseda University. Available online: http://www.laurenceanthony.net/software.

Behrens, B. (2017), 'Processing Possessives in Translation between Unequal Systems. An Exploratory Study', *Oslo Studies in Language (OSLa)*, 9 (2): 105–136.

Bergh, G. and S. Ohlander (2012), 'Free Kicks, Dribblers and WAGs. Exploring the Language of "the People's Game"', *Moderna spark*, 106 (1): 11–46.

Bergh, G. and S. Ohlander (2016), 'Iniesta Passed and Messi Finished Clinically: Football Verbs and Transitivity', *Nordic Journal of English Studies*, 15 (2): 19–38.

Ebeling, J. and S. O. Ebeling (2013), *Patterns in Contrast*, Amsterdam: John Benjamins.

Ebeling, S. O. and J. Ebeling (2017), 'A Cross-linguistic Comparison of Recurrent Word Combinations in a Comparable Corpus of English and Norwegian Fiction', in M. Janebová, E. Lapshinova-Koltunski and M. Martinková (eds), *Contrasting English and Other Languages through Corpora*, 2–31, Newcastle: Cambridge Scholars Publishing.

Ebeling, J., S. O. Ebeling and H. Hasselgård (2013), 'Using Recurrent Word-combinations to Explore Cross-linguistic Differences', in K. Aijmer and B. Altenberg (eds), *Advances in Corpus-based Contrastive Linguistics: Studies in Honour of Stig Johansson*, 177–199, Amsterdam: John Benjamins.

Granger, S. (2014), 'A Lexical Bundle Approach to Comparing Languages: Stems in English and French', in M.-A. Lefer and S. Vogeleer (eds), *Genre- and Register-related Discourse Features in Contrast, Special Issue of Languages in Contrast*, 14 (1): 58–72.

Gries, St. Th. (2009), *Quantitative Corpus Linguistics with R. A Practical Introduction*, New York/London: Routledge.

Hasselgård, H. (2017), 'Temporal Expressions in English and Norwegian', in M. Janebová, E. Lapshinova-Koltunski and M. Martinková (eds), *Contrasting English and Other Languages through Corpora*, 75–101, Newcastle: Cambridge Scholars Publishing.

Johansson, S. (2007), *Seeing through Multilingual Corpora. On the Use of Corpora in Contrastive Studies*, Amsterdam: John Benjamins Publishing Company.

Kuiper, K. (1996), *Smooth Talkers: The Linguistic Performance of Auctioneers and Sportcasters*, Mahwah, NJ: L. Erlbaum Associates.

Lavric, E. (2008), 'Introduction', in E. Lavric, G. Pisek, A. Skinner and W. Stadler (eds), *The Linguistics of Football*, 5–8, Tübingen: Günter Narr.

Lavric, E., G. Pisek, A. Skinner and W. Stadler, eds. (2008), *The Linguistics of Football*, Tübingen: Günter Narr.

Levin, M. (2008), '"Hitting the Back of the Net Just before the Final Whistle": High-frequency Phrases in Football Reporting', in E. Lavric, G. Pisek, A. Skinner and W. Stadler (eds), *The Linguistics of Football*, 143–155, Tübingen: Narr.

Meier, S. (2017), 'Korpora zur Fußballlinguistik – eine Mehrsprachige Forschungsressource zur Sprache der Fußballberichterstattung', *Zeitschrift für Germanistische Linguistik*, 42 (2): 345–349.

Richard, A. (2008), 'Televised Football Commentaries: Descriptions, Narrations and Representations of a Non-victory. The European Club Championship Final 1996

(Bayern Munich vs AS Saint-Étienne)', in E. Lavric, G. Pisek, A. Skinner and W. Stadler (eds), *The Linguistics of Football*, 193–203, Tübingen: Günter Narr.

Sinclair, J. (1996), 'The Search for Units of Meaning', *Textus*, IX: 75–106.

Sinclair, J. (1998), 'The Lexical Item', in E. Weigand (ed.), *Contrastive Lexical Semantics*, 1–24, Amsterdam/Philadelphia, PA: John Benjamins.

Stubbs, M. (2013), 'Sequence and Order. The Neo-Firthian Tradition of Corpus Semantics', in H. Hasselgård, J. Ebeling and S.O. Ebeling (eds), *Corpus Perspectives on Patterns of Lexis*, 13–24, Amsterdam/Philadelphia, PA: John Benjamins.

Appendix

Table A Overview of premiership teams, URLs and tokens in the individual corpus files

Corpus id./ Club abbr.[14]	Team	URL	# of words in ENMaRC (AntConc counts)
AFC	Arsenal	http://www.arsenal.com/	32,892
AFCB	Bournemouth	http://www.afcb.co.uk/	24,107
BFC	Burnley	http://www.burnleyfootballclub.com/	29,342
CFC	Chelsea	https://www.chelseafc.com/	35,998
CPFC	Crystal Palace	http://www.cpfc.co.uk/	24,664
EFC	Everton	http://www.evertonfc.com/	38,223
HC	Hull City	http://www.hullcitytigers.com/	24,475
LC	Leicester City	http://www.lcfc.com/	23,412
LFC	Liverpool	http://www.liverpoolfc.com/	25,845
MC	Manchester City	http://www.mancity.com/	26,668
MU	Manchester United	http://www.manutd.com/	25,886
MFC	Middlesbrough	http://www.mfc.co.uk/	25,161
SFC	Southampton	https://southamptonfc.com/	23,316
SC	Stoke City	http://www.stokecityfc.com/	22,423

Corpus id./ Club abbr.[14]	Team	URL	# of words in ENMaRC (AntConc counts)
SAFC	Sunderland	https://www.safc.com/	27,202
SCAFC	Swansea City	http://www.swanseacity.net/	29,276
TH	Tottenham Hotspur	http://www.tottenhamhotspur.com/	31,171
WFC	Watford	https://www.watfordfc.com/	23,113
WBA	West Bromwich Albion[a]	http://www.wba.co.uk/	12,076
WHU	West Ham United[b]	http://www.whufc.com/	18,134
			Total: 523,384 (9,599 types)

[a] two games: no report.
[b] six games: no report.

Table B Overview of *Eliteserie* teams, URLs and tokens in the individual corpus files[15]

Corpus id./ Club abbr.[16]	Team	URL	# of tokens in ENMaRC (AntConc counts)
AaFK	Aalesund	http://www.aafk.no/	16,903
KBK	Kristiansund	http://www.kristiansundbk.no/	13,767
LSK	Lillestrøm	http://www.lsk.no/	11,932
OBK	Odd	http://www.odd.no/	12,100
RBK	Rosenborg	http://www.rbk.no/	8,585
SaF	Sandefjord	http://www.sandefjordfotball.no/	8,821
S08	Sarpsborg 08	http://www.sarpsborg08.no/	12,653
SoF	Sogndal	http://www.sogndalfotball.no/	4,901
STB	Stabæk	http://www.stabak.no	9,567

Corpus id./ Club abbr.[16]	Team	URL	# of tokens in ENMaRC (AntConc counts)
SIF	Strømsgodset	http://www.godset.no/	11,999
TIL	Tromsø	http://www.til.no/	13,481
VFK	Viking	http://www.viking-fk.no/	17,551
VIF	Vålerenga	http://www.vif-fotball.no/	12,487
			154,747 (8,815 types)

Table C Win keywords in the English and Norwegian match reports (shaded cells contain proper nouns)

English				Norwegian				
Rank	Freq.	LL	keyword	Rank	Freq.	LL	keyword	gloss
1	602	321.291	we	1	121	75.72	seier	victory
2	399	211.13	our	2	82	40.188	eliteserien	
3	399	102.569	win	3	44	37.494	seieren	the victory
4	260	102.419	victory	4	25	34.176	deilig	wonderful
5	172	88.197	mins	5	165	25.846	tre	three
6	127	76.87	dele	6	21	24.081	borteseier	away victory
7	299	69.681	blues	7	28	23.684	sikret	secured
8	167	68.49	diego	8	19	20.769	spennende	exciting
9	200	65.948	hazard	9	31	18.147	publikum	audience
10	1349	58.357	goal	10	20	17.763	jubel	cheer
11	163	54.784	alexis	11	13	16.305	enga	
12	360	44.862	points	12	19	16.279	sterk	strong
13	200	44.142	kane	13	11	16.254	feire	celebrate
14	146	43.15	pedro	14	33	15.625	helland	
15	60	41.467	kante	15	434	15.507	han	he
16	115	41.15	us	16	17	15.303	strake	straight/in a row
17	425	39.617	this	17	26	14.669	viktige	important
18	97	36.65	willian	18	51	14.465	plass	place

English				Norwegian				
Rank	Freq.	LL	keyword	Rank	Freq.	LL	keyword	gloss
19	92	35.355	fabregas	19	7	14.148	trepoenger	a three-point game
20	1662	32.491	it	20	41	13.306	bassel	
21	130	32.163	son	21	18	13.069	fjerde	fourth
22	248	27.584	goals	22	11	12.881	pangstart	flying start
23	295	27.365	team	23	23	12.344	tabellen	the table
24	45	27.038	style	24	26	12.277	rad	row
25	676	26.788	league	25	38	12.173	år	year
26	96	26.77	has	26	6	12.127	magi	magic
27	65	25.897	wins	27	6	12.127	pris	appreciate[17]
28	102	25.512	is	28	12	11.957	tokki	
29	5192	25.503	and	29	162	11.775	odd	
30	23	24.638	ovation	30	63	11.2	nå	now
31	32	24.281	memorable					
32	173	24.068	costa					
33	77	23.989	see					
34	78	23.877	alonso					
35	42	23.602	sheet					
36	28	23.499	ways					
37	87	23.089	moses					
38	72	22.632	conte					
39	389	21.098	season					
40	220	20.998	reds					
41	93	20.41	perfect					
42	173	19.955	what					
43	447	19.85	three					
44	50	19.741	matic					
45	163	19.594	so					
46	26	18.692	nervy					
47	46	18.255	dembele					
48	101	18.218	table					
49	24	18.211	welcome					
50	55	17.835	news					

English				Norwegian				
Rank	Freq.	LL	keyword	Rank	Freq.	LL	keyword	gloss
51	320	17.16	th					
52	147	17.056	swansea					
53	47	16.94	sissoko					
54	143	16.911	move					
55	3812	16.902	in					
56	482	16.855	premier					
57	138	16.735	eriksen					
58	335	16.478	all					
59	21	16.477	capped					
60	13	16.476	special					
61	86	15.616	control					
62	53	15.2	secured					
63	20	15.176	marked					
64	40	14.883	seal					
65	60	14.72	cahill					
66	27	14.617	trippier					
67	8	13.904	hennessy					
68	8	13.904	small					
69	29	13.877	batshuayi					
70	35	13.587	adding					
71	27	13.158	total					
72	13	12.988	merited					
73	28	12.842	kieran					
74	21	12.618	truly					
75	86	12.577	player					
76	1102	12.53	he					
77	46	12.228	you					
78	7	12.166	absolute					
79	7	12.166	spoken					
80	16	12.141	wembley					
81	22	12.139	gibbs					
82	31	12.1	yaya					
83	214	11.882	him					
84	97	11.828	winning					
85	62	11.72	luiz					

English				Norwegian				
Rank	Freq.	LL	keyword	Rank	Freq.	LL	keyword	gloss
86	97	11.334	deserved					
87	92	11.157	year					
88	64	11.068	fifth					
89	21	11.034	celebrated					
90	21	11.034	emphatic					
91	21	11.034	standing					
92	39	11.015	dominant					
93	83	10.867	performance					

Table D Loss keywords in the English and Norwegian match reports (shaded cells contain proper nouns)

English				Norwegian				
Rank	Freq.	LL	keyword	Rank	Freq.	LL	keyword	gloss
1	250	221.15	defeat	1	102	132.569	tap	loss/defeat
2	90	57.338	sanchez	2	45	48.668	tapte	lost
3	44	51.353	disappointing	3	180	30.198	viking	
4	275	48.832	swans	4	25	27.038	vif	
5	155	48.635	tigers	5	29	26.137	desverre	unfortunately
6	2003	44.256	as	6	451	22.845	ikke	not
7	61	43.633	suffered	7	17	19.488	verst	worse/worst
8	126	41.56	cats	8	138	17.751	hjemmelaget	home team
9	180	36.901	clarets	9	16	15.334	reise	travel
10	129	36.412	black	10	486	15.334	vi	we
11	576	35.661	they	11	14	14.622	wichne	
12	39	33.898	worse	12	23	14.288	kwarasey	
13	91	33.232	beaten	13	12	14.098	ajeti	
14	57	31.344	clucas	14	20	13.478	håp	hope
15	60	27.736	blow	15	20	11.989	amund	
16	94	27.731	tottenham	16	6	11.86	gabrielsen	
17	102	27.243	unable	17	6	11.86	håland	
18	242	26.787	chelsea	18	32	11.631	ingebrigtsen	
19	201	23.885	change	19	25	11.53	norø	
20	17	23.315	mountain	20	16	11.431	uheldig	unlucky
21	21	21.435	undone	21	42	10.855	lite	little

English				Norwegian				
Rank	Freq.	LL	keyword	Rank	Freq.	LL	keyword	gloss
22	1217	20.528	minutes					
23	51	19.306	moyes					
24	222	18.853	sunderland					
25	52	18.482	routledge					
26	9	18.152	hernández					
27	32	17.956	borja					
28	37	17.75	comeback					
29	41	15.831	hope					
30	27	15.807	eleven					
31	107	15.776	gray					
32	479	15.734	box					
33	30	15.587	markovic					
34	34	15.537	empty					
35	79	15.107	llorente					
36	12	14.534	wounds					
37	35	14.53	deficit					
38	28	14.468	abel					
39	10	14.374	condemn					
40	10	14.374	salt					
41	570	14.274	made					
42	347	14.267	saw					
43	20	14.095	defeated					
44	73	13.657	allowed					
45	34	13.499	hopes					
46	150	13.41	fell					
47	309	13.251	later					
48	111	12.9	failed					
49	135	12.657	once					
50	9	12.558	avert					
51	21	12.444	fray					
52	15	12.297	cruel					
53	23	12.275	montero					
54	6	12.101	holmesdale					
55	6	12.101	tasked					
56	16	11.933	unfortunately					

English				Norwegian				
Rank	Freq.	LL	keyword	Rank	Freq.	LL	keyword	gloss
57	124	11.786	despite					
58	169	11.611	get					
59	25	11.11	phelan					
60	25	11.11	reduced					
61	771	11.056	their					
62	14	10.873	miserable					
63	14	10.873	spirited					

4

Lexical Features of Football Reports: Computer- vs. Human-mediated Language

Rita Juknevičienė and Paulius Viluckas

1. Introduction

Sports discourse, as any other variety of language, is inevitably influenced by interactions between computers and human language. Computer games represent an area in which computer-mediated communication is an important aspect. Sports software packages are developed to cover all aspects of real sports events, which, among other elements, include verbal sports reports. One such video gaming platform is 'Football Manager 2017' (henceforth: FM), a licensed football video game developed and released by Sports Interactive Limited. It is a typical example of computer-mediated communication: having played a video match, the player may instantly read an automatically generated report of that match. Similarly, real-life matches are reported in the media, the only difference being the authorship, i.e. they are originally written by real sports reporters. As any traditional match reports, FM linguistic output covers key events of the match with brief comments on the progress of the game. FM reports could thus be seen as examples of computer-mediated football language which imitates texts written by professional sports reporters. Yet how similar those reports are to human-mediated football language remains unknown.

The present study was undertaken to analyse the language of football in computer- vs. human-mediated reports by using the corpus-driven approach (Tognini-Bonelli 2001). The two modes of football reports are represented in this study by FM reports and real football language published on a sports news portal. FM was chosen subjectively by the authors as a computerized football game that generates the largest amount of language in comparison to any other sports gaming platform. To match its linguistic output, the BBC online football reports were used as an example of authentic English-mediated football discourse. The BBC website covers a wide range of matches played in different football leagues rather than events within one national football association, and in this respect BBC reports are comparable to FM reports, which made them the most suitable source of human-mediated football reports for the purposes of this study.

Linguistic research into football language has experienced a considerable growth in the last decade with quite a few studies published on football discourse in different languages. Cross-linguistic and cross-cultural studies in this field seem to represent the most extensive research strand (e.g. Anchimbe 2008; Jung 2008; Bergh and Ohlander 2012a; Lewandowski 2013; Rossing and Skrubbeltrang 2016). As for English, it is rightly noted by Bergh and Ohlander that linguistic research into the language of the so-called 'people's game', or one of the most popular sports in the world invented by the English, remains surprisingly limited, especially in comparison to other fields of English for specific purposes (2012a: 19–21). Even if research into football discourse produced in English has not been extensive, several studies report that the English language is exerting a substantial influence with a number of English football terms used in other languages (Sępek 2008; Bergh and Ohlander 2012b; Balteiro 2018). As regards computer games, the English version is usually developed for most products available on the market, so research into linguistic features of computer-game English is an area that may be expected to grow.

Football vocabulary has been the focus of several studies which could be ascribed to one of the two major research directions. Some studies deal with specific terms expressed by single lexemes, e.g. action verbs (Uchechukwu 2008), fatal events (Fortington et al. 2018), proper names and nicknames (Calderón 2008). Yet there are studies which place multi-word units at the focus of attention, which possibly reflects the current interest in phraseology. Researchers have investigated different types of multi-word units, e.g. idioms (Matulina and Ćoralić 2008), metaphorical expressions (Nordin 2008; Vierkant 2008), semi-fixed phrases (Levin 2008), often investigated as realizations of metaphor and/or metonymy in language. Although these studies discuss the use of one pre-selected type of multi-word unit, they provide convincing evidence that there is a considerable degree of formulaicity in football discourse which might be interesting to investigate by the application of the corpus-driven approach.

Football language chosen for linguistic analyses represents different varieties and registers. For obvious reasons, for quite some time the choice of media was limited to TV and radio (e.g. Makarova 2008; Balzer-Siber 2015) which often involved spoken comments or written reports. Increasingly, however, computer-mediated communication is gaining attention. A good example of such discourse is a written online sports commentary which combines elements of spoken and written language. Several recent studies focus on real-time online football commentaries as a new specialized register and its cross-cultural features (Pérez-Sabater et al. 2008; Werner 2016) while others use it as a source for the analysis of specific linguistic phenomena (Jucker 2010; Bergh 2011). As regards the language of computerized sports games, to the best of our knowledge, none of the previous studies compared human- and computer-mediated football language, which is the niche that this study aims to fill in.

The present study focuses on the vocabulary of football reports and aims to shed light on those lexical features which can be captured through corpus-driven analyses. Firstly, two corpora of after-match football reports were compared for keywords. Secondly, the lexical bundle approach was used in order to establish to what extent computer- and human-mediated reporting is (dis)similar in terms of recurrent word sequences. The study is expected to answer the following research questions: (1) what are the keywords distinguishing one mode of football reporting from the other? (2) is there a relationship between the mode of football reporting and qualitative (structural and functional) features of lexical bundles?

2. Materials and methods

To compare human- and computer-generated football reports, two corpora of football match reports were compiled, each containing 200 texts. As mentioned above, after-match football reports are texts which give a chronological description of a football match and cover all major events that took place on the pitch. The following section will present a more detailed description of each corpus and research methods.

The first corpus used in this study and henceforth referred to as $Corpus_{FM}$ consists of reports generated by the video game 'Football Manager 2017' which has been developed by Sports Interactive Limited (http://www.footballmanager.com/games/football-manager-2017). The algorithm for match reporting in this game produces a coherent text at the end of each game which is supposed to replicate real-life football reports. Based on personal experience of the authors, FM reports were considered to be a suitable source of rather elaborate football language generated by a computerized sports game software. The key events reported by FM include (own) goals, yellow/red cards, injuries that force a player to leave the pitch, and penalties. A certain key event in the match triggers a string of text in the match report, for instance, a goal from a distance of 30 yards would be described as a *30-yard screamer* implying that the goal was scored by means of a very powerful long-range shot. It should also be noted that FM does not have a pre-set storyline, which means that the language algorithm generates each report anew and covers the main events of the last match played in the sequence in which these appeared on the computer screen. Furthermore, since FM reporting imitates football reporting in real life, each report starts with an opening paragraph and a brief mention of a few important background facts, such as names of players or a team manager who were playing against their former teams. Some reports contain a general evaluative statement about the match which summarizes all the events and informs the reader that the losing team actually dominated the match and its eventual loss went against the expected pattern of play. In total, $Corpus_{FM}$ consists of 21,341 tokens; 2,457 types. The average length of a report is 102.37 words, with moderate variance across the corpus (standard deviation 25.99).

Football match reports written by real football commentators were taken from the BBC sports website (http://www.bbc.com/sport/football) and cover the football season of 2016/2017. BBC reports are rather lengthy match reports, which have a consistent organizational pattern where the first part is the factual report of events on the pitch while the second contains the commentator's opinion and speculations, comments from team managers, individual players and so on. In order for BBC reports to match the material of FM, only one part of the originally published report was included into our second corpus (henceforth – $Corpus_{BBC}$). While most of the match reports cover English and Scottish domestic matches, there are a few covering matches from Italian, Spanish, French leagues, as well as European championships and other international games. The only exception in this respect was exclusion of match reports that deal with matches between national teams, since such events do not feature in FM and reports of national matches often include commentaries of national sports which are rather different from topics covered by FM. The total size of $Corpus_{BBC}$ is 19,810 tokens; 3,308 types. The average length of a report is 99.34 words, with the variance of length slightly higher (standard deviation 34.17) than in $Corpus_{FM}$.

All match reports were saved in plain text (txt) format. Texts included in $Corpus_{FM}$ had first to be keyboarded as they can be neither downloaded onto external files nor copied otherwise. The original punctuation and capitalization were kept, and each report was saved in a separate file. Two corpus analysis tools were used to extract data from the corpora: #LancsBox (Brezina et al. 2015) was used to obtain frequency counts (absolute and relative) for words and keywords; WordSmith Tools v. 5 (Scott 2010) was used to generate keywords and lists of recurrent lexical bundles. All statistical tests were performed using the program R (R Development Core Team 2008; RStudio Team 2015).

3. Results and discussion

The results of this study are reported in two sections, each covering two stages of analysis. Section 3.1 discusses keywords identified in the two corpora, whereas Section 3.2 presents a discussion of lexical bundles in terms of their structural and functional features.

3.1. Word forms and keywords in Corpus$_{FM}$ and Corpus$_{BBC}$

The analysis of word forms and keywords was undertaken to identify differences between the two corpora on the level of single words. Word frequency lists offer preliminary insights into a language variety based on the rankings of the most frequent words, while the analysis of keywords reveals distinctly frequently used words which usually reflect the 'aboutness' of a corpus (cf. Kilgariff 2009; O'Keeffe et al. 2007). First differences between the two corpora were observed from the frequency lists of individual word forms. The twenty most frequent words in Corpus$_{BBC}$ represent for the most part function words among which prepositions account for the majority of types. Only three words among the most frequent twenty words in this corpus are lexical words, namely, the nouns *league*, *half* and *goal*. In contrast, out of the top twenty words in Corpus$_{FM}$, eight items are lexical words (in the sequence of decreasing frequency: *minutes, range, close, finish, minute, strike, lead, then*). A closer examination of the most frequent function words reveals a number of other interesting differences. For example, in Corpus$_{FM}$, the most frequent prepositions are *with* (normalized frequency 284 per 10,000 words), *from* (252), *on* (208) and *in* (183), whereas in Corpus$_{BBC}$ a different set of most frequent prepositions was found, namely, *in* (238), *from* (128), *of* (117) and *on* (107). The highest-ranking conjunction in the frequency list of Corpus$_{FM}$ is *as* (61, including *as* used as a conjunction but excluding prepositional uses e.g. *as an expert*) occupying the twenty-second position in the list which is distinctly different from Corpus$_{BBC}$ where the conjunction *and* appears as the sixth most frequent word (cf. *and* ranked as low as the sixty-seventh frequent word in Corpus$_{FM}$). The preliminary comparison of the two wordlists also shows that Corpus$_{FM}$ contains fewer lemma types and all of them occur in much higher frequencies than individual lemma types in Corpus$_{BBC}$. Our observations from the frequency lists suggest that the computer-mediated reports contain many more repetitively used lexical words, which might be expected in a computer game using a limited pre-installed vocabulary. Differences in the rankings of prepositions and other function words also show that the two corpora are different in terms of lexical words as different complementation patterns of, for example, verbs or nouns may account for differences in the frequencies of individual prepositions.

The keyword analysis was undertaken in order to identify individual word types that significantly differentiate one mode of football reports from the other. Keywords are understood as words which are significantly more frequent in one corpus in comparison to the other (Scott 1997). Keyness of individual word types can be measured by applying a number of statistical procedures that are available in most corpus analysis tools. The statistical technique of keyword analysis in WordSmith Tools (Scott 2010) is based on chi-squared or log-likelihood statistics, while #LancsBox (Brezina et al. 2015) offers five solutions for the extraction of keywords, all of which are based on different statistical procedures and thus yield different output. Having extracted the list of keywords on the basis of so-called 'simple-maths' procedure proposed by Kilgariff (2009), we compared it against lists obtained through the other statistical solutions and filtered out those keywords that appear in at least three lists extracted through application of the other statistical measures. Table 4.1 presents the top twenty keywords extracted from our material listed in the order of decreasing keyness value.

What is instantly obvious from the keyword lists is the dominance of football-specific lexical words in Corpus$_{FM}$ and a range of high-frequency function words in Corpus$_{BBC}$. As already observed above, the use of functional words seems to be particularly noteworthy for the comparison of the two corpora. For example, quite a few conjunctions appear in the keyword list of Corpus$_{BBC}$, namely, *and*, *before*, *when*, *but*. In contrast, they are rather infrequent in the computer-generated football reports (Corpus$_{FM}$). Apparently, text cohesion is given less importance or is more difficult to achieve in the automated language generation which explains why linking words are underused in Corpus$_{FM}$. Although the reporting of important events in FM does follow the chronology of each match, the reports consist of isolated declarative statements with no explicit marking of logical relations between consecutive ideas. Contrast, for instance,

Table 4.1 Keywords in Corpus$_{FM}$ and Corpus$_{BBC}$

	Corpus$_{FM}$	Corpus$_{BBC}$
1	# (number)	and
2	Range	first
3	finish	home
4	Close	before
5	minutes	second
6	With	league
7	placed	when
8	Timed	but
9	striker	hosts
10	flyer	points
11	deftly	time
12	accurate	who
13	executed	win
14	midfielder	premier
15	a	half
16	from	championship
17	then	last
18	got	headed
19	yards	ball
20	experienced	opponent

can be expressed by the conjunction *but*, yet its use requires interpretation of the context, which, for better or worse, still remains the property of human commentators, for example:

(1) Bradley Johnson almost equalized later on but his header hit the bar.
 <BBC66.txt>

Here the commentator gives a specific detail ('header hit the bar') in order to explain why the player failed to equalize, and it creates a contrast to an 'almost equalized' situation of the match. Interestingly, in FM reports, specific details to create contrast in *but*-clauses are not used at all. Instead, the use of *but* seems to be limited to situations where no detailed or context-dependent information is required in order to express contrast, for instance:

(2) Hibernian were nearly gifted a goal on 49 minutes through David Abraham's lapse in concentration but they failed to capitalise on the opportunity presented to them. <FM126.txt>

(3) Carrick put Livingston back with a shout on 78 minutes with a close range finish into the bottom right corner but it was too little, too late. <FM125.txt>

Both underlined clauses with *but* in examples (2) and (3) express negative comments on the final failure of the teams despite some positive development described in the preceding clauses. Differently from (1) where the *but*-clause contains a specific detail observed by the commentator, clauses in (2) and (3) may refer to any situation when a team loses a match despite scoring a goal. Interestingly, this is the only pattern in which *but* is used in $Corpus_{FM}$ where its normalized frequency is nearly six times lower than in $Corpus_{BBC}$ (9 vs. 60 instances).

The only three function words that are more frequent in $Corpus_{FM}$ in relation to $Corpus_{BBC}$ are the indefinite article and prepositions *with* and *from*. On the one hand, the high frequency of the article indicates the fact that countable nouns in the singular are often used with the indefinite article which in human-generated reports might be substituted by a number of other determiners, for instance, personal pronouns. Another explanation for the high frequency of the indefinite article, as the analysis of concordance lines revealed, is related to the use of prepositional phrases with the two frequently used prepositions, i.e. *with* and *from*. Over half (56 per cent) of all cases of *a* are realizations of the following pattern including *with*:

(4) Wonderkid Ousmane Dembele completed the rout with a free kick from the edge of the area on 70 minutes. <FM95.txt>

The underlined prepositional phrase in example (4) is used as an adverbial which is a rather loose constituent of a sentence that is easier to process and incorporate in a coherent text than a strictly governed structure, e.g. a complement. It is this use of adverbial phrases that largely accounts for the overuse of *with* and *from* in $Corpus_{FM}$.

Apart from function words, the two corpora also differ in their lexical keywords. Quite a few activity verbs found in $Corpus_{FM}$, predominantly in the Past Simple tense, refer to the players' actions on the pitch. The other distinct group of keywords contains football-specific references to the movement of the ball (*flyer*) or players (*striker*). Lastly, there are words that refer to time in the match which is evidenced by the number symbol (#) identified as the top keyword in Corpus$_{FM}$. In most cases, it refers to a specific point in time (*23rd minute*) or the score of the game. In contrast, football-related keywords in Corpus$_{BBC}$ are not directly relevant to the actual match but rather refer to the broader context outside the pitch, e.g. *league, championship, premier*. Such references are absent in Corpus$_{FM}$ where the focus of attention is the actual match rather than some external aspects.

Lastly, the comparison of the two corpora on the level of single word forms was supplemented with the analysis of the so-called lockwords which are generated by #LancsBox (Brezina et al. 2015). Lockwords are defined as words that do not distinguish corpora because they appear in similar frequencies in both corpora under study (Baker 2011). Hence lockwords provide the opposite evidence of keyword analysis and reveal which words make the two corpora alike. All lockwords in our data turned out to be proper names that refer to individual players, for instance, *Aleksandar, Alston, Anderson, Bacca*. Since the reports chosen for this study covered the same time span and season, the same players' names featured both in real sports commentaries and in the computer game.

3.2. Lexical bundles in football reports

The second stage of the analysis was focused on recurrent multi-word units, known in linguistics as lexical bundles (Biber et al. 1999; Biber et al. 2004; Hyland 2008; Cortes 2015). A frequency list of lexical bundles was generated using the cluster function of WordSmith Tools (Scott 2010). The decision to analyse four-word lexical bundles rather than longer or shorter sequences was based on findings from previous research which suggests that it is the optimal length in order to retrieve a sample of the most salient lexical bundles in terms of their meaning and form (cf. Cortes 2015: 204). As our pilot study showed, two- or three-word lexical bundles are often parts of the longer ones, e.g. *a close range* and *close range finish* are parts of the four-word bundle *a close range finish*, whereas the longer ones are infrequent in our corpora. Therefore the length of four words was chosen as the most suitable for this study. The software was set to retrieve four-word sequences that appear at least twice in two different texts. It produced a list of 1,925 types in Corpus$_{FM}$ and 1,426 in Corpus$_{BBC}$. Frequencies of individual lexical bundles differed greatly (cf. a list of the top twenty items in Table 4.2), and it made operationalizing the definition of lexical bundles on the basis of normalized frequency and dispersion rather difficult, because by application of the same normalized cut-off point, two samples of very different sizes would be obtained. It was thus decided to choose for this analysis the 200 most frequent lexical bundles from each corpus. Admittedly, these samples do not represent lexical bundles of similar currency in both corpora, but they still allow us to capture the most typical recurrent lexical patterns in our data.

Manual revision of the automatically generated lists was minimal: there were a handful of cases where the software misread punctuation marks and counted compounds, e.g. *build-up*, as two words rather than one. Such items were excluded from the study sample. On the other hand, it was decided to keep those lexical bundles which had numerals. As seen from Table 4.2, the corpus analysis tool replaced all digits with the number symbol (#). Numerals in lexical bundles refer either to the exact time during the match (*in the 23rd minute*), duration (*after just 4 minutes*), or goals (*37th goal of the season*) and scores (*made it 2–0*).

Table 4.2 Twenty most frequent lexical bundles in the corpora with normalized frequency per 10,000 words

Corpus$_{FM}$	Corpus$_{BBC}$
in the # minute (105)	*in the premier league* (9)
# minutes with a (69)	*at the top of* (8)
after # minutes with (53)	*in the second half* (8)
the # minute with (43)	*came from behind to* (7)
# minute with a (37)	*goal of the season* (7)
a flyer by scoring (36)	*of the premier league* (7)
off to a flyer (36)	*made it # #* (6)
to a flyer by (36)	*the top of the* (6)
with a close range (34)	*in the # minute* (5)
finish from close range (33)	*# goal of the* (5)
the lead with a (33)	*clear at the top* (5)
on # minutes with (32)	*from behind to beat* (5)
a close range finish (30)	*from the penalty spot* (5)
a deftly executed finish (30)	*in the first half* (5)
finish into the bottom (30)	*points clear at the* (4)
flyer by scoring a (28)	*at the back post* (4)
deftly executed finish from (28)	*from # # down* (4)
a placed shot from (27)	*on the stroke of* (4)
an accurate finish from (27)	*stroke of half time* (4)
with a placed shot (25)	*the stroke of half* (4)

Since such references are an important aspect of football reporting, lexical bundles incorporating the # symbol were kept in the study samples.

The initial analysis revealed that computer-generated football reports have very few shared lexical bundles with those recurring in real-life football reports. Out of the top 200 lexical bundles from each corpus, only eleven items occur in both samples, albeit with varying frequencies (see Table 4.3). While this finding may indicate that football reports generated by FM have little in common with real football reports, it might also point to the fact that the language algorithm of FM is limited in its range and virtually represents one or two language users with their idiosyncratic language use. In contrast, Corpus$_{BBC}$ contains texts written by different reporters which, as a consequence, involve a much broader range of vocabulary. It is then not very surprising to find that one 'commentator', i.e. the virtual FM reporter, does not possess in its lexical repertoire many of the phrases characteristic to other reporters.

The shared lexical bundles could be described as basic stock expressions of football commentators which may be used to describe any football match. As seen from Table 4.3, they refer to positions of the players at the moment of an important move (*from the edge of, from the spot after*), time (*in the # minute, on # minutes with*) and describe how the goals were scored (*a close range finish, into the bottom corner*). One of the shared lexical bundles (*took the lead when*) describes an important moment in the progress of the match when one of the

Table 4.3 Shared lexical bundles and their normalized frequencies per 10,000 words

Shared lexical bundles	Frequency	
	Corpus$_{BBC}$	Corpus$_{FM}$
# goal of the	8	4
a close range finish	35	2
from the edge of	7	2
from the spot after	7	2
his # goal of	7	3
in the # minute	38	5
into the bottom corner	23	3
into the top corner	17	2
on # minutes with	7	2
the edge of the	6	3
took the lead when	8	2

teams scores a goal. It is obvious that all of the shared lexical bundles are more frequent in Corpus$_{FM,}$ and the most frequent ones are those referring to time and place.

In addition to shared sequences, another four lexical bundles were established with three words out of four overlapping and one variable slot (underlined in the list below), namely

goal of the game (Corpus$_{FM}$) vs. *goal of the season* (Corpus$_{BBC}$);
edge of the area (Corpus$_{FM}$) vs. *edge of the box* (Corpus$_{BBC}$);
from close range in/on/which (Corpus$_{FM)}$ vs. *from close range after* (Corpus$_{BBC}$);
the # minute to/with (Corpus$_{FM}$) vs. *the # minute when* (Corpus$_{BBC}$).

The first two pairs of lexical bundles given above could be interpreted as having similar referents, namely, the best goals in their given contexts (*goal of the game/ season*) and the location of a player (*edge of the area/box*). Arguably, their variable slots reflect the mode of reporting, as it would be difficult to nominate the best goal of a season in the computer game environment. As to *area*, it is a more general word than *box* which probably makes it a safer option to refer to location in FM. Variable slots after *from close range* and *the # minute*, interestingly, reveal a different specificity of FM reports as they are related to the use of function words. For example, *from close range* is followed by *after* in Corpus$_{BBC}$ (*from close range finish after the break*), yet there are three types of function words in this slot in Corpus$_{FM}$ which realize three possibilities:

(5) a deftly executed finish from close range in the 29th minute <FM27.txt>
(6) a deftly executed finish from close range on 53 minutes <FM28.txt>
(7) a deftly executed finish from close range which found its target via the post <FM20.txt>

Variable slots appear at the boundary of recurrent lexical sequences where another sequence is added to form a longer stretch of text. Examples (5) and (6) illustrate time adverbials whereas (7) exemplifies a relative clause. The occurrence of a variable slot here indicates that in Corpus$_{FM}$ the sequence *a deftly executed finish from close range* is typically followed by one of the three recurrent patterns, namely, two prepositional phrases and a *wh*-clause. In contrast, in Corpus$_{BBC}$, as evidenced by the single slot-filler *after* in this particular lexical bundle, there is only one recurrent pattern (e.g. *from close range after the break*) and a plenitude of other expressions, none of which recurs in identical form. The lexical bundles approach, thus, reveals text processing steps and allows us to understand how a computer algorithm captures events and converts them into coherent verbal output.

3.2.1. Structural features

Both samples of lexical bundles were analysed quantitatively and qualitatively. The structural analysis of lexical bundles largely draws on the classification presented in Biber et al. (2004) and Biber (2006) which was adapted to the data of this study in order to obtain a more fine-grained picture of morphological differences between the two varieties of football language. Bearing in mind our observations from the analysis of single word forms, the following structural types were identified:

1. lexical bundles incorporating noun phrases (NP), e.g. *premier league relegation zone, the first half and*;
2. lexical bundles incorporating prepositional phrases (PP), e.g. *in the Champions league, at the back post*;
3. lexical bundles incorporating verb phrases (VP), e.g. *gave away a penalty, hit the inside of*;
4. lexical bundles incorporating adjectival/adverbial phrases (AdP), e.g. *clear at the top, early in the second*;
5. lexical bundles incorporating dependent clauses (DepCl), e.g. *after being played in, to open the scoring*.

Bar plots in Figure 4.1 present the distribution of lexical bundle types across the five structural types. NP-based lexical bundles, as seen from the bar plots, account for the greatest proportion of lexical bundles in both corpora, namely, 56 per cent of all lexical bundles in Corpus$_{FM}$ and 45 per cent in Corpus$_{BBC}$. The proportion of bundles incorporating PP-based bundles in Corpus$_{FM}$ is the second

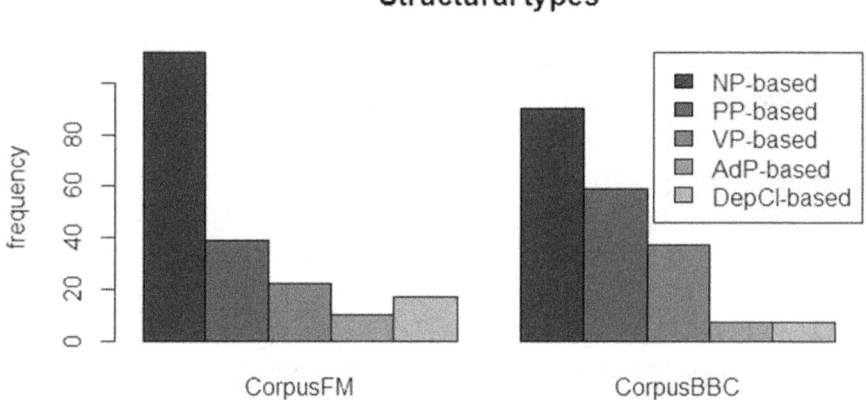

Figure 4.1 Distribution of lexical bundles across structural types.

most prominent category in the sample (29.5 per cent of all lexical bundles in this corpus). The effect size, however, is small (Cramér's V: 0.194). To test the statistical significance of differences between the two corpora, the χ^2 test was run (χ^2 = 14.9873, df = 4, *p*-value = 0.004728). The obtained *p* value confirms that differences in the distribution of structural types in the two samples are statistically significant, which suggests that the structural categories and the mode of reporting are dependent. To establish which structural types have the greatest influence on the differences, we checked the residuals. It was found that the two categories which contribute to the statistical differences mostly are lexical bundles incorporating dependent clauses (DepCl) in Corpus$_{FM}$ and PP-based lexical bundles in Corpus$_{BBC}$.

A closer qualitative examination of structural features of lexical bundles in the study sample offered some explanation for the quantitative findings. Among DepCl-based bundles, infinitive clauses are predominant in the sample from Corpus$_{BBC}$, e.g. *to hit the target, to move out, to open the scoring, to double the lead*. In Corpus$_{FM}$ the range of clause types is much broader. In addition to several infinite clauses (e.g. *to extend the lead, to be the winner*), there are also lexical bundles with segments of adverbial *-ing* clauses (e.g. *before crossing the line*) and finite clauses (e.g. *as they showed their*). Most importantly, this structural category shows the role of postmodification in computer-generated reports – half of the DepCl-based lexical bundles (9 out of 18 types) incorporate (non-)finite postmodifying clauses, for example:

(8) Striker Sabin then clinched a late winner on 90 minutes with an accurate volley which found its way in off the post. <FM39.txt>
(9) (…) an accurate finish from inside the penalty area which went in off the post. <FM104.txt>

Another markedly different structural category in the sample is lexical bundles that incorporate a segment of prepositional phrases. While their overall frequency is higher in Corpus$_{BBC}$, the two types of reports, as already observed in the discussion of keywords, prefer different prepositions. For instance, one of the frequently used prepositions in Corpus$_{FM}$ is *with* which recurs in lexical bundles that have an identical pattern, namely, *with+indefinite article+noun phrase*, e.g. *with a free kick, with a good header*. All of them function as adverbials and quite often, as will be discussed later, express stance. It is obvious that such syntactically loose chunks of texts are easier to process for the language algorithm because they are easier to incorporate into a sentence than any strictly governed element of the sentence. Possibly, it explains why lexical bundles with *with* are more frequent in Corpus$_{FM}$ in comparison to Corpus$_{BBC}$. Interestingly, only two lexical bundles in the sample retrieved from Corpus$_{BBC}$ include this preposition, namely, *with # minutes left* and *with a # #*. On the other hand, certain types of PP-based lexical bundles are almost totally absent in the Corpus$_{FM}$ sample and very prominent in Corpus$_{BBC}$. The most obvious cases are lexical bundles with *in* and *of*, most of them referring to football leagues, championships, cups, ranking lists, seasons, etc., all of which is largely irrelevant in the FM game environment. For instance, such lexical bundles as *in the champions league, in the first leg, of the FA cup, of the premier league* refer to concrete realistic contexts. This is an aspect that the developers of the FM game might be deliberately disregarding in order to ensure that the game represents a more decontextualized football world.

The structural analysis also revealed a number of specific features of football discourse that are common to both modes of reporting under study. Firstly, verb forms in lexical bundles are predominantly used in the Past Simple tense, which is to be expected in after-match reporting where time references point to the past. It was also found that there are several multi-word verbs (phrasal and prepositional) which recur in both modes of reporting and could perhaps be seen as characteristic attributes of football reports, for instance

(10) Sanchez, predictably, emerged as a substitute at the start of the second half and set up a goal for Danny Welbeck. <FM40.txt>
(11) Maxi Periera was sent off for handball. <BBC113.txt>

To obtain a fuller picture of how lexical bundles may contribute to the study of football discourse, a functional analysis was undertaken, the results of which are reported in the following section.

3.2.2. Functional features

In contrast to structural properties of lexical bundles, the quantitative analysis of functional categories of lexical bundles, whose definitions draw on the functional classification proposed by Biber et al. (2004) and Biber (2006), gave a different picture. Out of three major functional types identified in the literature, only two were found in our data. It is referential lexical bundles which refer to entities, processes, events, etc. and stance lexical bundles which express authorial stance, attitudes, modality, etc. None of the bundles was ascribed to the discourse-organizing function, which is the third major functional type discussed in the literature. Distributions across the two functional types established in our data were found to be rather similar in both corpora (see Figure 4.2) which was further confirmed by the χ^2 significance test ($\chi^2 = 0.5833$,

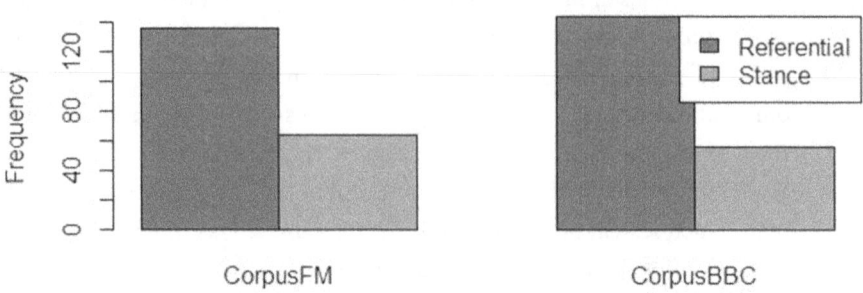

Figure 4.2 Distribution of lexical bundles across functional types.

df = 1, *p*-value = 0.445). So it is possible to argue that there is no dependence between the mode of reporting and functional features of lexical bundles as the statistical difference is insignificant.

The proportions of referential and stance lexical bundles in both corpus samples are indeed similar, namely, 68 per cent were categorized as referential and 32 per cent stance in Corpus$_{FM}$ and 72 and 28 per cent, respectively, in Corpus$_{BBC}$. A few interesting corpus-specific features, however, were captured through the qualitative analysis of the samples.
Referential lexical bundles were subdivided into subtypes on the basis of their meaning as follows:

1. References to moves and actions on the pitch, e.g. *cleared off the line, free kick from the, was sent off for*;
2. References to the position or place on the pitch, e.g. *from outside the box, into the bottom corner, the edge of the*;
3. References to goals and/or the ball, e.g. *a close range header; a flyer by scoring; his first goal for*;
4. References to time, e.g. *after # minutes with; just before the break; on the stroke of*;
5. References to match-related matters beyond the pitch, e.g. *top of the championship; FA cup # round; premier league relegation zone*;
6. References to scores and ranks of teams, e.g. *the bottom of the; within # points of; from # # down*;
7. Other references, e.g. *the hosts went ahead; against his former club*.

Out of the seven referential subtypes, the sample of lexical bundles representing Corpus$_{FM}$ has the first four subtypes with references to moves and actions of the players being the most numerous subtype (32 per cent of all referential bundles in this sample). References to the players' positions on the pitch or locations of goals and kicks account for 30 per cent in this corpus whereas the remaining lexical bundles are references to the ball (25 per cent), e.g. *# goal of the, finish into the bottom, kick from the edge*, as well as time references and other bundles. The distribution of lexical bundles across the referential subtypes in the Corpus$_{BBC}$ sample is much more varied. The most striking difference is the fifth subtype—it accounts for 25 per cent of all referential bundles extracted from Corpus$_{BBC}$ and none in Corpus$_{FM}$. Clearly, references to football leagues and championships provide an important context in the reports and give a broader background in which the match is to be situated. All of this contextual information is largely absent in FM. Similarly, references to overall results and ranks of teams (subtype 6) are also a typical feature of Corpus$_{BBC}$ as references to issues that are not directly visible on the pitch are probably less relevant for the player of the computer game.

As regards expressions of stance, it was unexpected to find that they are used with similar frequencies in both corpora. Yet again, while in Corpus$_{FM}$ authorial stance is explicitly marked in such lexical bundles as *a fine spring evening, finally a well-timed close finish, deftly executed finish from*, many of which express evaluation of a successfully manipulated ball or other events on the pitch, the focus of attention in Corpus$_{BBC}$ is predominantly on the rank of the team in question (e.g. *clear at the top, the champions league knockout*), overall progress of the match (e.g. *a hard fought victory, win of the season*). It could also be argued that expression of stance is rather different in the two corpora, for example

(12) Flamboyant midfielder Mesut Ozil got Arsenal off to a flyer by scoring a powerful close range diving header on 6 minutes. <FM180.txt>
(13) Atletico Madrid missed a chance to go top of La Liga (…) <BBC18.txt>

Example (12) from Corpus$_{FM}$ contains explicit expressions of evaluation which makes categorizing, for instance, the bundle *a powerful close range* as an expression of stance fairly straightforward. In the same sentence, there is another evaluative adjective, i.e. *flamboyant*. The lexical bundle exemplified in sentence (13), however, requires a broader context for the interpretation of its function. In other words, the vocabulary used in the FM game contains a number of overtly subjective lexical bundles with such lexemes as *deftly, forced, impeccably, fine, good, powerful, accurate* that are probably meant to add a more individualized tone to the automatically generated reports. Expression of stance in Corpus$_{BBC}$, in contrast, is less explicit or euphoric which, in comparison to FM reports, creates a more reserved and moderate tone of the reports.

4. Conclusion

While the language of football has been the focus of a number of studies, research into computer-generated sports language remains rather scarce. This research project was undertaken to compare two varieties of football discourse, i.e. computer-mediated reports and online reports written by real football commentators. The design of the study allowed us to capture several specific features of the two modes of football reports.

The analysis of frequency lists of single word forms and keywords showed that the two modes of reporting have a number of differences in terms of individual lexemes, and these differences are particularly prominent among function words. Furthermore, the analysis of four-word lexical bundles revealed that only eleven lexical bundles among the 200 most frequent are shared by both corpora. The qualitative analysis of lexical bundles in terms of their structural and functional types provided further insights into the (dis)similarity of the two types of football reports. It was found that lexical bundles retrieved from Corpus$_{FM}$ and Corpus$_{BBC}$ have a number of structural differences, but both corpora are similar in the prevalent functional types, namely, referential lexical bundles account for the majority of recurrent sequences in both analysed samples.

One of the major differences between the two modes of football reports observed in this study is related to text cohesion. The limited use of conjunctions in the computer-mediated football reports partly explains why the language generated by the computer game does not give the impression of a naturally flowing text but is rather perceived as a string of isolated statements, even though FM reports do present chronologically accurate accounts of the matches. As this study shows, the expression of text cohesion and the use of linking devices, conjunctions among them, are rather limited in the computer-generated football reports. Arguably, a handful of strong evaluative adjectives recurring in lexical bundles in Corpus$_{FM}$ partly help to redress the imbalance caused by the lack of naturally expressed human reasoning and are most probably expected to create the impression of live reactions to the matches. Even so, in many respects FM reports are indeed comparable to real football reports.

The findings of this study are not devoid of certain limitations, largely owing to the small size of the corpora analysed. Hopefully, future research based on a larger corpus of football language will corroborate some of our observations and offer new insights into the specificity of computer-mediated football language. The ongoing development of computer games based on sports will continue to provide linguists with opportunities to contrast human- and computer-generated language and contribute to a better understanding of natural language production.

Acknowledgements

The authors would like to thank two anonymous reviewers for their constructive and insightful comments. This study was partly supported by a grant of the Lithuanian Research Council (project No 09.3.3-LMT-K-712-07-0008) within a project implemented under the action program 'The development of research competence and cooperation through the exchange of scientific ideas and study visits to/from Lithuania'.

References

Anchimbe, E. A. (2008), 'Bend It Like a Banana?: Representing the Ecology in Live Football Commentaries', in E. Lavric, G. Pisek, A. Skinner and W. Stadler (eds), *The Linguistics of Football*, 133–142, Tübingen: Narr Francke Attempto Verlag.

Baker, P. (2011), 'Times May Change but We'll Always Have Money: A Corpus Driven Examination of Vocabulary Change in Four Diachronic Corpora', *Journal of English Linguistics*, 39: 65–88.

Balteiro, I. (2018), 'Oh Wait: English Pragmatic Markers in Spanish Football Chatspeak', *Journal of Pragmatics*, 133: 123–133.

Balzer-Siber, M. (2015), 'Functional and Stylistic Features of Sports Announcer Talk: A Discourse Analysis of the Register of Major League Soccer Television Broadcasts', MA diss., East Tennessee State University.

Bergh, G. (2011), 'Football Is War. A Case Study of Minute by Minute Football Commentary', *Veredas*, 15 (2): 83–93.

Bergh, G. and S. Ohlander (2012a), 'Free Kicks, Dribblers and WAGs. Exploring the Language of "the People's Game"', *Moderna Språk*, 106 (1): 11–46.

Bergh, G. and S. Ohlander (2012b), 'English Direct Loans in European Football Lexis', in C. Furiassi, V. Pulcini and F. Rodríguez González (eds), *The Anglicization of European Lexis*, 281–304, Amsterdam: John Benjamins Publishing Company.

Biber, D. (2006), *University Language: A Corpus-Based Study of Spoken and Written Registers*, Amsterdam/Philadelphia: John Benjamins Publishing.

Biber, D., S. Johansson, G. Leech, S. Conrad and E. Finegan (1999), *Longman Grammar of Spoken and Written English*, Harlow: Pearson Education Limited.

Biber, D., S. Conrad and V. Cortes (2004), 'If You Look at ... : Lexical Bundles in University Teaching and Textbooks', *Applied Linguistics*, 25 (3): 371–405.

Brezina, V., T. McEnery and S. Wattam (2015), 'Collocations in Context: A New Perspective on Collocation Networks', *International Journal of Corpus Linguistics*, 20 (2): 139–173.

Calderón, M. (2008), '*Kakj, Gallinas, Gent Blaugrana* and Other Soccer-related Onymic Phenomena in the Teaching of Onomastics', in E. Lavric, G. Pisek, A. Skinner and W. Stadler (eds), *The Linguistics of Football*, 157–170, Tübingen: Narr Francke Attempto Verlag.

Cortes, V. (2015), 'Situating Lexical Bundles in the Formulaic Language Spectrum: Origins and Functional Analysis Developments', in V. Cortes and E. Csomay (eds), *Corpus-based Research in Applied Linguistics: Studies in Honor of Doug Biber*, 197–216, Amsterdam: John Benjamins Publishing Company.

Fortington, L. V., S. Bekker and C. F. Finch (2018), 'Online News Media Reporting of Football-related Fatalities in Australia: A Matter of Life and Death', *Journal of Science and Medicine in Sport*, 21 (3): 245–249.

Hyland, K. (2008), 'As Can Be Seen: Lexical Bundles and Disciplinary Variation', *English for Specific Purposes*, 27: 4–21.

Jucker, A. H. (2010), '"Audacious, Brilliant!! What a Strike!" Live Text Commentaries on the Internet as Real-time Narratives', in Ch. R. Hoffmann (ed.), *Narrative Revisited. Telling a Story in the Age of New Media*, 57–78, Amsterdam: Benjamins

Jung, K. (2008), 'World Cup Football Live on Spanish and Argentine Television: The Spectacle of Language', in E. Lavric, G. Pisek, A. Skinner and W. Stadler (eds), *The Linguistics of Football*, 343–358, Tübingen: Narr Francke Attempto Verlag.

Kilgariff, A. (2009), 'Simple Maths for Keywords', in M. Mahlberg, V. González-Díazand and C. Smith (eds), *Proceedings of the Corpus Linguistics Conference*, 20–23 July 2009, Liverpool: University of Liverpool. Available at: http://ucrel.lancs.ac.uk/publications/cl2009/.

Levin, M. (2008), '"Hitting the Back of the Net Just before the Final Whistle": High-frequency Phrases in Football Reporting', in E. Lavric, G. Pisek, A. Skinner and W. Stadler (eds), *The Linguistics of Football*, 143–155, Tübingen: Narr.

Lewandowski, M. (2013), *The Language of Football: An English-Polish Contrastive Study*, Poznań: Wydawnictwo Naukowe UAM.

Makarova, A. (2008), 'Deviations in Sports Commentator Speech: Statistical and Linguistic Analysis', in E. Lavric, G. Pisek, A. Skinner and W. Stadler (eds), *The Linguistics of Football*, 305–316, Tübingen: Narr Francke Attempto Verlag.

Matulina, Ž. and Z. Ćoralić (2008), 'Idioms in Football Reporting', in E. Lavric, G. Pisek, A. Skinner and W. Stadler (eds), *The Linguistics of Football*, 101–112, Tübingen: Narr Francke Attempto Verlag.

Nordin, H. (2008), 'The Use of Conceptual Metaphors by Swedish and German Football Commentators. A Comparison', in E. Lavric, G. Pisek, A. Skinner and W. Stadler (eds), *The Linguistics of Football*, 113–120, Tübingen: Narr Francke Attempto Verlag.

O'Keeffe, A., M. McCarthy and R. Carter (2007), *From Corpus to Classroom: Language Use and Language Teaching*, Cambridge: Cambridge University Press.

Pérez-Sabater, C., G. Peña-Martínez, E. Turney and E. Montero-Fleta (2008), 'A Spoken Genre Gets Written: Online Football Commentaries in English, French and Spanish', *Written Communication*, 25 (2): 235–261.

R Development Core Team. (2008), *R: A Language and Environment for Statistical Computing. R Foundation for Statistical Computing, Vienna, Austria.* Available at: http://www.R-project.org.

Rossing, N. N. and L. S. Skrubbeltrang (2016), 'The Language of Football: A Cultural Analysis of Selected World Cup Nations', *Sport in Society*, 20(5–6): 599–611.

RStudio Team. (2015), *RStudio: Integrated Development for R. RStudio, Inc., Boston, MA.* Available at: http://www.rstudio.com/.

Scott, M. (1997), 'PC Analysis of Key Words – and Key Key Words', *System*, 25 (2): 233–245.

Scott, M. (2010), *WordSmith Tools (v. 5)*, Oxford: Oxford University Press.

Sępek, S. (2008), 'Is English Injuring Polish? An Analysis of the Spread of English Terminology in (and through) Polish football', in E. Lavric, G. Pisek, A. Skinner and W. Stadler (eds), *The Linguistics of Football*, 53–62, Tübingen: Narr Francke Attempto Verlag.

Tognini-Bonelli, E. (2001), *Corpus Linguistics at Work*, Amsterdam/Philadelphia, PA: John Benjamins Publishing Company.

Uchechukwu, Ch. (2008), 'Igbo Verb Roots and Their Realization of the "Root Schema" within the Football Domain'; in E. Lavric, G. Pisek, A. Skinner and W. Stadler (eds), *The Linguistics of Football*, 35–42, Tübingen: Narr Francke Attempto Verlag.

Vierkant, S. (2008), 'Metaphor and Live Radio Football Commentary', in E. Lavric, G. Pisek, A. Skinner and W. Stadler (eds), *The Linguistics of Football*, 121–132, Tübingen: Narr Francke Attempto Verlag.

Werner, V. (2016), 'Real-time Online Text Commentaries: A Cross-cultural Perspective', in Ch. Schubert and Ch. Sanchez-Stockhammer (eds), *Variational Text Linguistics. Revisiting Register in English*, 271–306, Berlin, Boston: De Gruyter.

Part Two

Media. Expanding the Scope of Research to New Contexts of Use

5

Such a Nice Guy Who Loved Racing His Bike: Framing in Media Accounts of Fatal Crashes Involving Competitive Cyclists

Turo Hiltunen

1. Introduction

Cycling has become increasingly popular globally, both as a leisure activity and as a spectator sport. While the sport has traditionally enjoyed great popularity across Continental Europe – in Spain, for example, it was practised by 39 per cent of the population in 2015 (MECD 2015: 38)[1] – its visibility has also increased in Anglophone countries. In part, this is due to the success of UK and Australian riders in continental European stage races (Fotheringham 2012; Ferrero-Regis 2018). Linked with health benefits and environmental sustainability, cycling has been widely hailed in the Anglo-American media as 'the new golf', due to its association with middle-class lifestyle (Falcous 2017), although the public image of road cycling as a sport has also suffered blows due to many high-profile cases of doping (Hambrick et al. 2015).

Despite the efforts of advocacy groups promoting the view of cycling as a 'relatively safe activity' (Cycling UK 2012), cycling is often seen as dangerous and accident-prone, and the perceived lack of security has been identified as a barrier for non-riders taking up cycling (Daley and Rissel 2011). Such attitudes are due to a variety of reasons and vary between people, but in general terms, along with personal experience, one factor that holds sway over the public view is media coverage of crashes where competitive cyclists are involved. A number of such incidents have unfortunately taken place in recent years, both on training rides and in races, and they have been widely covered in news and sports media globally. While riders may be able to quickly return to sport after a minor fall, a serious crash may lead to major injuries or even death, as in the case of Wouter Weylandt or Michele Scarponi.

This chapter uses a corpus-based approach to explore framing in news media accounts of cycling crashes. Framing is understood broadly to cover the process of choosing to highlight some aspects of the perceived reality at the cost of others (Scheufele and Tewksbury 2007). Despite some studies on the news reports of road traffic crashes (e.g. Connor and Wesolowski 2004), the language of cycling crash reports remains largely unexplored. The aims of this chapter are to identify the structure and functions of the texts, describe the ways different social actors are represented and investigate what is identified as the cause of the crash, and whether it is expressed neutrally or in such a way that it assigns blame to some party, either directly or indirectly.

Contrasting ways of describing the same event can be illustrated with quotes from reports about the death of Italian cyclist Michele Scarponi on 22 April 2017:

(1) Italian cyclist Michele Scarponi has died aged 37 after being **involved in a collision with a van** during a training ride.[2] (BBC 2017)
(2) Veteran Astana rider **hit by a van** near his home in central Italy. (Cycling News 2017)
(3) Pro rider Michele Scarponi – a former Giro d'Italia winner – **killed while training by inattentive truck driver**. (Reid 2017b)

These examples represent different types of media – mainstream, specialist and social – and there are clear differences in their wording. In example (1), quoted from a BBC story, Scarponi's death is described as having taken place after a collision where he was involved. No stand is taken as to who was responsible for the crash, whether Scarponi or the van, which is mentioned as the other participant in the incident. A somewhat similar reporting strategy is used in example (2), taken from *Cycling news*, an online medium specializing in competitive cycling. Although the van appears as the agent of a long passive construction, suggesting a more important role compared to example (1), the example simply identifies the other participant as *a van*, which downplays the human agency involved in the incident.

By contrast, a different version of the incident is offered in the social media report by Carlton Reid, cycling journalist and author. Reid's tweet (example 3) explicitly mentions the truck driver, and by describing him as *inattentive*, Reid implies that the truck driver is to blame for the crash. Reid's choice of words was also one of the topics in a roundtable podcast panel show which aired the following day (Reid 2017a), where it was suggested that even talking about 'an inattentive driver' in the case of Scarponi's death may have been too soft and could be replaced by 'a negligent driver' (Reid 2017a). Although Twitter posts and contributions to roundtable discussions are not directly comparable to news articles – they are more ephemeral and represent more clearly the journalist's personal point of view rather than that of a newspaper – these three examples illustrate that the same incident can be framed in various ways. The kind of meta-commentary found in (3) served as the impetus for the present study, but the main focus is on the type of texts represented by the first two examples.

Reid's statement in (3) echoes the message of the campaigns such as #CrashNotAccident,[3] which argue using the word 'accident' trivializes the fact that what are referred to as 'accidents' are most often caused by human error (see Liao 2015; Richtel 2016). Giddings (2015) argues that articles about bike crashes are also often guilty of implicit 'victim-blaming', where the responsibility is shifted to the cyclist even before all the facts are known.[4] On the other hand, journalists also have the responsibility to respect principle of 'presumption of innocence' (e.g. Laitila 2005), which influences the representation of different social actors in the text. In addition, Connor and Wesolowski (2004) are critical of journalists' tendency to represent crashes as mini-dramas involving innocent victims and clearly defined villains, arguing that such narratives are designed to give readers easy answers even when such answers are not supported by actual facts. This being the case, adopting a neutral stance regarding the responsibility of the parties involved in the crash may also reflect journalistic caution and deliberate avoidance of hasty conclusions and moral judgements that might turn out to be unfounded when more information becomes available at a later stage.

To empirically approach the issue of representation in the context of accident reporting, this chapter aims to provide a systematic analysis of a sizeable corpus of news articles about crashes leading to the death of a competitive cyclist. It adopts a discourse-analytical perspective to determine the main rhetorical and structural patterns of reporting about such crashes, in particular how the crashes are framed, how different actors are represented and what lexico-grammatical patterns are used in the reporting. The study does not aim to comment on factuality of individual stories, but to study the framing in the data on a general level.

A corpus linguistic approach is particularly well suited for this task, as it enables the combination of a top-down analysis of rhetorical structure with a bottom-up analysis of language patterns using large corpora. The present analysis is based on a specialized corpus compiled for this study. The corpus is a convenience sample of news reports on crashes involving professional and competitive cyclists, collected specifically for this study from various English-language sports and news media. This sample is analysed inductively (Huckin 2004: 16) to explore what frames are used, what aspects of the crash they foreground and how they are realized linguistically. Along with the analysis of text structure, the words and patterns related to specific frames in the convenience sample are further investigated in terms of their co-occurrence patterns and semantic associations.

2. Theoretical background

I use the term *crash report* to refer to media reports on crashes which resulted in the death of a competitive cyclist, either during training or in a race. The reports represent crashes of different types, also those not involving a motor vehicle. Following the recommendation of Giddings (2015) and others, I consistently use the term *crash* in lieu of *accident*, although the latter term occurs in both the primary data and some previous academic studies.

2.1. Framing

The point of departure of the present study on the framing of crash reports, like studies on news and media discourse in general, is the premise that descriptions are never fully neutral and objective, but always highlight some things and background others. In other words, descriptions offer different '*representations* of events' (Baker et al. 2013: 3) and display different socially shared organizing principles, or *frames*, which 'work *symbolically* to meaningfully structure the social world' (Reese 2001: 11). Both terms are linked to issues of ideology and power, as well as other concerns like journalistic preference and the amount of available space. I use here the term *framing*, and while there are differences between the meanings of these terms, the analysis below is largely compatible with the term *representation*.

For Entman (1993), the act of framing a story consists of two components: selecting some aspects of reality and foregrounding them to make them salient in the text. Functions associated with framing may involve defining problems, identifying their causes, evaluating (morally) the agents involved in the event, as well as suggesting solutions and predicting their effects (1993: 52). Kitziger (2007: 139) notes that framing research often considers alternative or opposing frames, such as whether the shooting down of an aircraft is represented as *an unwarranted act of war* or *an unfortunate accident*.

In my analysis of framing, I also draw on (critical) discourse analysis, particularly Van Leeuwen's *Social Actors approach* (1996, 2016) and Reisigl and Wodak's *Discourse-historical approach* (2016), both of which are clearly related to Entman's view of framing. For example, many of the representation alternatives described in Van Leeuwen (1996) (e.g. *nomination* and *functionalization*) offer ways of foregrounding some discourse participants and backgrounding others. The concept of framing also exhibits obvious affinities with the discursive strategies described in Reisigl and Wodak (2016): for example, *predication* refers to 'characteristics, qualities and features attributed to social actors, objects, phenomena, events, and processes' and *perspectivization* to the positioning of the writer's perspective and the expression of involvement and distance (Reisigl and Wodak 2016: 43).

Previous studies of media reports on accidents have investigated such aspects as the representation of the parties involved, the possible causes of the accident and their economic consequences (Beullens et al. 2008). Daniels et al. (2010) compared official crash data to media reports to determine what factors contribute to the accident being covered in the media.[5] Analysing the coverage of fatal motor-vehicle crashes in the United States from a public health perspective, Connor and Wesolowski (2004) criticize local newspapers for inaccurate and one-sided representation of risks to vehicle occupants (e.g. related to seat belt use) and also missing good opportunities to provide health information to the public that could make a real difference. In the context of cycling, Rissel et al. (2010) studied how cycling and cyclists were represented in major newspapers in Australia. While they did not focus on crash reporting per se, they found that 'cycling' as an activity was generally framed in positive terms, whereas 'cyclists' as actors were often represented in negative rather than positive terms. They also noted that the most frequently chosen 'news angles' in the articles were *injury to* and *death of cyclist*, suggesting that crashes are indeed a major way in which cycling receives media attention (2010: 3–6). This is consistent with Bednarek and Caple's analysis of newspaper articles about cycling, which also found negativity to be the most typically constructed news value, established through the use of negative lexis in reports of crashes (2017: 166). The term *framing* is not limited to academic studies but is frequently used in journalistic meta-commentary; for example, Giddings has used it in her article for the *Bicycling* magazine, entitled 'Five Cyclist-Blaming Headlines – And How to Reframe Them' (Giddings 2015). Using the terms in Brossard (2010: 310), the present analysis focuses on frame building (the process of producing the frames) rather than frame setting (how the frames are interpreted by the audiences).

3. Material and method

3.1. The corpus

Like any register, newspaper sports reporting can be studied on different levels of specificity. Newspapers cover a wide range of sports and sports-related topics, ranging from scores and results to and athletes' private lives and economy (Fest 2016: 190). The corpus used in the present study represents a very specific subregister of sports news, namely, news items that describe fatal crashes involving competitive cyclists. This corpus, referred to in this study as the *Crash report corpus*, is a convenience sample, collected from texts available on the internet. It aims to represent how cycling crashes are covered globally in different English-language news media, which are accordingly not limited in terms of location, type or readership unlike some other studies on framing (e.g. Rissel et al. 2010).

To select texts for the corpus, I compiled a list of riders who had died in cycling-related crashes, both in races and during training. The list was based on the Wikipedia article 'List of cyclists with a cycling-related death' (2010), which contains separate lists for training and race-related crashes; this distinction is also followed in the construction of the corpus. The corpus covers the period starting with the death of Fabio Casartelli in the 1995 Tour de France and ending in 2017 with the crashes of Michele Scarponi and Jason Lowndes.[6] The *Crash report corpus* is thus a small and specialized corpus, containing 230 reports involving forty incidents, with a total size of 79,000 words.

The news reports were located with Google searches, using as search terms the names of riders and, where necessary, appropriate context words like *death, accident* or *crash*. For this reason, the articles represent a variety of sources, ranging from major international news outlets and news agencies (e.g. the BBC, *The Guardian*, the *New York Times* and Reuters) to specialized online news platforms dedicated to cycling (e.g. *Cycling Weekly, Velonews, road.cc*). Only articles in English were included in the sample, which results in an obvious over-representation of riders from Anglophone countries. In many cases, there were many more reports about a specific incident written in the language of the rider's country of origin than English-language reports. The data is also skewed towards successful and well-known riders, since incidents involving them are more newsworthy. As shown in Table 5.1, reports about the fifteen most frequently covered incidents account for two-thirds of the total number of reports. For this reason, the corpus is clearly not representative of crash reporting as a whole, but given its specificity, it is assumed to represent reasonably well the

Table 5.1 Most 'newsworthy' crashes included in the corpus

Rider	Number of reports
Antoine Demoitié	18
Jason Lowndes	17
Michele Scarponi	13
Burry Stander	10
Annefleur Kalvenhaar	10
Junior Heffernan	9
Chad Young	9
Victor Cabedo	8
JoAnne Nell	8
Carly Hibbert	8
Amy Dombroski	7
Wouter Weylandt	7
Casey Saunders	7
Mike Hall	7
Randall Fox	7
Iñaki Lejarreta	7
Other riders	78
Total	**230**

kind of material that an English-speaking reader is likely to come across (cf. the discussion in Connor and Wesolowski 2004: 151).

The *Crash report corpus* only contains articles on the actual crashes written immediately or very soon after they took place. Other types of articles are accordingly left out; these may include reports of later investigations on the causes of crash and court decisions determining responsibility, in which the social actors may be represent differently from crash report. Similarly excluded were news articles on memorial rides organized to pay homage to deceased cyclists and call attention to road safety, as well as articles about deaths that were not due to a crash.

The selected reports were downloaded, and the HTML boilerplate was removed. The corpus files only include the headline and the main body of the article, thus excluding embedded images, captions and reader comments. Especially the most recent articles contain embedded social media content from Twitter or Instagram, which was also removed.

The texts were converted into TEI-compatible XML, which enables the addition of further layers of annotation. To facilitate searches for grammatical patterns, the corpus was automatically POS-tagged using CLAWS (Garside and Smith 1997).

3.2. Method of analysis

As a first step towards the analysis of framing, a basic bottom-up content analysis was carried out at the sentence level.[7] In other words, each sentence in the corpus was qualitatively assigned into a category indicating its basic function in the article. While these functions could be seen as broadly similar to 'rhetorical moves' in the Swalesian sense (Swales 1990), the present study is not intended as a comprehensive genre analysis. For the same reason, each sentence was assigned its own label, even if it was clearly part of the same 'macrostructure' as the previous or subsequent sentences. The process of categorizing the sentences was iterative, starting few basic categories and modifying them and adding new ones during the analysis. Some examples of the categories are given in Table 5.2.

The functional categories are meant to be as broad and illustrative as possible to keep the analysis maximally straightforward and minimally subject to interpretation, even if it potentially means sacrificing some of the more nuanced distinctions between individual sentences. This approach is in line with the overall objective of the study, which is the description of the framing of crashes, not a full appraisal of the genre characteristics of the crash report. The classifications were recorded in the XML file to enable the detection of any thematic, organizational and rhetorical patterns in the corpus (cf. Huckin 2004), as well as comparisons of lexico-grammatical patterns across different functional categories.

Table 5.2 Examples of functional categories

Category	Example
Report of fatal crash	Dutch mountain biker Annefleur Kalvenhaar dies following World Cup crash.
Description of crash	It seems that Hall was hit by a vehicle in the early hours of the morning and died at the scene.
Description of rider	Demoitie was also recently married.
Link to previous crash	Weylandt was the first rider killed in a crash in one of cycling's three main tours since Italian rider Fabio Casartelli in the 1995 Tour de France.

As the *Crash report corpus* is an unbalanced convenience sample, frequency information needs to be used with great caution when making generalizations. For example, it is possible to determine how many times descriptions of crashes refer to other cyclists. However, this figure is not useful in isolation, since some crashes described in the corpus involved other cyclists whereas others did not, and the number of texts on a specific crash also varies. In other words, the number of opportunities for such statements (and many others) to occur varies across texts. In many cases, it can also be seen that the articles also use very similar turns of phrases when quoting or paraphrasing statements, press releases and news agency reports. For this reason, frequency data is mainly used for the analysis of collocational/colligational patterning. At the text-structural level, frequency information is only used to describe the structure of the crash report on a macro-level – what the core/optional constituents are – and to explore the extent of formal variation in specific categories across texts – for example, what characteristics are typically invoked when describing the deceased rider (Section 4.3) – with the help of relative frequencies.

After coding the data, scripts were written to extract information from the corpus for content analysis. The word and sentence counts were determined for individual texts and functional categories across texts, which were used to arrive at a schematic description of text structure. The functional categories were also used for a closer linguistic and sociosemantic analysis of specific discourse types to determine how crashes were framed and how riders and other social actors were represented. This exploratory process involved carrying out corpus searches within a particular functional category of texts – e.g. description of crash, description of rider – identifying core vocabulary items and sentence frames used in describing crashes, cyclists and other participants in discourse, drawing on Halliday's (2004) description 'material processes' and Van Leeuwen's (1996) work on social actors.

4. Analysis

In what follows, I shall first describe the structure of the crash report at a general level, identifying the core components and describing the degree of variation between texts. Then, I shall provide a more detailed assessment two main discourse topics – description of crashes (4.2) and representation of actors (4.3), and illustrate their linguistic characteristics.

4.1. Structure of crash report

Given that each incident described in the corpus is different, it is not surprising to find variation in the news reports that describe them. At the same time, we also find a great deal of topical and structural similarity, showing that irrespective of the characteristics of individual incidents, there are many recurrent elements that the reports have in common. The structure of a prototypical crash report in the corpus can be summarized as a hierarchical concept map (Figure 5.1), similar to what Brown and Yule (1983: 75) refer to as a 'topic framework', a framework within which the crash being reported is constituted. The concept map shows the main topics, their constituents, and hierarchical relations between them, but does not specify the order in which they appear in the texts.

Some of the elements are near-obligatory, in that they occur in virtually all the reports, whereas others are optional, and their inclusion is dependent on a multitude of factors, including the characteristics of the crash, the availability of information at the time of writing, as well as journalistic choices. The best example of an obligatory element is the **report of fatal crash**. It is a definitional constituent of the whole genre, which opens most reports in the corpus. Along with mentioning the fatality, such statements typically identify the rider, provide some additional details like their nationality (as in example 4), and

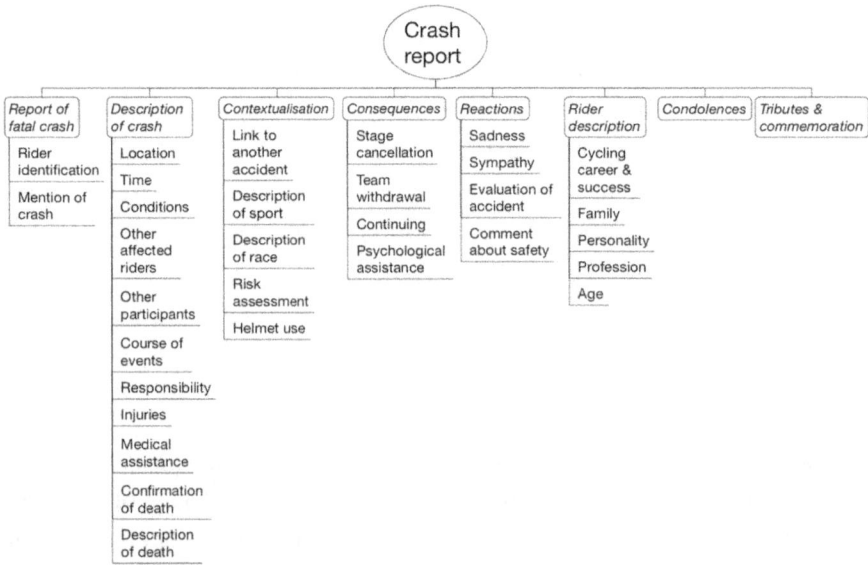

Figure 5.1 Topic framework of crash report.

give some information about the crash, like the location (example 5). These statements provide the core of the report, and they are included even in the shortest texts.

(4) American rider Chad Young, 21, dies of crash injuries.
(5) Aussie cycling star Carly Hibberd dies in crash in Italy.

More specific information of the crash is usually provided in separate sentences later in the article, which form another main component of these stories. These **descriptions of crashes** may span several sentences in the article and provide many different kinds of details, and what is included obviously varies greatly between the articles. Examples 6 and 7 illustrate the range of variation in the statements.

(6) The accident occurred on a section of road that sloped gently downhill, the State Patrol reported.
(7) According to official reports, Mathieu hit the windscreen of a passing ambulance that was at that moment, coming from the opposite direction.

These statements may include some characterization of the deceased rider, usually in reference to their nationality or age. In addition, the articles frequently contain separate **descriptions of riders** (see the third row of Table 5.2), which are discussed more fully below (Section 4.3).

Many articles contain sentences that provide a **contextualization** for the crash. This label refers to statements describing the race, assessing the safety of cycling as a sport or linking the crash being described to another deadly incident in the recent history of the sport. This last type of statement (illustrated on the last row of Table 5.2) is particularly frequent across texts, but it is not rare to encounter sentences describing the relevant category of cycle sport, which is likely to be unfamiliar to the reader (example 8).

(8) Keirin is an event where cyclists start out behind a small motorbike.

These statement types can be treated as the core constituent of crash reports, given that they occur in the majority of the texts in the corpus. In addition to these, we find a number of optional constituents, including the reporting of **reactions** from fellow riders, governing bodies for cycling, and the like; descriptions of actions taken as responses to the crash (termed **consequences** in Figure 5.1) like the cancellation of a stage; expression of **condolences** to the rider's friends and family and the organization of tributes for them. The inclusion of these constituents clearly depends on the characteristics of the incident being reported (e.g. whether a stage was cancelled or not), and one notable division within the corpus can be found between crashes that took place during training as opposed to in a race.

To provide a birds-eye view of the structure of the data, Figure 5.2 shows the distribution of sentences categorized as representing nine functional categories which are most important for the crash report (the other sentences are subsumed together under 'OTHER'). Each bar on the y-axis corresponds to one text in the *Crash report corpus*, and the length of the bar on the horizontal axis indicates the number of sentences contained. The shades correspond to functions of sentences, but they do not indicate in what order they appear in individual text.

As can be seen, there is ample variation in the length of text: the median length is 15 sentences (IQR 9–23), but the number of sentences ranges from 3 to 64. But despite this variation, we also find structural similarity across texts: nearly all the texts contain one to three sentences reporting the death of the rider (black colour), and most devote one or more sentences to describing the crash (dark grey) and the rider (light grey). For our purposes, one key question is obviously what sets the longer texts apart from the shorter ones. Based on the figure, longer texts are primarily characterized by three factors: they contain

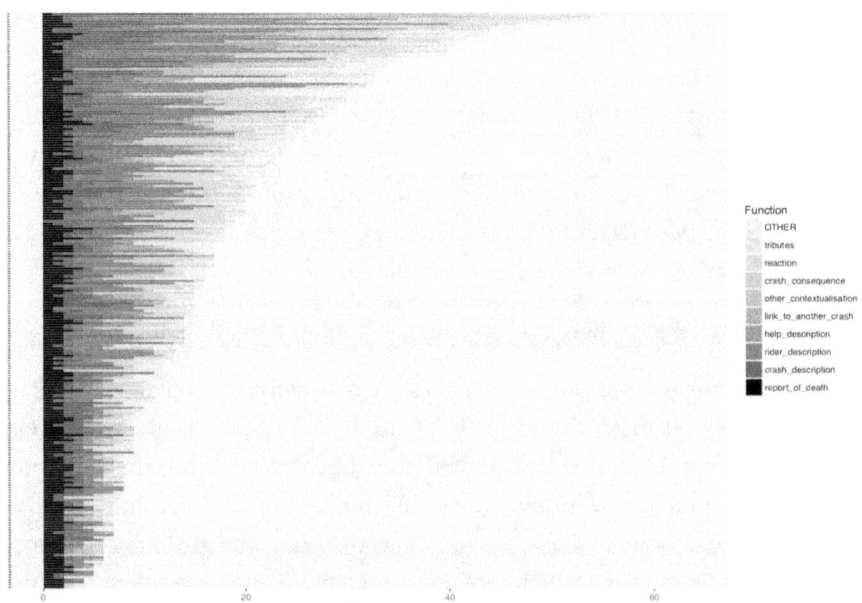

Figure 5.2 Main functional categories across texts in the *Crash report corpus*.

more detailed descriptions of the riders and crashes spanning many sentences, they devote several sentences to providing a contextualization of the crash, and they quote reactions typically from riders and other people involved in cycle sport. Both contextualizations and reactions are generally missing from short articles, whereas in longer articles they make up a large proportion of sentences.

For example, the fourth longest article in the corpus is an account of Michele Scarponi's crash published in the *Bicycling* magazine in 2016 (fifty-two sentences). It devotes eight sentences to the crash and thirteen to Scarponi, describes the reactions from the peloton in sixteen sentences and the tributes to the rider in seven. The extent of structural variation is further illustrated in Table 5.3, which shows some select examples both short and long texts.

To sum up, as far as text structure is concerned, we find both differences and similarities across corpus texts as far as their structure is concerned. This macro-level analysis is indicative of how fatal crashes are framed in media reports, but to get an insight into what aspects are highlighted and how different social actors are represented, we shall next look at individual categories in more detail.

Table 5.3 Some examples of text structure

Rider	Media	Length (sentences)	Structure
Lejarreta	ESPN	6	Report of crash (2)
			Crash description (1)
			Rider description (3)
Young	Reuters	15	Report of crash (2)
			Crash description (5)
			Rider description (4)
			Reaction (3)
			Tributes (1)
Casartelli	NY Times	64	Report of crash (1)
			Crash description (14)
			Rider description (6)
			Help description (4)
			Contextualization (14)
			Other consequences (1)
			Reaction (4)
			Other (20)[a]

[a] Mostly descriptions of other incidents in the stage.

4.2. Description and contextualization of crashes

While most initial statements reporting rider's death are short, crashes are often described in more detail in later sentences, mentioning environmental and human factors contributing to the crash such as road conditions, speed and other riders involved, as summarized in Figure 5.1.[8] The kind of medical assistance provided to the rider is also frequently described and appraised. Overall, the degree of detail provided indicates that accuracy and balance are clearly major concerns in these texts, and especially the longer texts in the corpus attempt to reconstruct the course of events as fully as possible.

Central to the question of representation and framing of crashes are labels used in the texts, as they may be indicative of journalistic angle and even bias (e.g. Kitziger 2007: 148). To shed light on this aspect of frame building, Table 5.4 lists the nouns applied to crashes and their frequencies in the corpus. As can be seen, *crash* and *accident* are by far the most common nouns in the data, whereas the other terms are used much more rarely.

A comparison of frequencies at the level of individual texts suggests that writers do not categorically choose between *crash* and *accident*, but they seem to be used almost interchangeably. The exception is *Bicycling* magazine, whose texts do not contain a single occurrence of *accident*. But elsewhere, these two terms occur in largely similar sentence configurations – typically as prepositional complements (example 9) or clause subjects (10 and 11), and in different parts of the text – and there does not appear to be any deliberate attempt to diminish anyone's responsibility.

Table 5.4 Nouns used in describing crashes

Noun	Frequency
crash	266
accident	222
collision	103
incident	51
fall	33
smash	5
wreck	3
mishap	1
Total	**678**

(9) The circumstances of the **accident** are under investigation.
(10) Police said the **accident** occurred before sunrise.
(11) The AFP reported the **crash** occurred in Sainte-Marie-Cappel, France.

This finding is similar to that of Connor and Wesolowski (2004: 152), who observe that even if *accident* has the connotation of an 'unavoidable act of fate', journalists frequently used the term while assigning blame to a specific party.

Another, related aspect of framing through labelling is manifested through the choice of verbs used to describe the crash that led to the death of the rider. These verbs represent what Halliday (2004) calls material processes, which unfold in time and have a separate final phase and outcome (2004: 228), and their usage in the corpus thus provides information about how crashes are represented in the data. Table 5.5 lists the most frequent verbs in material clauses in the data.

The most frequent verb in the table, *die*, occurs in intransitive clauses where the only participant is the rider. By contrast, most top verbs in the table are transitive verbs, representing the rider as a participant who is impacted by some other participant – 'Goal' and 'Actor' in Halliday's terms (2004: 225–226). Although active transitive clauses can be attested in the data (examples 12 and 13), *kill, hit* and *strike* are predominantly found in passive clauses where the rider appears as the grammatical subject, and the agent that brought about the process being described is indicated in the *by*-phrase. These agents are predominantly represented impersonally though objectification by referring to vehicles (*car, van, motorbike*) instead of humans driving them (examples 14 and 15; see also example 3 above). This usage illustrates what Van Leeuwen calls

Table 5.5 Verbs in material clauses describing crashes

Verb	Frequency
die	266
kill	215
hit	172
crash	104
strike	88
fall	50
collide	34
knock	10
plough	5
total	**678**

instrumentalisation, representation through an instrument associated with the activity, which can be used to background the role and identity of social actors (Van Leeuwen 1996: 59).

(12) They were riding along and **a car** came over the white line and hit them head-on.
(13) Lowndes, who had turned 23 last week, was riding to meet someone on Sedgwick Rd, Mandurang, when **a car** struck him from behind about 10.15 am on Friday.
(14) Belgian rider was struck **by motorcycle** after fall.
(15) She was hit **by a truck** while motorpacing in Belgium.
(16) **His bike** had collided with a car travelling in the opposite direction.

The prevalence of this strategy in the data lends credence to the idea that news reports routinely downplay the role of human agency in crashes involving cyclists and motor vehicles. This is further emphasized by the fact that instrumentalization is very seldom applied to cyclists; only one example was found in the corpus (16). However, despite the frequency at which this discourse strategy can be attested in the data, it cannot be attributed solely to deliberate or inadvertent victim-blaming, since other factors are also at play. For one, downplaying the influence of poor judgement or human error is not exclusively found in reports on crashes involving cyclists. Instead, as established by Connor and Wesolowski (2004), journalistic accounts frequently opt for simplistic and often factually inaccurate descriptions of traffic crashes and fail to represent the full complexity of the human factors involved. In addition, we also find multiple long passive clauses in the data that do provide information about the driver, and sometimes blame is indeed explicitly assigned to specific people (17 and 18).

(17) Robic was struck **by a car driven by a 55-year-old local resident**.
(18) Aus was reportedly hit from behind **by a drunk driver** and died from his injuries in the ambulance.

Based on these examples, together with the amount of other details provided in many texts, a more accurate conclusion is that the representation of motor vehicle drivers through instrumentalization is a feature of traffic crash reports in general and of cycling crash reports in particular. In addition, instrumentalization of car drivers is not always a deliberate attempt to exonerate them, but an expression of journalistic caution and the principle of presumption of innocence in a situation where conclusive evidence is not yet available for assigning responsibility.

4.3. Representing riders and other social actors

Mentions of the deceased riders are found in different places in the texts. Sentences reporting a rider's death typically identify them in terms of age and provenance (usually as premodifiers in a noun phrase), as previously illustrated in examples (1) to (5). Nationality is by far the most common category, which reflects the fact that the articles in the corpus are published online and are addressed to an international readership. That said, articles by local media outlets also use more specific locations (e.g. *Oregon cyclist*). Rider age seems to be foregrounded especially with young riders or veterans, which may indicate that these crashes are seen as particularly newsworthy (cf. Connor and Wesolowski 2004: 152; Beullens et al. 2008: 551). The actors are also often identified in functional terms, making reference to categories which are characteristic of sports and cycling discourse, such as the rider's success (e.g. *cycling star, a South African cyclist who won several college titles in the United States*), team affiliation (*Kelme rider*), and the type of rider (*Mountain biker, Spanish sprinter*). Compared to nationality, these functional categories are somewhat less frequently used in the data.

In addition to these sentences located in the beginning of texts, riders are commonly described in more detail in separate sentences later in the article. These descriptions take a different form compared to the previous examples. Two types stand out: about half of these descriptions refer to aspects of the rider's cycling career (example 19), which can be expected, but as many as one fourth praise their personality (examples 20–22).

(19) He represented South Africa at the UCI Track World Cup in Manchester in 2013.
(20) He was just a kind person who loved cycling and was always inspiring young cyclists.
(21) Such a nice guy who loved racing his bike.
(22) In a statement, Farrar called Weylandt one of the kindest, funniest and most admirable people I have ever had the opportunity to know.

Mentions of a rider's family, and other instances of relational identification (Van Leeuwen 1996: 56) are also present in the data.

(23) He leaves behind a wife and two children.
(24) Weylandt, whose girlfriend is pregnant, moved to the Leopard-Trek team at the start of the season after turning professional with Quick Step in 2005.

The frequent inclusion of laudations and mentions of rider's family suggest that in part, the *Crash report corpus* is generically similar to obituaries, whose communicative purpose is to commemorate a deceased person by highlighting 'what a society holds to be crucially important elements of one's life and death' (Moses and Marelli 2004: 124). Like obituaries, crash reports highlight the decedent's life accomplishments (usually related to cycling, though not exclusively) and personal history, of which family is a major component. The affinity between the genres is further emphasized by the inclusion of expressions of condolences in crash reports:

(25) British Cycling offered its condolences to the family and friends of the 23-year-old.
(26) Cyclingnews sends our condolences to Carly's family and friends.

While most texts report condolences expressed by some community or individual riders (25), some specialist media articles offer condolences in their own name (26).

5. Discussion

Media coverage of cycling crashes is important because it shapes the public understanding of the issues and may influence behaviour (Rissel et al. 2010: 2). This study has documented the characteristics of media reports of crashes which result in the death of a competitive cyclist. Crash reports were shown to employ similar textual strategies for framing the crash and representing the social actors involved, although the emphasis given to specific aspects varies between the texts, as can be expected. While the shortest texts merely report the occurrence of a fatal crash and identify the rider by name, most other texts include detailed and contextualized accounts of the crash. The analysis of labelling, nomination and categorization further shows how the deceased riders' profiles are discursively constructed in the texts and what strategies are used to meet the rhetorical goals (Reisigl and Wodak 2016: 94): many texts provide extensive information about the rider's professional trajectory and personal history, framed in terms similar to obituaries by highlighting the accomplishments and personal life.

But is there evidence in the data of negative framing or even 'victim-blaming'? Such evidence could potentially consist of consistent portrayal of riders in a negative light, or misrepresentations of crashes as unavoidable incidents in cases where in reality human factors like error of judgment clearly contributed to them. While the study did not explore whether the 'facts' of each incident were accurately reported, the analysis highlighted clear differences in the representation of riders and drivers of motor vehicles involved in the crash: the former were individualized whereas the latter were routinely impersonalized. This finding, coupled with the frequent occurrence of the term *accident*, could reasonably be interpreted as evidence for the existence of the kind of media bias against cycling identified and criticized particularly by cycling journalists and pundits (Giddings 2015; Reid 2017a). On the other hand, similar criticisms have been made about motor crash reporting more broadly (Connor and Wesolowski 2004), and the fact that the descriptions in the *Crash report corpus* are otherwise detailed and consider different perspectives suggest that the observed patterns could be attributed to journalistic conventions and the aim to respect the presumption of innocence and ensure that the right to fair trial is not undermined. The set of variables influencing the process of framing is complex, and the present study is just one step towards answering this question. More detailed investigations of additional corpus data and other evidence, such as information about what cultural norms and practices are involved in the production of crash reports and how they are received and interpreted by audiences are clearly needed.

Reports of crashes involving high-profile cyclists represent a special kind of writing, distinct both from other kinds of sports reporting and from crash reporting involving people riding a bicycle for recreation or transport. While the analysis of the latter type of text may be more relevant for public health and injury prevention, texts in the *Crash report corpus* offer valuable material for the understanding of discourse and language of sports. They shape to the image of cycling as a sport, and, by highlighting aspects of deceases cyclists public and private life, offer an insight into the social construction of cycling as a way of life.

Appendix: Names of cyclists in the corpus

Death in training: Lauri Aus, Victor Cabedo, Claudio Clarindo, Amy Dombroski, Amy Gillet, Kristof Goddaert, Luke Harrop, Carly Hibberd, Iñaki Lejarreta, Jason Lowndes, Anders Nilsson, Ricardo Otxoa, Jure Robic, Michele Scarponi, Burry Stander, Carla Swart

Death in race: Juan Barrero, Bob Breedlove, Thomas Casarotto, Fabio Casartelli, Antoine Demoitie, Randall Fox, Isaac Galvez, Bahman Golbarnezhad, Mike Hall, Junior Heffernan, Annefleur Kalvenhaar, Andrei Kivilev, Brett Malin, Dejan Maric, Jéanne Nell, Will Olson, Tim Pauwels, Nicole Reinhart, Mathieu Riebel, Casey Saunders, Diego Suta, Wouter Weylandt, Chad Young, Eslam Nasser Zaki.

Notes

1 As noted by the European cyclists' federation (ECF), comparing the cycling record across different countries is extremely difficult due to different metrics used. The ECF's cycling barometer, based on five EU-wide surveys, is topped by Denmark, the Netherlands and Sweden, with the Netherlands scoring highest for cycling usage (ECF 2015).
2 Emphasis mine.
3 https://www.crashnotaccident.com/
4 The Associated Press (2016: 51) recommends avoiding the term 'accident' when 'negligence is claimed or proved[,]… which can be read by some as a term exonerating the person responsible'.
5 Daniels et al. (2010: 1474) focus on 'agenda-setting' and do not consider how the reports are framed or how they were received. See further Adams (1992) on 'newsworthiness' in relation to risk communication.
6 A full list of the cyclists is given in the Appendix.
7 Sentence boundaries were detected by CLAWS.
8 The relative absence of references to helmet wearing, identified in previous work as correlating with the severity of injury in cycling crashes (e.g. Robartes and Chen 2017), is due to the corpus focusing on professional and competitive cycling, where the wearing of helmets was made compulsory in 2003.

References

Adams, W. C. (1992), 'The Role of Media Relations in Risk Communication', *Public Relations Quarterly*, 37 (4): 28–32.

Baker, P. C. Gabrielatos and T. McEnery (2013), *Discourse Analysis and Media Attitudes: The Representation of Islam in the British Press*, Cambridge: Cambridge University Press.

BBC (2017), 'Michele Scarponi: Italian Cyclist Dies in Training Crash', Available at: https://www.bbc.com/sport/cycling/39677856 (accessed on 22 April 2017).

Bednarek, M. and H. Caple (2017). *The Discourse of News Values: How News Organizations Create Newsworthiness*. Oxford: Oxford University Press.

Beullens, K., K. Roe and J. Van Den Bulck (2008), 'Television News' Coverage of Motor-vehicle Crashes', *Journal of Safety Research*, 39 (5): 547–553.

Brossard, D. (2010), 'Framing and Priming in Science Communication', in S. Hornig Priest (ed.), *Encyclopedia of Science and Technology Communication*, 309–311, Thousand Oaks, CA: SAGE Publications, Inc.

Brown, G. and G. Yule (1983), *Discourse Analysis*, Cambridge: Cambridge University Press.

Connor, S. M. and K. Wesolowski (2004), 'Newspaper Framing of Fatal Motor Vehicle Crashes in Four Midwestern Cities in the United States, 1999-2000', *Injury Prevention*, 10: 149–153.

Cycling News (2017), '*Michele Scarponi Killed in Training*', Available at: http://www.cyclingnews.com/news/michele-scarponi-killed-in-training/ (accessed on 22 April 2017).

Cycling UK (2012), 'Cycling UK's Cycling Statistics', Available at: https://www.cyclinguk.org/resources/cycling-uk-cycling-statistics.

Daley, M. and C. Rissel (2011), 'Perspectives and Images of Cycling as a Barrier or Facilitator of Cycling', *Transport Policy*, 18 (1): 211–216.

Daniels, S., T. Brijs and D. Keunen (2010), 'Official Reporting and Newspaper Coverage of Road Crashes: A Case Study', *Safety Science*, 48 (10): 1469–1476.

ECF (2015), 'ECF Cycling Barometer. Brussels: European Cyclists' Federation', Available at: https://ecf.com/resources/cycling-facts-and-figures.

Entman, R. M. (1993), 'Framing: Toward Clarification of a Fractured Paradigm', *Journal of Communication*, 43 (4): 51–58.

Falcous, M. (2017), 'Why We Ride: Road Cyclists, Meaning, and Lifestyles', *Journal of Sport and Social Issues*, 41 (3): 239–255.

Ferrero-Regis, T. (2018), 'Twenty-first Century Dandyism: Fancy Lycra® on Two Wheels', *Annals of Leisure Research*, 21(1): 95–112.

Fest, J. (2016), 'Register of Sports News around the World. A Quantitative Study of Field in Newspaper Sports Coverage', in D. Caldwell, J. Walsh, E. W. Vine and J. Jureidini (eds), *The Discourse of Sport: Analyses from Social Linguistics*, 190–208, London: Taylor & Francis.

Fotheringham, W. (2012), 'How Britain Became a Cycling Nation', *The Observer*, June: 14.

Garside, R. and N. Smith (1997), 'A Hybrid Grammatical Tagger: CLAWS4', in R. Garside, G. Leech and A. McEnery (eds), *Corpus Annotation: Linguistic Information from Computer Text Corpora*, 102–121, London: Longman.

Giddings, C. (2015), 'Five Cyclist-Blaming Headlines – And How to Reframe Them', *Bicycling*, 11 November. Available at: https://www.bicycling.com/news/a20049939/five-cyclist-blaming-headlines-and-how-to-reframe-them/ (accessed on 23 May 2018).

Halliday, M. A. K. (2004), *An Introduction to Functional Grammar*, 4th edn, London: Routledge.
Hambrick, M.E., E. L. Frederick and J. Sanderson (2015), 'From Yellow to Blue: Exploring Lance Armstrong's Image Repair Strategies across Traditional and Social Media', *Communication & Sport*, 3 (2): 196–218.
Huckin, T. (2004), 'Content Analysis: What Texts Talk About', in C. Bazerman and P. Prior (eds), *What Writing Does and How It Does It*, 13–32, Hillsdale: Lawrence Erlbaum Associates, Publishers.
Kitziger, J. (2007), 'Framing and Frame Analysis', in E. Deveraux (ed.), *Media Studies. Key Issues and Debates*, 134–161, London: Sage.
Laitila, T. (2005). 'Journalistic Codes of Ethics in Europe', in E. de Bens, P. Golding and D. McQuail (eds), *Communication Theory and Research*, 191–204, London: SAGE Publications Ltd.
Liao, H. (2015), 'Stop Calling My Daughter's Death a Car Accident', *WIRED*, 4 October. Available on: https://www.wired.com/2015/10/stop-calling-daughters-death-car-accident/ (accessed on 22 May 2018).
List of Cyclists with a Cycling-related Death (2010), 'List of Cyclists with a Cycling-related death – Wikipedia, The Free Encyclopedia'. Available at: https://en.wikipedia.org/wiki/List_of_cyclists_with_a_cycling-related_death (accessed on 9 April 2018).
MECD (2015), *Encuesta de Hábitos Deportivos en España 2015*, Madrid: Ministerio de Educación, Cultura y Deporte.
Moses, R. A. and G. D. Marelli (2004), 'Obituaries and Discursive Construction of Dying and Living', *Texas Linguistic Forum*, 47: 123–130.
Reese, S. D. (2001), 'Prologue – Framing Public Life: A Bridging Model for Media Research', in A. E. Grant, S. D. Reese and O. H. Gandy Jr. (eds), *Framing Public Life. Perspectives on Media and Our Understanding of the Social World*, 1–32, Mahwah, NJ: Lawrence Erlbaum Associates.
Reid, C. (2017a), 'Episode 157: The Prodigal Podcaster', *The Spokesmen Cycling Roundtable Podcast*. Available at: http://www.the-spokesmen.com/wordpress?p=637.
Reid, C. (2017b), *Tweet posted 22 April 2017 8.32 AM*. Available at: https://twitter.com/carltonreid/status/855731076278497280.
Reisigl, M. and R. Wodak (2016), 'The Discourse-historical Approach (DHA)', in R. Wodak and M. Meyer (eds), *Methods of Critical Discourse Studies*, 87–121, London: Sage.
Richtel, M. (2016), 'It's No Accident: Advocates Want to Speak of Car "Crashes" Instead', *New York Times*, May: 23.
Rissel, C., C. Bonfiglioli, A. Emilsen and B. J. Smith (2010), 'Representations of Cycling in Metropolitan Newspapers – Changes Over Time and Differences between Sydney and Melbourne, Australia', *BMC Public Health*, 10 (1): 371.
Robartes, E. and T. D. Chen (2017), 'The Effect of Crash Characteristics on Cyclist Injuries: An Analysis of Virginia Automobile-bicycle Crash Data', *Accident Analysis & Prevention*, 104: 165–173.

Scheufele, D. A. and D. Tewksbury (2007), 'Framing, Agenda Setting, and Priming: The Evolution of Three Media Effects Models', *Journal of Communication*, 57 (1): 9–20.

Swales, J. M. (1990), *Genre Analysis: English in Academic and Research Settings*, Cambridge: Cambridge University Press.

The Associated Press (2016), *The Associated Press Stylebook 2016*, New York, NY: Basic Books.

Van Leeuwen, T. (1996). 'The Representation of Social Actors', in C. R. Caldas-Coulthard and M. Coulthard (eds), *Texts and Practices. Readings in Critical Discourse Analysis*, 13–32, London: Routledge.

Van Leeuwen, T. (2016), 'Discourse as the Recontextualization of Social Practice – A Guide', in R. Wodak and M. Meyer (eds), *Methods of Critical Discourse Studies*, 23–61, London: Sage.

6

When Did I Do Dangerous Driving Then?: Structures and Functions of Formula One Race Radio Messages

Jukka Tyrkkö and Hanna Limatius

1. Introduction

Formula One is widely regarded as the pinnacle of all motor racing sports. With the highest team budgets, the most sophisticated automotive technology and an estimated worldwide television audience of more than 400 million for each Grand Prix (GP), Formula One is one of the world's premier spectator sports and also a truly multimodal experience. In addition to the race itself, which is filmed from every possible angle and enhanced by a wide range of analytical graphics, additional media content is provided in the form of live qualifying sessions, interviews, behind-the-scenes tours, mobile apps and commentary by racing experts, among many other things.

A relatively recent feature has been the public broadcasting of the radio dialogues between drivers and pit crews that take place during a race. By providing a glimpse into team tactics, these broadcasts are of particular interest because they allow the viewers at home to hear the drivers' live comments on the performance of their car, their own and other drivers' actions, other events during the race and the emotional highs and lows that take place in the heat of battle (see Real 2012). From the linguistics perspective, the language of race radio can be approached as a specialized form of synchronically transmitted dialogic discourse under paradigms such as Language for Specific Purposes and Communities of Practice (see Billings and Hardin 2014; Caldwell et al. 2016; Wenger 1998; Jucker and Kopaczyk 2013; Fazio 2012; Tyrkkö and Limatius 2018).

However, race radio interactions also present a unique opportunity for a specialized case study of language use under extreme pressure (see Saslow et al. 2014). In this chapter we analyse a newly compiled corpus of transcripts of all team radio messages broadcast over the 2016 and 2017 seasons of Formula One (see Collantine 2013–). Our primary research question concerns the complexity features, understood as a combination of syntactical and stylometric parameters, in both the drivers' and the race engineers' language. Noting that the dialogue between driver and team mostly takes place as the driver is handling a race car going at extreme speeds and thus undergoing considerable physical – and cognitive – pressure, our hypothesis is that the drivers' language will display signs of stress particularly as the race progresses, and that these signs can be quantified in the form of reduced turn and sentence length, a tendency to use shorter words and an altered pattern of lexical choices that shows signs of reduced complexity. To test the hypothesis, we apply corpus-based quantitative and qualitative methods to investigate the dialogic turns for structure and complexity, and present a breakdown analysis of the stylometric markers of both driver and team broadcasts. To our knowledge there are no previous linguistic studies of race radio interactions or of any other similar context of language use.

2. Background: Formula One racing and race radio

According to Formula One journalist and author Joe Saward (2016), while the race radio excerpts heard in the TV broadcasts are often chosen with the intention of adding 'drama', radio messages are 'not meant for the public'. Radio communication is used to exchange information – e.g. pit stop strategy, the state of the tires, weather reports – between the drivers and their race engineers, but as they are monitored and recorded by the FIA (Federation International de L'automobile; the governing body of the Formula One world championship, as well as Rally, Touring car, Endurance and Rallycross championships), radio messages are also a way for drivers to report incidents to Race Control. Other teams also listen to the broadcasts, and can inform their drivers if, for example, another driver is experiencing technical difficulties with their car (see Saward 2016). In Example (1) from the 2017 Singapore GP, Kimi Raikkonen (KR) and his race engineer discuss the latest weather report right before the race begins.

(1) To KR: Kimi we're going to go for inters. If they cancel the start to go behind the Safety Car it'll be [full wets] but for now I think if we just get a normal start we have to do inters.[1]

From KR: Do we expect that it's going to rain like this? Cause it's not going to take long before it's full wets.

To KR: It's not going to rain like this for very long.

At the beginning of the 2016 season, the FIA enforced new, more restricted rules for the use of team radio during the race. Their goal was to adhere to Article 20.1 of F1's Sporting Regulations: 'The driver must drive the car alone and unaided' (Noble 2016). As a result, only certain types of radio messages were allowed (from teams to drivers) during the first half of the 2016 season, until the ban was lifted 'at the request of the teams and commercial rights holder' in July 2016 (see Collantine 2016). The effects of these short-lived radio restrictions can also be observed in our data, as illustrated by the exchange in (2) between Lewis Hamilton (LH) and his race engineer during the 2016 Australian GP.

(2) From LH: How do I turn the alarm off?
 To LH: I'm afraid I can't say, Lewis.

Here, 'can't' clearly refers to permission instead of ability – while the engineer most likely had all the necessary information to tell Hamilton how to turn off the alarm, under the FIA regulations in place at the time, he was not allowed to do so.

On the fastest tracks (e.g. Autódromo Hermanos Rodríguez in México), Formula One racing cars can reach up to 370 km/h speed on the straights. The combination of handling a high-speed vehicle, the high temperature in the cockpit and the exposure to g-forces makes the race an extremely physically demanding experience for the driver – not to mention the added emotional stress of competition. The communications that are transmitted over the team radio thus take place in rather challenging circumstances, and the driver and the race engineer need to have a mutual understanding of what constitutes efficient communication. As our data demonstrates, this goal is not always reached – there are times during a race when the driver simply has to request radio silence. The exchange in (3) took place between Valtteri Bottas and his engineer during the 2017 British GP:

(3) To VB: Good job.
 From VB: Copy. Minimal talking.

Even though the engineer is offering encouragement here, Bottas replies bluntly by requesting 'minimal talking' to be able to concentrate fully on the race. This exchange took place in the closing laps of the race, during which Bottas attempted – and succeeded – to close in on the two competing cars in front of him.

During the race, a driver usually communicates with his race engineer, though other members of the team can listen to the exchange as well and may occasionally participate.[2] All the drivers communicate with their pit crews primarily in English, although some may use another language on occasion. Drivers who are fluent in several languages, such as Sebastian Vettel and Nico Rosberg, occasionally switch to their team's native language, particularly when thanking them during the victory lap. Although these exchanges are usually restricted to a few set phrases, they nevertheless signal a particular affinity between the driver and the pit crew. In example (4) Sebastian Vettel thanks his team (Ferrari) in Italian.

(4) From SV: Dai un'altra bandiera a Maranello. Vai! Grazie! Forza Ferrari. Grazie mille. Grazie ragazzi. Grande lavoro.

The number of radio messages broadcast during the live transmissions appears to reflect the respective drivers' status, which means that less prominent drivers' communications tend to be underrepresented in the dataset. Consequently, we were very careful not to compare individual drivers with one another except when it comes to anecdotal evidence or when an individual driver is particularly well represented in the corpus. In the 2016 season, twenty-four drivers drove for eleven teams, and in 2017, twenty-three drivers drove for ten teams. Thus, not all drivers in the data participated in all of the races; it is not unheard of for the teams to switch drivers in the middle of a season, and changes between seasons are common, as the drivers' contracts are usually negotiated on a yearly basis. During the seasons under investigation in this study, Mercedes, Red Bull and Ferrari were the teams with the most successful drivers. (See Appendix 1 for a complete list of drivers.)

The stressors affecting a Formula One driver during a GP are both physical and cognitive Physically, a driver's heart rate is consistently elevated, they endure prolonged exposure to temperatures of up to 60 degree centigrade and their bodies have to cope with repeated momentary g-forces of up to 5 or 6 Gs depending on the circuit. While this is happening, the driver is concentrating on piloting a car that accelerates from 0 to 100 kilometres per hour in 2.1 to 2.7 seconds and reaches top speeds of 370 kilometres per hour, focusing not only on driving but also on race strategy and the mechanical performance of the car, which must be discussed with the pit crew and adjusted by the driver. The fact that the drivers demonstrably manage to perform under these circumstances in relative safety demonstrates that with experience these stressors can be overcome to a considerable degree. It is worth noting that the thematic scope of communication during a race is intensively focused only to matters of relevance to the race. Our data does not show a single instance of driver and race engineer engaging in discussion of anything unrelated to the race. Nevertheless, our hypothesis is that the multitude of stressors over the course of a race will have an effect on a driver's and possibly also a race engineer's linguistic performance.

2.2. Linguistic complexity and spoken language under stress

Linguistic studies of complexity are most typically carried out in the context of genre and register analysis, and perhaps most often focusing on formal registers such as academic and legal writing (see, e.g., Lehto 2013; Biber et al. 2013, 2016). In the present study, we apply the concept of complexity to the investigation of spoken performance under considerable physical and cognitive stress, arguing that the task of maintaining radio communication while driving a race car can be approached from the theoretical perspective as an analysis of the effects of task complexity on linguistic performance (see, e.g., Salimi and Dadashpour 2012). In the present study, the stress-inducing task itself is not a linguistic one,[3] but instead we attempt to observe how highly stressful conditions may affect a speaker's linguistic performance (see Pennebaker and Lay 2002; Cohn et al. 2004). Our hypothesis is that a driver's language will show a significant reduction in complexity features during a race, that this reduction of features will intensify as the race progresses, and furthermore that these effects will be less pronounced in the more experienced drivers' language use. While linguistic performance under specialized circumstances is most accurately studied under laboratory conditions, it would be impossible to recreate this level of stress in a more controlled environment.[4]

The effects of acute stress on linguistic performance and the physiochemical mechanisms involved have been studied under a variety of theoretical frameworks. According to the disruptive stress hypothesis (Suedfeld and Rank 1976; Suedfeld and Coren 1992), increasing stress can impair cognitive functions and narrow the scope of performance. Although much of the research has focused on general cognitive performance, some recent work has also explored the effects of stress on linguistic performance. According to Saslow et al. (2014: 261–263), changes in a subject's heart rate are reflected in linguistic cognitive complexity and physiological reactions may be especially central to the impact of stress on language. The effects of stress can be observed in language production as a decrease in features associated with linguistically complex speech, such as exclusive words (e.g. *but, except, however, unless*), tentative words (e.g. *maybe, perhaps, hesitant, guess*), negations (e.g. *never, neither, without, cannot*) and discrepancies (e.g. *should, would, ought, wish*).[5] As the analysis will show, this effect can be observed in the Formula One drivers' messages as well.

Most studies of linguistic complexity focus on either clausal or phrasal complexity features, following either the T-unit tradition (e.g. Norris and Ortega 2009; Crossley and McNamara 2014) or the register analysis tradition of analysis (e.g. Parkinson and Musgrave 2014; Staples et al. 2016). However, many of these established approaches are challenging to implement directly in the present study because the communicative scenario examined produces turns that are extremely short and structurally very simple. As an alternative, we opted to measure complexity from a stylometric or so-called shallow text perspective,[6] focusing on the established metrics of turn length, sentence length and word length (see Lewis and Frank 2016), as well as two additional easily quantifiable features, namely, the proportion of interrogative sentences and the proportional distribution of word classes. Similar measures have been used in a variety of fields such as automatic genre recognition and authorship attribution (see Stamatatos et al. 2002; Lim et al. 2005; Lex et al. 2010; Tyrkkö 2013; Lijffijt and Nevalainen 2017). The word class distribution not only allows us to identify similarities between subsets of the corpus, but also to obtain a general impression of the frequencies at which word classes associated with complex language, such as coordinating and subordinating conjunctions, occur in the different subsets. More detailed analyses of the lexical, phraseological and syntactic aspects of complexity in race radio interactions had to be left out due to restrictions of space, but they will be discussed in follow-up studies (Tyrkkö and Limatius 2018).

3. Material and methods

3.1. The corpus

The primary data for this study consists of the radio transcripts of the 2016 and 2017 seasons of Formula One, as broadcast across the world. An important caveat to this study is that the data comes from the official television broadcasts, which are a professionally edited part of a commercial product. This means, among other things, that instances of swearing are edited out of the transmissions. As a result, our data does not include all radio communications that took place during a race but only those that make it into the television feed, and the data is disproportionately representative of the more popular and successful drivers and their teams. We openly acknowledge that the sampling method is opportunistic and thus far from ideal, and that further studies under more controlled circumstances and with more data will be needed.

Altogether thirty-nine individual races were included, twenty in the year 2016 and nineteen in 2017. The transcripts were harvested from the Formula One fan website http://www.f1fanatic.co.uk, the messages between the drivers and the pit crews having been transcribed by Keith Collantine, a contributor to the website (see Collantine 2013–).[7] The transcripts are first live tweeted on the f1fanatic twitter account (@f1fanatic) during Grand Prix weekends and subsequently posted on the website. The accuracy of the transcripts was randomly verified by comparing them to official race recordings and they were generally found to be of good quality.

The transcript corpus consists of 5,432 individual messages, or 63,183 word tokens, of which 24,193 come from the drivers and 38,990 from the teams. The dataset includes messages sent between thirty individual drivers belonging to twelve teams (see Appendix 1). The drivers represent eighteen different nationalities. Seven of them are native speakers of English, and all are able to communicate in English, most of them reasonably fluently.[8] The original data includes the name of the driver, the direction of the message (to or from the driver), the lap during which a message was delivered and the message itself. The metadata was manually edited and systematized for corpus use. This processing involved correcting typos, removing occasional meta comments included in the original transcripts,[9] and resolving some cases where the direction of the message – whether to or from the driver – was unclear. There were 157 instances in which one or more words were unavailable because they had been censored by Formula One Management, the corporation that owns the television rights to the sport. These were annotated in the original transcription as '[censored by FOM]'.

A series of preliminary steps was needed prior to the stylometric analysis. The number of sentences was counted relying on the sentence delimiters provided in the transcript, assigning the sentence count of one to messages that did not include a single item of standard sentence-final punctuation. Word length was calculated by character count, with hyphenated words and contracted forms being calculated as single words.[10]

Finally, the corpus was part-of-speech tagged using the widely known tool Treetagger (see Schmid 1994). Although the tagging of spoken language is notably problematic, this was not an issue here because there are no overlapping turns and the messages are generally short and the sentence structures very simple. Contracted forms were expanded prior to the tagging (e.g. *can't -> cannot, he'll -> he will*) and some systematic tagging mistakes were manually corrected[11]; for example, the tags of *OK* and *yeah* were changed from adjectives or nouns into interjections in nearly 85 per cent of the cases, typically when occurring in turn-initial positions). As a final step, Treetagger's 58-tag tagset was simplified by collapsing most of the detailed tags under the main tag; for example, we used only one tag for nouns, one for adjectives, one for lexical verbs and so on. This procedure makes sense with the present data, because the subsets of data are relatively small and a very fine-grained analysis would give excessive weight to items that occur very rarely in the data, such as comparative forms of adjectives, plural proper nouns or the past participle forms of *do*.

A typical Formula One race is between seventy and seventy-five laps long and takes approximately 90 minutes to complete. The original metadata provides lap numbers, in addition to which some messages were labelled PR (pre-race), FL (final lap) and VL (victory lap). During PR the drivers sit in their cars in the starting grid and the victory lap takes place after the actual race is over. To streamline our analysis of the timeline and to facilitate the analysis of races of different durations, we divided each race into three sections of equal length labelled beginning, middle and end, collapsing the final lap into the third section. We retained the original labels pre-race and victory lap (see Table 6.1).

Finally, in order to access the possible effects of experience and skill on language, we categorized the drivers into three tiers based on their ranking in the 2016 and 2017 GPs as well as earlier career history. Ten drivers were classified as being top tier, five as middle tier and fifteen as bottom tier (see Appendix 1).

Table 6.1 Messages during different parts of the race

Part of the race	Messages from drivers	Messages to drivers	Words
pre-race	94	141	3,079
beginning of race	883	1,165	22,616
middle of race	668	1,049	19,181
end of race	283	374	7,014
victory lap	329	457	11,288
total	**2,257**	**3,186**	**63,183**

3.2. Methods

The analysis presented here is largely based on an investigation of quantitative variables obtained from the data. The main statistical method used in the multivariate analysis is decision tree partitioning, also known as recursive partitioning (Strobl et al. 2009; Lijffijt and Nevalainen 2017; Tyrkkö and Nurmi 2017).[12] Decision tree methods provide an alternative to regression models, which can be difficult to interpret. By contrast, decision trees produce results that read like a flowchart, where each iterative split into two new branches can be interpreted as a decision and each node that follows provides values (count, mean, standard deviation) that are directly relevant to the task at hand. As with all multivariate methods, the objective of the analysis is to evaluate the effect of a number of predictor variables on an outcome variable, distinguishing between those that have a significant effect and those that do not, as well as measuring the size of the effect.

The procedure of partitioning is straightforward to explain. First, we select a response variable and several predictor variables. All possible ways of splitting the data into two are then tested for statistical significance; this includes testing the split by every predictor, as well as by every level of predictors that have more than two levels. When all possible splits using all the predictors and all their levels have been tested, the dataset is split into two by the one that gives the highest statistical significance.[13] This produces the first split or branching in the decision tree, with the two newly created nodes or leafs representing new subsections of the dataset. With the data now in two parts, new tests are run on both parts using all the remaining variables and their remaining levels to find out where to split the data next. This procedure is carried out in a stepwise fashion until all the predictor variables have been used, no more statistically significant splits can be made or the pre-determined minimum number of observations per leaf has been reached.[14] In the tree diagram, each leaf is represented by a box giving the number of observations (count), the mean value of the outcome variable (mean) and its internal distribution (standard deviation) and, in the case of leafs that are further split, the statistical significance (LogWorth) of the split and difference between the means of the next two leafs (difference).

We also use hierarchical cluster analysis in our investigation of word class distributions. Cluster analysis is one of several types of exploratory data analysis aimed at identifying similarities and dissimilarities between objects such as texts or groups of texts based on finite sets of variables. Similar items can be organized into clusters based on a wide variety of different methods, each of which has its own strengths and shortcomings (see e.g. Tyrkkö 2013). The methods are well documented in literature, but in short we standardized the variables to avoid skewing in the direction of variables that occur at naturally higher frequencies (e.g. nouns vs. *wh*-pronouns) and employed Ward's method for clustering.

4. Findings

The findings will be discussed in three sections. First, a breakdown is provided of the basic quantitative features of the messages in the corpus. Next, the stylometric variables are analysed using a series of statistical analyses on factors affecting linguistic performance. Finally, the distribution of word classes across specific subsets of the corpus is used to identify notable tendencies.

4.1. Basic quantitative indicators

For an overview of the data before proceeding to closer analysis, we use a heatmap to visualize the distribution of counts of the mean turn lengths and word lengths grouped by part of the race and the driver tier; Figure 6.1 shows messages from the race engineers to the drivers and Figure 6.2 messages from the drivers to the

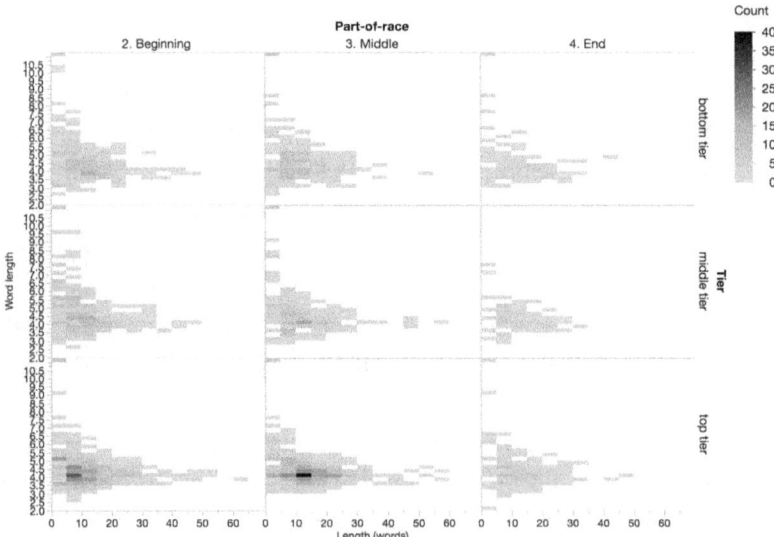

Figure 6.1 Distribution heatmap of turn and word length in teams' messages by part-of-race and driver tier.

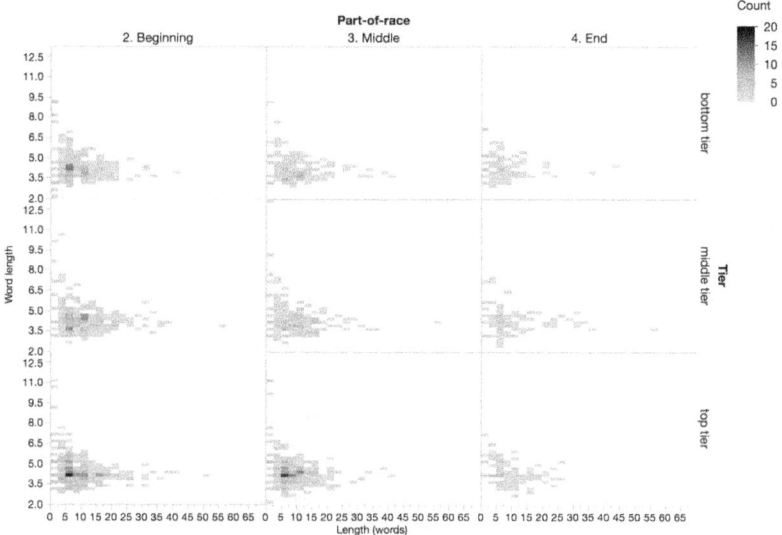

Figure 6.2 Distribution heatmap of turn and word length in drivers' messages by part-of-race and driver tier.

race engineers. The pre-race and victory lap subsets of the data have been left out of the visualization to put more focus on the actual race language. As the figures show, although there are occasionally turns of fifteen words of longer, the vast majority of messages fall within the five- to fifteen-word range in length. The typical word length falls at 4.4 letters, with some occasional words of up to twelve letters. The observed overall difference between the teams' and drivers' mean turn lengths, sentence lengths and word lengths are all statistically significant, each showing that the drivers' messages are somewhat simpler and briefer than the race engineers' (see Table 6.2).[15]

Table 6.2 Basic descriptive statistics

Source of message	Turn length (words)			Sentence length (words)			Word length (letters)		
	Mean	SD	Median	Mean	SD	Median	Mean	SD	Median
Drivers	10.71	8.72	8	6.70	3.97	6	4.35	1.01	4.18
Race engineers	12.28	9.49	10	7.28	4.49	6.33	4.55	1.18	4.31

4.2 Stylometric features

To test the hypothesis that the part of the race and the individual driver's experience level affect turn and sentence length, we used decision tree partitioning as discussed in section 'Methods'. In addition to the two factors mentioned, we also included the direction of the message in the model to investigate differences in production between drivers and their race engineers. All three predictors are categorical variables, with the levels given in Table 6.3.

Applying a decision tree model to the data with turn length as outcome variable and part-of-race, direction-of-message and tier as predictors, we see that the most significant predictor is part-of-race, with a split between radio messages during the actual race and messages either before or after the race (mean 11.06 vs. 14.11; see Figure 6.3). During the race, the direction of the communication is the most important predictor, with messages from the drivers being shorter than those of the teams (mean 9.72 vs. 12.01). Top- and middle-tier drivers' messages are longer than those of bottom-tier drivers (mean 10.18 vs. 7.69), while the race engineers of top-tier drivers communicate in longer turns than bottom- and middle-tier drivers' (mean 12.6 vs. 10.93). Before and after the actual race,

Table 6.3 Predictor variables and levels in the decision tree partitioning

Predictor	Levels
Part-of-race	pre-race, beginning, middle, end, victory lap
Tier	bottom, middle, top
Direction of message	from driver, to driver

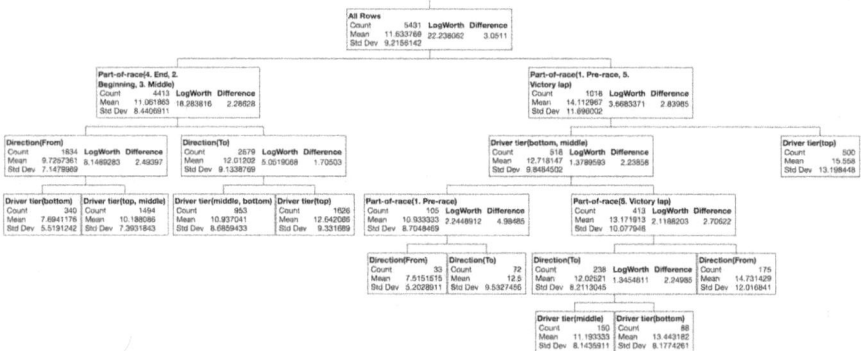

Figure 6.3 Decision tree for turn length.

the driver's tier is the most significant predictor, with the messages of top-tier drivers and their teams being the longest (mean 15.58 vs. 12.71), which is to be expected considering that they are the most likely to engage in celebratory discourse after the race.

The following exchange between Daniel Ricciardo and his race engineer during a heated moment in the 2017 Abu Dhabi GP, one of the longest in the corpus, illustrates the varying turn lengths (Example 5).

(5) To DR: It will be close to Raikkonen but you should be clear. We will be close.
    From DR: OK. I don't know if something in the front broke. I'll let you know.
    From DR: I've got a puncture, boxing. Sorry. Something felt wrong on the front.
    To DR: No worries. Just push on the way out.
    From DR: I think so. Just down at 19 felt weird.
    To DR: All feel OK with the car question?
    From DR: Something on the front still feels weird.
    To DR: OK mate. We've got a hydraulic problem. Go mode one and switch off mate. I can see what you're doing, just pull as far off the track as you can. You were doing a really good job until that point. You were quicker than Raikkonen behind you. Go to P0.
    From DR: Want me to stay in sixth? It's gone, it's gone.
    To DR: OK understood. Do not shift gear if you can.
    From DR: I think I'm losing power steering.

A similar analysis of sentence length shows that pre-race sentences are significantly longer than those spoken during the rest of the rest (mean 8.70 vs. 6.97; see Figure 6.4). Given that pre-race is the period where the car is sitting on

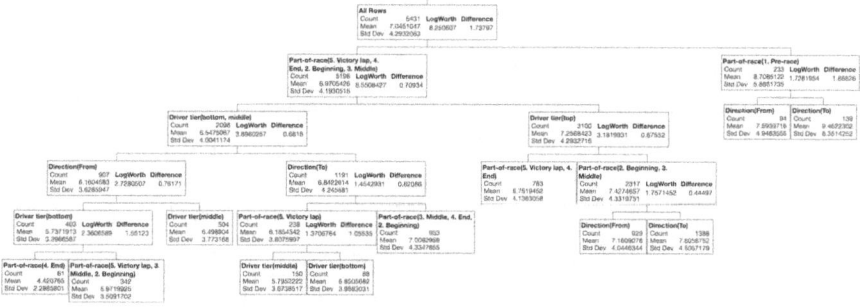

Figure 6.4 Decision tree for sentence length.

the track and the race is not yet on, this is unsurprising. The next split is based on the drivers' tier during the race and on direction of message during the pre-race period. During the race, top-tier drivers and their teams communicate in longer sentences than bottom-tier and middle-tier drivers and teams (mean 7.25 vs. 6.54), while during pre-race, race engineers' sentences are longer than drivers' sentences (mean 9.46 vs. 7.59). When it comes to communication during the race, the longest sentences are produced by top-tier drivers' teams during the beginning and middle of the race (mean 7.60) while the shortest sentences are produced by bottom-tier drivers during the end of the race (4.42).

Focusing on the possible effects of stress on speech production, we see that the drivers' experience appears to correlate with sentence length. The bottom-tier drivers' mean sentence length during the race is 5.73 words per sentence, the middle-tier drivers' is 6.48 and top-tier drivers' is 7.25. The bottom-tier drivers appear to be particularly strongly affected by stress as the race progresses, as seen in the drop of their mean sentence length from 5.97 during the beginning and middle of the race to only 4.42 words during the last third of the race. The middle-tier and top-tier drivers' sentences also get marginally shorter, but the differences are not statistically significant.

At this point it may be asked, why, if we are interested in performance, did we opt to use the somewhat crude category of tier instead of looking at drivers individually? The reason is simple: there is not enough evidence from individual drivers to allow statistically well-argued observations. Although some of the top drivers like Kimi Raikkonen, Nico Rosberg and Sebastian Vettel are featured frequently in the broadcasts, we do not have enough evidence from most of the drivers to allow us to include the individual drivers in the statistical model. However, what we can do is to compare these top drivers with the others and with their race engineers (Figure 6.5).

Figure 6.5 gives box plots of five top drivers' turn lengths and sentence lengths during the actual race (beginning, middle and end). As the figure shows, the former World Champions Kimi Raikkonen and Sebastian Vettel stand out as particularly talkative, both speaking in longer turns and sentences than their race engineers; the other top drivers' language does not differ from the average. Raikkonen's mean turn length is 12.88 words and mean sentence length is 9.02, while Vettel's mean turn is 11.35 words long and his mean sentence length is 6.69 words. Notably, if Raikkonen's own messages are removed from the dataset, the other drivers' mean turn length is 9.46 and mean sentence length is 6.50, which means that Raikkonen's mean turn is 36 per cent longer than the other drivers' on average and his sentences are 38 per cent longer.[16] Both differences

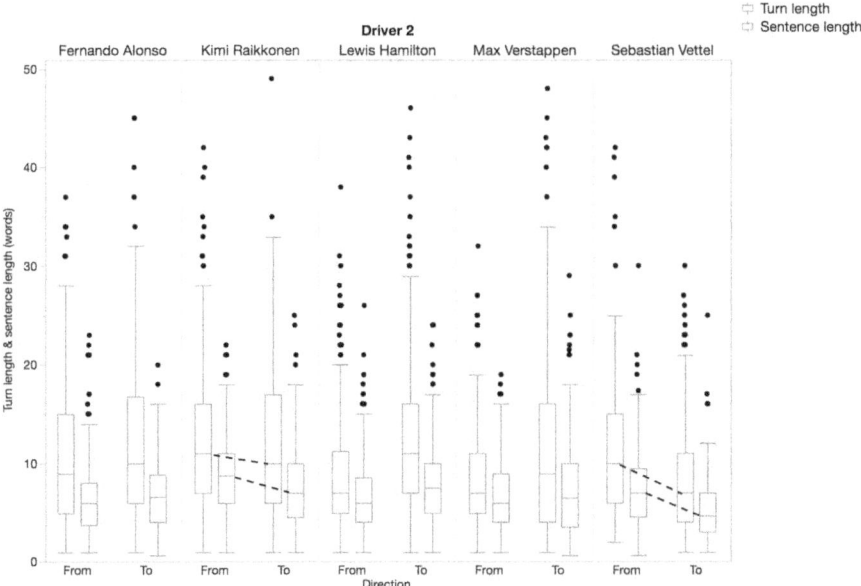

Figure 6.5 Box plot of select drivers' and their race engineers' turn and sentence lengths.

are statistically highly significant (ANOVA F=8.09, p=*** and F=33.31, p=***, respectively). For Vettel, only sentence length is the significant difference compared to the other drivers (ANOVA F=16.15, p=***).

Returning to the full dataset, Figure 6.6 shows that the most significant factor is the direction of the message, with the drivers using slightly shorter words than the race engineers (mean 4.35 vs. 4.55 characters). The drivers also use longer words outside of the race (4.50 characters) than during a race (4.31 characters), but no significant differences can be observed between different sections of the race. Notably, no statistically significant difference can be observed when it comes to the race engineers' word choices before, during or after the race. Comparing this information with the fact that drivers' words are shorter during the race supports the hypothesis that stress during racing conditions affects the drivers' language.

In addition to analysing word length by means of a mean length, we can also investigate the feature by looking at the proportional distributions of words of different lengths. Based on the previous finding, we focus only on messages from the drivers to see precisely how pre-race and victory lap differ from the actual race. For convenience and to reduce the number of potential levels, we bin

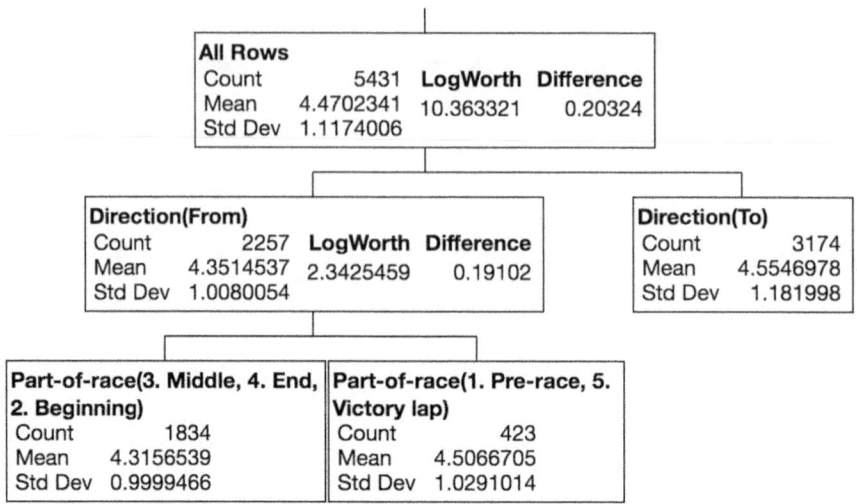

Figure 6.6 Decision tree for word length.

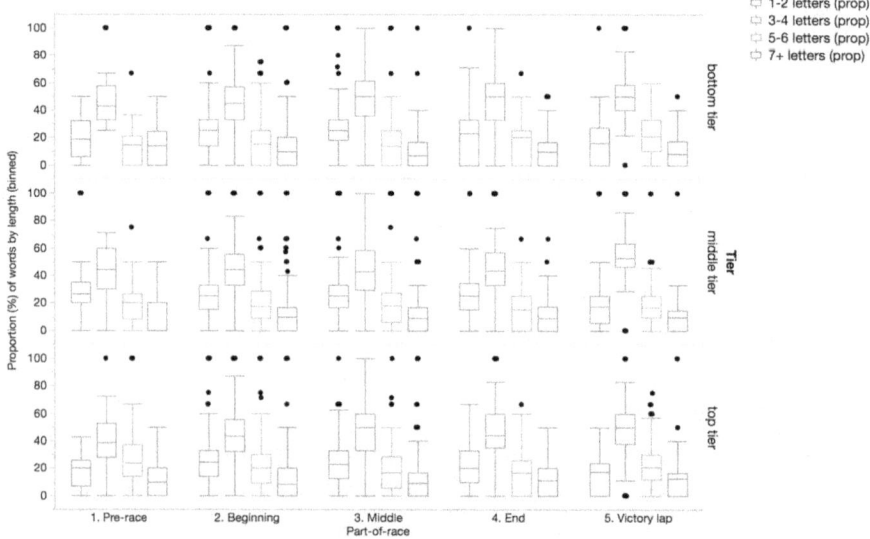

Figure 6.7 Box plot of binned word lengths (%) by part-of-race and driver tier.

the lengths of words into five groups: words of one or two letters, three or four letters, five or six letters and finally words of seven letters or more. As Figure 6.7 shows, the distributional profiles of word lengths are remarkably similar during the actual race: the three sections of the race hardly differ at all, and the driver's tier also has no significant effect. The tier-by-tier differences during pre-race and victory lap are not entirely consistent, but it appears that the middle- and top-tier drivers use longer words (five letters or more) during that period than during the race, as expected.

Another factor that may also be affected by processing constraints under stress is the amount of question-and-answer interaction between the drivers and engineers. Given that one of the main functions of race radio is to allow the driver and team to discuss ongoing events, it is natural that questions feature in the communication. Treating the inclusion of a question in the message as a categorical outcome variable with the levels 'yes' or 'no', and using the same three predictor variables as before, we ran another decision tree model (Figure 6.8).

The result shows that the direction of communication is the most significant factor affecting questions. Drivers ask questions in 20 per cent of their messages, while race engineers do so only 6 per cent of the time. The drivers' questions come primarily during the pre-race, the middle and the end of the race with 26 per cent of the messages containing one (or more), while the race engineers ask the most questions during the beginning of the race (9.5 per cent of all messages). Importantly, considering our hypothesis, the top-tier and middle-tier drivers ask significantly more questions than the bottom-tier drivers after the beginning of the race (28.3 vs. 18.3 per cent), while the top-tier drivers' teams ask the least questions with only 3 per cent of their messages containing a question. This suggests that top-tier teams avoid distracting their drivers with questions during the final stages of the race. The overall results thus point in the same direction as the previous ones, namely, that top-tier and middle-tier drivers maintain their

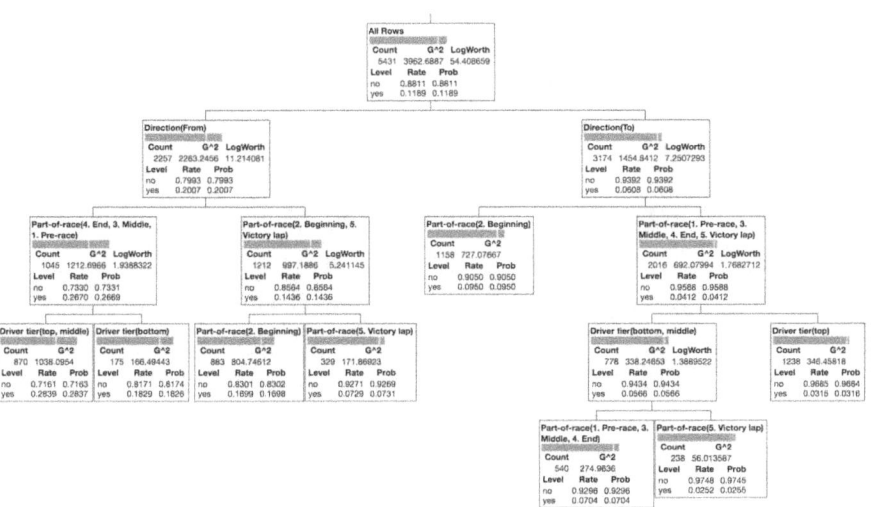

Figure 6.8 Decision tree for proportion of interrogative sentences.

ability to communicate effectively throughout the race, while this appears to be more difficult for bottom-tier drivers.

4.3. Word class distribution

Finally, we carried out a simple stylometric analysis of word class distributions to obtain a general overview of whether or not there are notable grammatical differences between different parts of the race and the two groups of speakers. Using the Treetagged version of the corpus as a starting point (see section 'The corpus'), we first pruned the tag list by removing sentence tags, list tags, symbol tags and foreign word tags. We then retrieved the standardized frequencies of each tag in each of the five parts of the race, keeping messages from the drivers and the race engineers separate. This gave ten groupings indicating the direction of the message in relation to the driver and the part of the race: for example, 'To 1. Middle' or 'From 5. Victory'. The frequencies of each tag were then standardized, which is a necessary procedure to ensure that the inherent frequency differences of the variables do not affect the clustering; for example, while nouns are always much more frequent than *to*-infinitive markers, the important factor here would be the relative frequencies of nouns across the subsets. A hierarchical cluster analysis using Ward's method was then carried out to group the different subsets of the data together according to similarity of overall tag distributions. In Figure 6.9, both the colour of the subset label (left-hand side of heatmap)

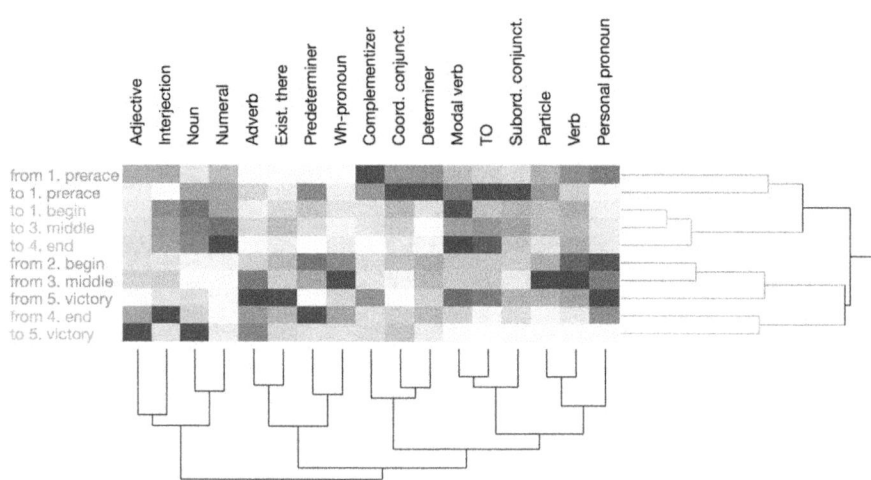

Figure 6.9 Hierarchical cluster dendrogram of part-of-speech distributions by part of race and message direction.

and the dendrogram (right-hand side) indicate the clusters, and the heatmap shows which tags are particularly frequent (dark blue) or infrequent (white) in the respective subset. Note that the colours in the heatmap are indicative of frequencies compared to the range of frequencies for that tag, and that the lighter colours do not mean that the tag in question would not appear in the data at all, simply that the frequency is lower there. The two-way clustering also includes a dendrogram for the tags below the treemap.

As Figure 6.9 shows, we identified four high-frequency clusters, which are: (i) pre-race messages from drivers and teams, (ii) messages from race engineers during the race (iii) messages from drivers during the beginning and middle of the race, and during the victory lap and (iv) messages from drivers at the end of a race and from teams during the victory lap. The statistical breakdown of the data appears to supports our hypothesis, but there are some seemingly surprising results, which will be addressed below.

Firstly, the fact that the messages of drivers and their race engineers in terms of POS used are very similar during the pre-race period is entirely expected. The clustering shows that the high-frequency items are complementizers, determiners, coordinating conjunctions and modal verbs or, in other words, markers of more complex language. The race engineers also use *to*-infinitive markers and subordinating conjunctions at this point, the latter of which are otherwise very rare in the corpus. The race engineers' more complex language is illustrated by Example (6), one of the longest turns in the dataset, in which Kimi Raikkonen's race engineer briefs him on important technical issues during the pre-race period of the 2017 Brazilian GP.

(6) OK Kimi, I'll go through the normal stuff in a second but just to bring you up to speed where we are, the reason why all the fuss earlier was we saw an issue with the telemetry signal being a bit weak so we're worried we might lose telemetry in the race. We did then have problems connecting to the car but that seems to have resolved itself. So the only thing to remind you of in the event we do have a problem with telemetry is to look after your fuel. You've got your display, you know how to use it.

Moving on to the next cluster, we see that the race engineers' messages during the race feature comparatively high frequencies of interjections, nouns and numerals, as well as modal verbs. This is explained by the engineers' role of provide feedback to their drivers about race positions, when to come in for a pit stop and, in the case on interjections, the repeated use of turn-initial discourse markers *yeah* and *ok*, which typically initiate a new message. Extremely common phrases in the engineers' messages include *at the moment, at the end* and *going to* (Tyrkkö and Limatius 2018). The engineers frequently address the drivers by name, while the drivers rarely reciprocate.

The drivers' language during the race is characterized by the use of adjectives, personal pronouns and verbs, as well as pre-determiners and *wh*-pronouns; on the other hand, their language is low on modal verbs, nouns, numerals and coordinating conjunctions during the race. The drivers use personal pronouns at a high frequency, typically either the first-person singular or the third-person singular. By contrast, the race engineers very rarely use the first-person singular and instead use either the second-person singular or the first-person plural. The use of adverbs and verbs is related to the fact that the drivers' language is typically descriptive, commenting on the performance of the car or of the other drivers'; high-frequency phrases include 'I don't know', 'a little bit', and 'a lot of'. In Example (7) from the 2017 Abu Dhabi GP, Nico Hulkenberg and Sergio Perez express their differing views on events taking place on the track.

(7) From SP: Hulkenberg cut the corner.
    From NH: He pushed me off the track, he made me run wide there.
    To NH: OK Nico understood.

For the drivers, the victory lap is similar to the first two-thirds of the race when it comes to word class usage. Although the driver is still tired, the stress of the race performance is over and, especially for the winners, the excitement of a successful race frequently comes out. This is illustrated by Lewis Hamilton's short speech after confirming his fourth championship title in the 2017 Mexican GP as shown in Example (8).

(8) From LH: I'd like to say a big thanks to everyone in this team. What you've done the past couple of years is just remarkable and I'm just so grateful for all your hard work this year. God bless you.
    To LH: Thank you Lewis mate. Great to have you in the team.
    From LH: Never gave up, man.

The seemingly surprising finding here is that drivers' messages towards the end of the race resemble the race engineers' messages during the victory lap. For the drivers, the final laps are the most stressful and thus their linguistic performance is the most strained, which leads to shorter messages, as discussed above. They use adjectives and adverbs, interjections, pre-determiners and personal pronouns, while the frequencies of complexity-related features are very low. When it comes to the race engineers, they speak relatively little during the victory lap, letting the drivers express emotions and mostly responding with short and simple congratulatory expressions. The similarity between these two subsets of the data demonstrates how different discourse functions can lead to choices that superficially resemble each other.

5. Tentative conclusions

The findings of this pilot study support the argument that the effects of stress can indeed be observed in the Formula One race radio messages by examining the linguistic markers selected. On average, the drivers' turns and sentences become shorter as the race progresses and both are significantly shorter than turns and sentences produced by the race engineers. Notably, while these differences grow more pronounced over the course of a race, they cannot be observed either before or after the actual race. Word length was found not to be a particularly useful indicator. The stylometric analysis of word class distributions further confirmed that the drivers' and race engineers' messages are significantly different in terms of grammatical realization. Most importantly, the analysis confirmed that word classes associated with more complex syntactic structures appear primarily, if not exclusively, during the pre-race period and thereafter only in the race engineers' messages. By contrast, the physical and mental strain that the drivers experience appears to result in a substantial reduction in complexity-related word classes during the race.

In addition to the overall differences between drivers and teams, the results also show that the more experienced drivers produce longer turns and sentences than less experienced drivers, and they initiated more question-and-answer interactions. A likely reason for the differences between drivers is the fact that bottom-tier drivers have, overall, less racing experience and therefore may find it more difficult and stressful to engage in dialogue during the race as they need to focus more on the driving itself. The world of Formula One is notorious for its ruthless competition – for a rookie driver, making a mistake in a couple of subsequent races could prove disastrous, as evidenced by the case of Daniil Kvyat, who was first demoted from Reb Bull Racing to Toro Rosso, and later asked to leave Toro Rosso as well. The role of the car should not be overlooked either, as top-tier drivers are probably driving a technically superior car in a team with a higher financial budget. Formula One racing is, after all, a 'combination of man and machine' (Couldwell 2003: 9). However, if we take the performance of the car into account, it seems somewhat surprising that the bottom-tier drivers initiated less interrogative interactions, as they are considered more likely to experience technical issues with the car, and thus ask questions on how to solve these issues.

This chapter should be considered a pilot study into the language of Formula One during the actual race. Further studies are in preparation on the factors that affect the linguistic practices of race drivers, including qualitative studies that focus on the in-group dynamics of the Formula One world at large, as well as the individual teams specifically, as communities of practice (e.g. Wenger 1998) with shared goals of achieving the best possible result both on the race level (wins, podiums, points) and on the season level (drivers' and constructors' championships) (Tyrkkö and Limatius 2018). The authors plan to expand the dataset and also to carry out contrastive analyses with reference corpora, which would allow us to measure the drivers' linguistics performance more accurately and in greater detail.

Notes

1 The term *inters* refers to intermediate tyres (used for driving in wet conditions when there is light standing water on the track). Formula One cars have a selection of tyres available, each suitable for different conditions. The selection of the right type of tyre has a fundamental impact on the car's performance.
2 We will use 'team' and 'race engineer' interchangeably throughout the paper.
3 Unlike some other studies of the effect of stress on language, where the source of stress has been a language-related task such as public speaking, in our case the speakers are highly unlikely to pay any attention to or worry about their language.
4 It may be added that standard ethics rules governing scientific research prohibit exposing test subjects to life-threatening situations.
5 The features were identified and grouped by Pennebaker and King (1999).
6 Stylometric analysis can be described as a shallow approach to linguistic analysis because the metrics used measure linguistic performance at a relatively superficial level.
7 The authors gratefully acknowledge that the present study would not have been possible without Mr Collantine's generous work for the good of the Formula One fan community. As of 2018, he has changed the name of the website to *RaceFans. net* (https://www.racefans.net/). As of 18 October 2018, it appears that race radio transcripts are not available for the 2018 season.

8   The effects of the drivers' first languages and general language proficiencies will be discussed in follow-up studies. Preliminary results discussed in Tyrkkö and Limatius (2018) suggest that native speaker drivers do not produce language significantly differently, but the race engineers appear to produce longer turns when communicating with native speakers.
9   Descriptive meta comments had been added by the transcriber to some entries to help readers understand the context in which that particular message was delivered. Examples include significant race event occurring right before or at the moment the message was delivered, or notes about problems with the clarity of the radio message.
10 Syllable count would arguably be a more appropriate measure in the case of spoken language, but we opted against syllable counting because the speakers' actual pronunciation could not be verified at this time.
11 The argument can be made that contracted forms out to be preserved as single units for reasons of processing speed. We calculated contracted forms as single items in the stylometric analysis, but they were expanded for the part-of-speech analysis. We aim to explore the effects of the two approaches in follow-up studies.
12 The analysis was carried out using the statistical tool JMP13. Recursive partitioning is fairly well supported in statistical software. In R, use the library rpart.
13 The decision tree model in JMP uses the statistic LogWorth for measuring statistical significance. LogWorth is defined as $-\log10(p\text{-value})$, where a LogWorth of 1.30 corresponds with the conventional threshold value of $p = 0.05$. The p-value used in calculating LogWorth takes into account the multiple comparison problem inherent to the task of comparing multiple splits. An unadjusted p-value would favour predictors with a high number of levels and the conventional Bonferroni correction would favour variables with few levels. For full details, see Sall (2002).
14 A potential problem with decision tree partitioning is so-called overfitting, which in this context means carrying out the splitting past the point where further splits cease to produce statistically significant results. In the present study, we used LogWorth 1.30 as the minimum threshold for splitting.
15 Inferential tests carried out using independent samples t-test assuming unequal variances, null hypothesis of equal means. For turn length, $d = 1.56$, $t = 6.27$, $p = ***$; for sentence length, $d = 0.58$, $t = 5.07$, $p = ***$; for word length, $d = 0.20$, $t = 6.81$, $p = ***$.
16 This detail is interesting because Raikkonen is famous in the Formula One world as a man of few words during interviews and other public events, while Vettel is known as one of the most talkative drivers.

References

Biber, D., B. Gray and K. Poonpon (2013), 'Pay Attention to the Phrasal Structures: Going beyond T-units – A Response to WeiWei Yang', *TESOL Quarterly*, 47: 192–201.

Biber, D., B. Gray and S. Staples (2016), 'Predicting Patterns of Grammatical Complexity across Language Exam Task Types and Proficiency Levels', *Applied Linguistics*, 37 (5): 639–668.

Billings, A. C. and M. Hardin, eds (2014), *Routledge Handbook of Sport and New Media*, London and New York: Routledge.

Caldwell, D., J. Walsh, E. W. Vine and J. Jureidini, eds (2016), *The Discourse of Sport: Analyses from Social Linguistics*, New York: Taylor and Francis.

Cohn, M. A., M. R. Mehl and J. W. Pennebaker (2004), 'Linguistic Markers of Psychological Change Surrounding September 11, 2001', *Psychological Science*, 15: 687–693.

Collantine, K. (2013–), *Team radio transcript archive*. Available at: https://www.racefans.net/category/regular-features/team-radio-transcripts/.

Collantine, K. (2016), 'Radio Ban to Be lifted during Races'. Available at: https://www.racefans.net/2016/07/28/radio-ban-lifted-races/.

Couldwell, C. (2003), *Formula One: Made in Britain – The British Influence in Formula One*, London: Virgin Books.

Crossley, S. A. and D. McNamara (2014), 'Does Writing Development Equal Writing Quality? A Computational Investigation of Syntactic Complexity in L2 Learners', *Journal of Second Language Writing*, 26 (4): 66–79.

Fazio, A. (2012), *Analysing the Language of Sport and Related Sciences*, Roma: Edizioni Nuova Cultura.

Jucker, A. H. and J. Kopaczyk (2013), 'Communities of Practice as a Locus of Language Change', in J. Kopaczyk and A. H. Jucker (eds), *Communities of Practice in the History of English*, 1–16, Amsterdam and Philadelphia, PA: John Benjamins.

Lehto, A. (2013), 'Complexity and Genre Conventions: Text Structure and Coordination in Early Modern English Proclamations', in A. H. Jucker, D. Landert, A. Seiler and N. Studer-Joho (eds), *Meaning in the History of English: Words and Texts in Context*, 233–256, Amsterdam: John Benjamins.

Lewis, M. L. and M. C. Frank (2016), 'The Length of Words Reflects Their Conceptual Complexity', *Cognition*, 153: 182–195.

Lex, E., A. Juffinger and M. Granitzer (2010), 'A Comparison of Stylometric and Lexical Features for Web Genre Classification and Emotion Classification in Blogs', in *2010 Workshops on Database and Expert Systems Applications*. Available at: https://ieeexplore.ieee.org/abstract/document/5591976/.

Lijffijt, J. and T. Nevalainen (2017), 'A Simple Model for Recognizing Core Genres in the BNC', in T. Hiltunen, T. Säily and J. McVeigh (eds), *Big and Rich Data in English Corpus Linguistics: Methods and Explorations*. Available at: http://www.helsinki.fi/varieng/series/volumes/19/ (accessed 16 June 2018).

Lim, C. S., K. J. Lee and G. C. Kim (2005), 'Automatic Genre Detection of Web Documents', *Lecture Notes in Computer Science*, 3248: 310–319.

Noble, J. (2016), 'Analysis: The Full Scope of F1's 2016 Radio Ban'. Available at: https://www.motorsport.com/f1/news/analysis-the-full-scope-of-f1-s-2016-radio-ban-677934/

Norris, J. and L. Ortega (2009), 'Towards an Organic Approach to Investigating CAF in SLA: The Case of Complexity', *Applied Linguistics*, 30: 555–578.

Parkinson, J. and J. Musgrave (2014), 'Development of Noun Phrase Complexity in the Writing of English for Academic Purposes Students', *Journal of English for Academic Purposes*, 14: 48–59.

Pennebaker, J. W. and L. A. King (1999), 'Linguistic Styles: Language Use as an Individual Difference', *Journal of Personality and Social Psychology*, 77 (6): 1296.

Pennebaker, J. W. and T. C. Lay (2002), 'Language Use and Personality during Crises: Analyses of Mayor Rudolph Giuliani's Press Conferences', *J Res Pers*, 36: 271–282.

RaceFans.net (formerly *F1Fanatic.co.uk*). Website. Available at: https://www.racefans.net/ (accessed 16 June 2018).

Real, M. (2012), 'Theorizing the Sports-television Dream Marriage: Why Sports Fit Television So Well?', in A. C. Billings (ed.), *Sports Media: Transformation, Integration, Consumption*, 19–39, Amsterdam: John Benjamins.

Salimi, A. and S. Dadashpour (2012), 'Task Complexity and Language Production Dilemmas (Robinson's Cognition Hypothesis vs. Skehan's Trade-off Model)', *Social and Behavioral Sciences*, 46: 643–652.

Sall, J. (2002), 'Monte Carlo Calibration of Distributions of Partition Statistics', SAS Institute, Available at: http://www.jmp.com/content/dam/jmp/documents/en/white-papers/montecarlocal.pdf (accessed 16 June 2018).

Saslow, L. R., S. McCoy, I. van der Löwe, B. Cosley, A. Vartan, C. Oveis, D. Keltner, J. T. Moskowitz and E. S. Epel (2014), 'Speaking under Pressure: Low Linguistic Complexity Is Linked to High Physiological and Emotional Stress Reactivity', *Psychophysiology*, 51 (3): 257–266.

Saward, J. (2016), 'Understanding F1 Radio'. Available at: https://joesaward.wordpress.com/2016/11/03/understanding-f1-radio/ (accessed 16 June 2018).

Schmid, H. (1994), 'Probabilistic Part-of-Speech Tagging Using Decision Trees', *Proceedings of International Conference on New Methods in Language Processing*, Manchester.

Stamatatos, E., N. Fakotakis and G. Kokkinakis (2002), 'Text Genre Detection Using Common Word Frequencies', *Proceedings of the 18th Conference on Computational Linguistics*, 808–814.

Staples, S., J. Egbert, D. Biber and B. Gray (2016), 'Academic Writing Development at the University Level: Phrasal and Clausal Complexity across Level of Study, Discipline, and Genre', *Written Communication*, 33 (2): 149–183.

Strobl, C., J. Malley and G. Tutz (2009), 'An Introduction to Recursive Partitioning: Rationale, Application and Characteristics of Classification and Regression Trees, Bagging and Random Forests', *Psychological Methods*, 14 (4): 323–348.

Suedfeld, P. and D. Rank (1976), 'Revolutionary Leaders: Long-term Success as a Function of Changes in Conceptual Complexity', *Journal of Personality and Social Psychology*, 34 (2): 169.

Suedfeld, P. and S. Coren (1992), 'Cognitive Correlates of Conceptual Complexity', *Personality and Individual Differences*, 13 (11): 1193–1199.

Tyrkkö, J. (2013), 'Exploring Part-of-Speech Profiles and Authorship Attribution in Early Modern Medical Texts', in A. H. Jucker, D. Landert, A. Seiler and N. Studer (eds), *Meaning in the History of English: Words and Texts in Context. (Current Issues in Linguistics)*, 190–210, Amsterdam: John Benjamins.

Tyrkkö, J. and H. Limatius (2018), '"Box, Box Now": A Corpus-based Analysis of Formula One Radio Messages', *Conference Presentation at the 9th Inter-Varietal Applied Corpus Studies (IVACS) International Biennial Conference*, Malta, 13–15 June.

Tyrkkö, J. and A. Nurmi (2017), 'Analysing Multilingual Practices in Late Modern English: Parameter Selection and Recursive Partitioning in Focus', in S. A. Hoffmann and S. Arndt-Lappe (eds), *Exploring Recent Diachrony: Corpus Studies in Lexicogrammar and Language Practices in Late Modern English*, Helsinki: Varieng.

Wenger, E. (1998), *Communities of Practice: Learning, Meaning and Identity*, Cambridge: Cambridge University Press.

Appendix 1 Drivers, nationalities, team, assigned tiers and counts of messages

Driver	Nationality	Team(s)	Tier	From	To	F/T %	Total
Antonio Giovinazzi	Italian	Sauber Ferrari	bottom	2	–	100.0	2
Brendon Hartley	Kiwi	Toro Rosso	bottom	16	13	55.2	29
Carlos Sainz Jnr	Spanish	Renault & Toro Rosso Ferrari	middle	78	73	51.7	151
Daniel Ricciardo	Australian	Red Bull Racing Tag Heuer	top	315	122	72.1	437
Daniil Kvyat	Russian	Redbull, Toro Rosso & Toro Rosso Ferrari	bottom	104	81	56.2	185
Esteban Gutierrez	Mexican	Haas Ferrari	bottom	29	18	61.7	47
Esteban Ocon	French	Force India Mercedes & MRT Mercedes	middle	72	52	58.1	124
Felipe Massa	Brazilian	Williams Mercedes	top	78	66	54.2	144
Felipe Nasr	Brazilian	Sauber Ferrari	bottom	30	25	54.5	55
Fernando Alonso	Spanish	McLaren Honda	top	152	140	52.1	292
Jenson Button	British	McLaren Honda	top	49	57	46.2	106
Jolyon Palmer	British	Renault	bottom	60	54	52.6	114
Kevin Magnussen	Danish	Haas Ferrari & Renault	bottom	101	67	60.1	168
Kimi Raikkonen	Finnish	Ferrari	top	223	153	59.3	376
Lance Stroll	Canadian	Williams Mercedes	middle	58	51	53.2	109
Lewis Hamilton	British	Mercedes	top	428	343	55.5	771
Marcus Ericsson	Swedish	Sauber Ferrari	bottom	101	64	61.2	165

Driver	Nationality	Team(s)	Tier	From	To	F/T %	Total
Max Verstappen	Belgian-Dutch	Red Bull Racing Tag Heuer	top	279	200	58.2	479
Nico Hülkenberg	German	Force India Mercedes & Renault	middle	92	77	54.4	169
Nico Rosberg	German	Mercedes	top	87	39	69.0	126
Pascal Wehrlein	German-Mauritian	Sauber Ferrari	bottom	56	35	61.5	91
Pierre Gasly	French	Toro Rosso	bottom	15	4	78.9	19
Rio Haryanto	Indonesian	MRT Mercedes	bottom	2	1	66.7	3
Romain Grosjean	French-Swiss	Haas Ferrari	middle	114	88	56.4	202
Sebastian Vettel	German	Ferrari	top	182	149	55.0	331
Sergio Perez	Mexican	Force India Mercedes	middle	110	66	62.5	176
Stoffel Vandoorne	Belgian	McLaren Honda	bottom	69	38	64.5	107
Valtteri Bottas	Finnish	Mercedes & Williams Mercedes	top	134	64	67.7	198

7

The Emotional Content of English Swearwords in Football Chatspeak: *WTF* and Other Pragmatic Devices

Isabel Balteiro

1. Introduction

Despite the prominent role of English in football, especially in multilingual contexts (see Giera et al. 2008), football followers, who often support their local or national teams, seem to currently interact and express themselves in their own mother tongue (see Balteiro 2018). Still, in such situations highly expressive general English words and specialized football terms are used to refer to matches, game-specific issues or make comments on the game itself. Consequently, not only for its Anglo-Saxon origin, but also for present-day football players' multicultural and multilingual backgrounds, the global role and use of English as the lingua franca and its power to penetrate other cultures, as well as the influence of the media, the language of football outside English-speaking communities are full of English borrowings at different linguistic levels (see Lavric et al. 2008; Pintarić 2008; Bergh and Ohlander 2012b; Campos-Pardillos 2015; Balteiro 2018).

Anglicisms in the Spanish language of football include general and specialized terms but also phraseological units like discourse markers, catchphrases and other types of constructions with salient pragmatic implications, related to 'culturally influenced text patterns, discourse norms and speaker attitudes' (Fiedler 2017: 2; Balteiro 2018). In the new social media, hidden behind their nicknames, Spanish football followers, for example, when watching the game in Spanish, use English swearwords in their interactions in Spanish and they do it publicly, probably, among other reasons, because the level of offence is felt to be lower than in the native language. General tendencies are then reversed as swearwords, used primarily to give relief to surges of emotional energy (Crystal 2003: 173), tend to be used in the mother tongue or even in the local tongue in diglossic cultures (cf. Lantto 2014).

This chapter analyses the use of *fuck, fucking* and *wtf* in Spanish football chats, where they fulfil a pragmatic role of discourse support by connecting utterances, facilitating interaction, etc. (see Pons and Samaniego 1998: 12), but also and mainly they convey metapragmatic information (e.g. the speaker's position, opinions and attitude as regards the utterances and the context or orientation towards the listener).

The data for this qualitative study have been manually compiled from the comments sections and messages in chatrooms in the online version of the Spanish sports newspaper *Marca* (one of the most popular sports newspapers in Spanish). The corpus consists of over 390,500 authentic online messages and/or comments produced between 2007 and 2018 by Spanish football followers (and still available online in August 2018). In order to find hits of the expletives, a specific search was performed in such pages for each of the forms analysed. The number of cases and occurrences was surprisingly very low and rare: a total of 144 examples (28 examples of *fuck*, 16 examples of *fucking* and 100 examples of *wtf*) by 139 different users. Reasons for these low figures may be that administrators of online communities often set up 'filters' to censor and eliminate either inappropriate or offensive language (e.g. swearwords), and/or comments used by participants. Although McEnery and Xiao (2004: 236) found that the *f*-word often occurs in speech rather than writing because 'spoken language is not pre-planned and is more dynamic', *f*-words may be encountered in online comments and messages evidencing the oralized character of this language. For reasons of space, for their pragmatic importance and singularity and basically to avoid repetition of similar (almost identical) examples, this chapter explicitly mentions only forty-five instances of the 144 which have been analysed.

2. Football followers' chatspeak: Intrinsic features and cross-linguistic influence

The language of football is one of the specialized and professional languages or 'subsystems of general or standard language, mainly concerning lexis, by means of which a given social and cultural sphere is identified' (Medina Montero 2007: 197; my translation). It may also be defined as a 'public language' used by widespread and diverse individuals and contexts, i.e. by professionals, followers and journalists in different media and registers (see Bergh and Ohlander 2012a: 14), 'containing its own vocabulary, pragmatic conventions and idiomatic phrases' (Krone 2005: 9).

However, precisely for this wide range of football language users, their knowledge and use of football language, the lexis employed displays different degrees of technicality which depend on the users' activity (football as a professional concern or as entertainment), background, needs, interests, as well as the channel or medium used in their interactions. For example, the language of football followers in comments made during matches in online chats on the internet differs quite substantially from the language of football commentators, the former being lexically less technical and syntactically more spontaneous and creative, as will be explored below. Still, it seems that the boundary between football language (or any other specialized language) and general language is 'a blurred one, with a good deal of overlap' (see Lavric 2008: 5; Bergh and Ohlander 2012a: 16) and is 'arguably more porous than in the case of most other special languages' as 'it is impossible to talk or write about football without using ordinary general-language items' (Bergh and Ohlander 2012a: 15).

In addition, some scholars talk about an 'English bias' (Bergh and Ohlander 2012a:13) in today's international football language because of the influence of English football language in other European languages. This is especially visible in lexis (either as direct non-adapted borrowings, loan translations or calques, semantic loans or false borrowings; see Campos-Pardillos 2015; Bergh and Ohlander 2017), and lately also in the syntax and pragmatic uses of phrases and idiomatic expressions (Balteiro 2018 for expressions such as *oh wait!*). It is certainly true that many referents have no linguistic counterpart in the speakers' native language, which necessarily leads to borrowing, with various degrees of adaptation (e.g. Sp. *penalti* < E. 'penalty'; Sp. *gol* < 'goal'). Besides, it may also be the case that non-English speakers who deal with football are fully familiarized with the media, the genre, the style and with certain general English expressions occurring in (online) football interactions and use them to make their discourses more fluid, vivid, precise and concise.

Football followers in chats make real-time contributions, usually in a passionate manner, while matches are being played or within twenty-four hours following the publication of a news item. One of the most salient traits that apparently define Spanish football followers' oralized discourse in chats and their natural and spontaneous comments is the expressiveness achieved through the use of codeswitches that include swearwords or rather, the use of borrowed swearwords from English with remarkable pragmatic functions, as explained below.

Code-switching (understood as communicatively meaningful code alternation) in non-English football chats, for example, is probably a learned and planned stylistic device, typical of some online communities, as explained in Balteiro (2018). The use of English, which alternates with the L1, in our case Spanish, responds to multiple motivations: (1) 'the choice can be an extension of the participants' multilingual language practices offline', but (2) it can also be 'an outcome of an official or group-specific language policy or politics, specific to online communication', which (3) may serve as a 'semiotic strategy' for different purposes and effects such as 'the creation of stylistic and cultural effects, and for the negotiation of identity and communality' (Leppänen and Peuronen 2012: 390). Also, participants in football chats (4) 'initiate switches to construct and to broadcast a particular relationship between what is said and aspects of the conversation context' (Matras 2009: 115). Finally, the choices and alternations between languages (5) contribute to organizing the *sequentiality* of discourse (Li and Milroy 1995) and (6) are motivated and arranged according to social factors such as the interlocutors' identity and personal preferences, the relations between them, their expectations, as well as for formal, creative, communicative and expressive reasons.

The (un)marked presence of pragmatic borrowings[1] or pragmatic code-switches in Spanish football comments in chats, a prototypical linguistic feature of oralized written messages, may be the result of learned behaviours and, hence, regarded as stylistic copying or replication (cf. Pennycook 2007; Schneider 2011; Peterson 2017; Balteiro 2018).

3. Expletives and swearwords in football chatspeak

Despite being intrinsic to languages and cultures, expletives and swearwords are generally seen as 'anti-social' or offensive (Beers Fägersten 2000, 2007; Baruch and Jenkins 2006), and are often associated with lower levels of education, lower socioeconomic status, and non-standard language or slang. Nevertheless, within particular boundaries and contexts, such as social media (e.g. football chats), where expectations differ from general language, the impact of swearing[2] may be diminished: it may be used as a mark of group identity or social bonding (cf. de Klerk 1991; Stenström 1995, 2006 in relation to teenagers, or Ross 1969 and Montagu 1967/2001 for 'social swearing' vs. 'annoyance swearing') or have other communicative effects (see, for example, Brown and Levinson 1987; Daly et al. 2004; Dewaele 2004; Stenström 2006; Rogerson-Revell 2007; Jay and Janschewitz 2008; Johnson 2012; Christie 2013). Thus, Rieber et al. (1979), Jay and Janschewitz (2008), as well as Johnson and Lewis (2010) consider that using profanity in all contexts at all times is not equivalently offensive.

Jay (2000) suggests that swearing is often and primarily used to express the speaker's emotional state, especially anger, as a relief mechanism for stress and tension, creating communicative and interactional effects. However, it can also be employed to convey other emotions such as happiness, surprise, fear, confusion, etc. Stapleton (2003), for example, found that *fuck!* may be used to 'appear hard' to others within a peer group. Furthermore, 'most instances of swearing are conversational; they are not highly emotional, confrontational, rude or aggressive' (Jay and Janschewitz 2008: 268) but have a social function of bonding, increasing familiarity and expressing solidarity with the in-group. The use and (pragmatic) functions of swearing, particularly of some *f*-expressions (*fuck, fucking* and *wtf*), in Spanish football comments and chats are discussed in the following section. While the *f*-word has generally been described in the literature among the most offensive swearwords in British English (see McEnery 2006), this study attempts to prove whether this is also (or not) the effect caused when it is transferred, adopted or borrowed by other languages and by non-English speakers, especially in social media, in this case football chats.

4. *Fuck, fucking* and *wtf* in football followers' chatspeak

The use of *f*-words by football followers in comments and messages in chats among native Spanish speakers, though probably a kind of learned, copied or replicated stylistic behaviour, simulating competence in the foreign language, produces pragmatic switching/borrowing and has salient (meta)pragmatic implications in relation to the users' attitudes, feelings and emotions towards other participants, the messages, the development of matches, football circumstances, etc.

Different typologies to analyse functions of swearing can be found in the literature (see Montagu 1967/2001 or McEnery et al. 2000, amongst others). For the purposes of this study, Pinker (2007) and Ljung (2011) are followed. Pinker's (2007: 350) typology, for example, based on the way people swear, distinguishes: (1) Descriptive swearing, *Let's fuck!*; (2) Idiomatic swearing, *It's fucked up*; (3) Abusive swearing, *Fuck you, motherfucker!*; (4) Emphatic swearing, *It's fucking amazing*; and (5) Cathartic swearing, *Fuck!*.

Ljung (2011) categorizes the functions of swearwords into stand-alones and slot fillers. The stand-alone functions are expletive interjections (*Fuck!*), oaths (*For fuck's sake*), curses (*Fuck you!*), unfriendly suggestions (*Fuck off!*), affirmations (*Fuck hell it is!*), ritual insults (*Your sister's cunt!*) and name-calling (*Fucker*). The slot fillers are adverbial/adjectival intensifiers (*What a fucking idiot!*), adjectives of dislike (*I hate that fucking place*), emphasis (*Fuck of me!*), modal adverbials (*They fucking bought one drink between them*), anaphoric use of epithets (*Tell the motherfucker to mind his own business*) and noun supports (*Motherfucker*).

4.1. *Fuck, fuck off* and *fuck logic*

Only twenty-eight occurrences of the expletive or swearword *fuck* appeared in the corpus, either in isolation or combined with another word in idiomatic expressions (e.g. *fuck off* and *fuck logic*). Twenty-four different participants (football followers) in either comments or messages in chats used these forms (note that the first line in the examples corresponds to the user's nickname, the second provides information on the date and time of the message, and the third and following constitute the content of the message itself). All the cases are pragmatically salient and marked: nine (32 per cent) of them appeared in comments or messages which were fully in English, as in

(1) *GASAN; #11410.oct.2015 | 14:15*
    Fuck then and fuck their laws!! no Cesc?

whereas nineteen (68.86 per cent) were clear borrowings or code-switches, as in

(2) *Z0yBer; #611.mar.2010 | 10:47*
    #5Extasis desenfreno!! [...]jajajaja anda y k os fuck a los katalanes ombre fuera de españa ya
    (#5Ecstasy debauchery!! [...]hahahahaha you katalans go and get fucked, man, out of Spain right now)

Among the twenty-eight occurrences of *fuck*, five (18 per cent) appeared in idiomatic (verbal) expressions, namely, two *fuck off* and three *fuck logic*.

Fuck off, as in example (3), is used with what Ljung (2011) calls 'a stand-alone function' which actually indicates the speaker's emotional state and reaction towards others (football team or other chat users, respectively) and reflects an unfriendly suggestion of dismissal. Thus, this expression may present a destinational usage showing some kind of 'sentiment' directed at somebody, namely, anger, irritability or aggression. However, it may also be said, following Pinker (2007), that *fuck off* is employed as cathartic swearing; that is, the user feels some relief after saying or writing this expression. Therefore, it seems to have a provocative, disruptive or even offensive character proper to chat messages, where participants, hidden behind nicknames, express themselves without restrictions and resort to trolling or flaming strategies:

(3) chechurri; #1 01.Nov.2009 | 20:00
     Fuck off Rangers!!!

Quite similarly, *fuck logic* is used in the corpus as a curse but also as cathartic swearing to express anger, irritability, disappointment or disbelief. In (4), the user not only expresses his/her feelings but also provides metapragmatic information regarding position, opinion or attitude towards the previous utterance. The codeswitch also contributes to the sequentiality of discourse:

(4) 10_Champions_; #10525.oct.2015 | 11:39
     Cules cuando se intentó fichar a De Gea decían que Navas mucho mejor, ahora que Navas se esta saliendo con el Madrid dicen que De Gea mucho mejor ... Fuck Logic!! :)
     (Cules [Barcelona fans], when they tried to sign De Gea, they said Navas much better, now that Navas is doing great at Madrid, they say De Gea much better .... Fuck Logic!! :))

Only twenty-three occurrences correspond to the simple word form *fuck*, which was found in different grammatical categories and with varied (meta) pragmatic functions. First, as a noun (two cases in the corpus) in, for example,

(5) RaulJR7; #222/12/2017 | 16:29
     Es que acaso deberia incluirle? Overrated as fuck, siempre con el apoyo de la prensa, sin fundamentos. Benzema tiene que ser titular porque si, porque es Benzema, punto. En fin, que lacra tenemos los madridistas.
     (Should I include him, then? Overrated as fuck, always supported by the press, with no grounds. Benzema has to play just because, because he's Benzema, period. Conclusion: what a burden we Madrid fans have to put up with)

Fuck in *overrated as fuck*, though functioning as an intensifier, to some extent preserves its dysphemistic meaning (in Spanish '¡sobrevalorado que te cagas!') probably for humorous purposes but, paradoxically, also to indicate the user's anger, irritability or mainly disagreement in what Pinker (2007) qualifies as 'descriptive swearing'. In fact, the *f*-word, when used in conjunction with 'as', serves to describe a high degree of a quality or something; in this case, to say that a player is overrated.

Unlike the preceding example, in

(6) *machotrik; #8128.jul.2015 | 13:23*
@ANDONIBOK TESESA????? no fuck??

Fuck functions as an expletive interjection to express disbelief. The expression reads like a literal translation of the Spanish '¡no jodas!' but it may also be interpreted as an analogy of 'no shit!'. This use differs from the actual English language ones, which suggests that the participant may be either consciously playing with language, mixing English with Spanish elements, or using it by imitation and for in-group social bonding.

The remaining twenty-one cases in the sample correspond to fifteen transitive verbal uses and six interjections, primarily with the stand-alone functions (see Ljung's 2011 taxonomy and above) but with different (meta)pragmatic implications as to the speaker's attitudes, feelings and emotions.

The transitive examples of *fuck* identified in the corpus, are used as curses to express anger, irritability, dissatisfaction, dismissal or even humiliation (cf. abusive and cathartic swearing; Pinker 2007), as in examples (1) above and (7) below:

(7) *GASAN; #11410.oct.2015 | 14:15*
Fuck then and fuck their laws!! no Cesc?

Fuck also appears in the corpus as an expletive interjection, with a stand-alone function or a cathartic one (see Ljung 2011; Pinker 2007, respectively). The participant shows anger and irritability for the spelling mistake in 'Hasegura?' in (8); these emotions and regret, as in (9), or dismissal, as in (10):

(8) *louki; #104/02/2017 | 17:12*
Hasegura? Fuck
(Guarantees [with spelling mistake]? Fuck])
(9) *Florentino ChequesFlorentinoChequesz; #23331.jul.2014 | 05:33*
Tendré que empezar a invertir dinero en arbitros, fuck!
(I'll have to start to invest money on referees, fuck!)
(10) *palacios21_rs2; #1621.oct.2012 | 18:19*
@AndreaGuardini callate la boca fuck id.iot!!!
(@AndreaGuardini shut up fuck id.iot!!!)

Example (10) is a rare use of *fuck*. As it is, 'idiot' may be understood as a vocative. Probably the user wanted to mean 'fucking idiot' or 'fuck off, idiot' but, for some reason, possibly the writer's imperfect knowledge of the English language, he/she cannot produce it correctly.

Apart from those, *fuck* may also be used as a relief expression of affirmation and/or irritability, e.g.

(11)   *pablomad dijo* (pablomad said) | *22:38*
       fuck yea

In general, it may be argued that *fuck*, as a pragmatic code-switching device, clearly serves to provide saliency and sequentiality to the discourse and, most importantly, it allows speakers' to express their attitude and emotions towards other football followers, matches, teams, what is being said or commented on in the online chat, or any event or circumstance related to football that may simultaneously be taking place or not.

4.2. Fucking

The figures for *fucking* are still lower than those for *fuck*: only sixteen occurrences, produced by sixteen users, have been identified; all of them are expletives which fulfil, following Ljung (2011), a slot-filler function as intensifiers. Two of the occurrences are adverbs or disjuncts modifying either Spanish or English verbs (see (12) and (13), respectively) and express modality, as in

(12)   *HatoriHanso; #11 | 14:53*
       no me fuck-ing jodas …
       (don't you give me that fuck-ing shit)
(13)   *Beti_ErrealaaaaM; #1917/09/2017 | 12:30*
       @vivaelbarca92 #13 Vendidos? WTF??? Are u fucking kidding me? Somos un equipo humilde de casta y pelotas mas que de millones como vosotros y el madrid, los cuales acaparais mas del 50% de los derechos televisivos de toda la liga cosa q en otras ligas de europa como alemania ni de koña es asi. Siempre e simpatizado mas con el barça y su juego ya que también me gusta el futbol, pero con todos mis respetos cada vez me dan mas asco el farsa y el mandril
       (bribed? WTF??? Are u fucking kidding me? We are a modest team with bravery and balls, not loaded like you and madrid, who hoard more than 50% of the TV rights of the whole league, sth that would not bloody

happen in other European leagues such as Germany. I have always liked Barça and its game because I also like football, but with due respect, I find Barcelona and Madrid more and more disgusting.)

In these cases, as in the following ones, *fucking*, as a semantically empty filler, makes no contribution to the propositional meaning of the message but serves to enhance and give additional emotional context to the word it modifies (see Pinker's (2007) 'emphatic swearing').

In the other fourteen cases in the corpus, *fucking* is an adjective also with a slot-filler function and modifying either (English or Spanish) nouns or noun phrases. In five examples, *fucking* is followed by and modifies a noun phrase or Spanish noun with either positive (e.g. *fucking amo, fucking pikito de oro, fucking sporting*) or negative connotations (e.g. *fucking verguenza* [sic]), as in

(14) *fcRobarsa; #15831/08/2017 | 00:34*
@Fladrif #106 si si, que empiece a tapar bocas, lo que no se es como no estas tu mudo de sus 9 anios en el madrid. No mos va a callar una fucking jugada al anio.
(@Fladrif #106 yes yes, let him start shutting haters up, what I don't understand is why you don't shut up after his 9 years at Madrid. We won't shut up because of one single fucking move a year.)

Similarly, in nine uses it is followed by and modifying an English noun, also with either contextually positive-connotation nouns (e.g. *fucking beast, fucking Machine, fucking boss* or *fucking master*), or expressing negative emotions or dislike because of the negative sentence or noun that follows (e.g. *not a fucking chance, fucking racist*), as in

(15) *Gerhard34; #505/11/2017 | 21:17*
Otro buen partido del Girona. Ha dominado mas que el Levante jugando a domicilio. Lastima de parón porque estamos enchufadismos. Estamos a 25 puntos del objetivo que no es otro que la salvación. Hay que aprovechar ahora porque cuando empiece la segunda vuelta nos enfrentaremos a todos los grandes pero fuera de casa. Som hi Girona y viva Pablo the fucking Machine!!!
(Another good game by Girona. They were in control much more than Levante, even though they were playing away. Pity about the league interruption because we are on a great track. We are 25 points from our goal, which is avoiding relegation. The moment is now, because in the second leg, we'll be playing all the big ones, but away from home. Let's go [originally in Catalan] Girona, and hail Pablo the fucking Machine!!!)

where the speaker may also play with the language and its creative power (there is a word play as the coach's name is Pablo Machín).

Note that all these uses are marked and salient and have visible communicative intentions and emotional implications. The Spanish language has equivalent forms that would make these expressions lexically and semantically unnecessary but the (meta)pragmatic information and force that they convey is different, for example, for 'fucking amo' or 'fucking master', Spanish has the form 'puto amo', but the in-group feeling would not be the same.

4.3. wtf

One hundred occurrences of *wtf* have been identified in the corpus. In most of the cases, as we shall see, *wtf* functions as an expletive interjection with which football followers express different feelings and emotions. There is only one case in which the user conveys his/her attitude towards other participants' comments. In such an occurrence *wtf* has a somehow downgrading and humiliating function, similar to an adjective of dislike, completely different from its use in English, as in

(16)   *Fanatleti; #925/05/2017 | 15:44*
       WTF de comentarios …
       (WTF these remarks …)

Apart from that, only one case is used as an expletive interjection to express a combination of surprise towards a given football event and regret for the subject's former circumstances, e.g.

(17)   *TridenteCeleste; #1419.mar.2012 | 20:05*
       Ryduan? WTF pobre chaval … la de collejas que habrá soportado…
       bromas a parte, teniendo un padre con la experiancia de Martín,
       esperemos verlo pronto como un importante.
       (Ryduan? WTF poor kid … he must have put up with a lot of bitching, jokes aside, with a father with so much experience as Martin, let's hope he succeeds soon.)

In the remaining ninety-eight cases, participants use *wtf* to express surprise, mockery, anger, irritability, disappointment or criticism (usually a combination of two or more feelings or emotions) towards a given piece of news or football event (see example (18)), the journalist's opinion, point of view or abilities (see (19) and (20)), or a previous participant's message or comment (see examples (21) and (22)).

(18) UEOLOT; #60 | 19:15
   Kevin-Prince Boateng al Las Palmas??? Wtf
   (Kevin-Prince Boateng to Las Palmas??? Wtf)

(19) tohugo; #1115.jul.2013 | 00:36
   Wtf. si le das a la noticia de 'El fichaje de Samuel está pendiente de un mecenas' vas a la noticia de colotto. ¿Pero esto que es?
   (Wtf, if you click on the news 'Waiting for a sponsor to sign up Samuel', you get the one on colotto. What's going on here?)

(20) MM_93; #419/02/2017 | 16:13
   Que tiene que ver esto con el Real Madrid??!! WTF?? Sera que teneis muchas prisas por subir semejante exclusive
   (What does this have to do with Real Madrid??!! WTF?? You must be in a great hurry to upload this scoop)

(21) NoLimitsAgain; #125/08/2017 | 16:46
   Renovación de Pau desde la calma? WTF! O renueva ya o se intenta venderlo porque el año que viene se va gratis. No hay más.
   (Pau signing an extension with no hurry? WTF! Either he signs now, or we try to sell him, because next year he leaves for free. There's no more to it.)

(22) ravech12; #819/01/2017 | 20:16
   #6 Que Ronaldo Nazario nunca fue un 9??WTF es el mejor 9 de la historia,usaba esa velocidad endiablada
   (#6 What do you mean Ronaldo Nazario never was a 9??WTF he's the best 9 in history, he used that devilish speed)

In line with the preceding, a highly remarkable occurrence of *wtf* was found in the corpus. As shown in (23) below, *wtf* is used as synonym of 'fail' (a meaning which has not been reported in the literature, probably because this sense and/or use does not exist in English). It may be argued that either the frequent use of this word or expression to laugh at mistakes produced by *Marca* editors may have led to a semantic shift or new meaning, or rather the user has often seen *wtf* when there are mistakes and associates it to the mistake itself:

(23) #22 jufelu; 08.Jul.2010 | 15:12
   Bienvenido a Valencia!! Por cierto, en el apartado Altas Bajas, pone que es de argentina, y luego dicen que es valenciano, menudo WTF!! XD
   (Welcome to Valencia!! By the way, in the New Signings section, it says he's from argentina, and then they say he's valencian, what a WTF!! XD)

As suggested above, the expression of surprise is usually accompanied by an ingredient of either anger (e.g. (33) below), criticism (e.g. (24)) or mockery (e.g. (25)), or a combination of several emotions and/or attitudes, e.g. (26), where the speaker expresses surprise but also some criticism and mockery.

(24) *SLQH; #1 | 13:23*
 supercopa en diciembre? Wtf
 (supercup in December? Wtf)
(25) *desderlin; #221/05/2018 | 00:23*
 Dragones wtf? Los dragones son el Oporto hahaha
 (Dragons wtf? Oporto are the dragons hahaha)
(26) *RSG1905; #7520.nov.2013 | 02:51*
 Como es que los últimos comentarios en una noticia del Valencia, son hablando del Atletico de Madrid?? WTF?? Mira que nosotros algunas veces nos bombardean pero esto no lo había visto casi nunca jaja En estas cosas alguien del marca debería mirarlo mas, va a echarse a perder, y es una pena :(
 (How is it that the last comments on a news item on Valencia are about Atletico de Madrid?? WTF?? We do get bombarded sometimes, but I had almost never seen this haha Somebody at Marca should take care of these things, it's going to be ruined, and it's a pity :( )

Still, there are occurrences like (18) above or (27) below where *wtf* only expresses surprise, but it is also found in other users' posts to merely convey the speaker's disappointment (e.g. (28)), criticism (e.g. (29)), disbelief (e.g. (30)), or that they find something funny, in such a way that *wtf* is in this case used as an expletive interjection to mock others (e.g. (31)).

(27) *AKUKAMARE; #222/08/2017 | 08:59*
 ¿Vitolo cortesía? ¿WTF?
 (Vitolo courtesy? WTF?)
(28) *thriller1985; #78 | 14:06*
 Masato por favor, establece la diferencia entre vender y ceder que dices vender todo el rato al referirte a cesiones y confundes al personal (Pabón, Valdez). por ejemplo vender con opción de compra y haciéndose cargo de la ficha (WTF??) Gracias crack
 (Masato please, make a difference between selling and loaning, you talk about selling all the time when talking about loans, and you mix people up (Pabón, Valdez). For instance, selling with a sale option and paying for the player's salary (WTF??) Thanks genius)

(29) *mkpsycholoko; #2427.jul.2015 | 19:17*
se quedaran con los kilos gastados que este pavo no rinde al igual que todos los colombianos venden solo humo!! 4°Ranking y no hicieron nada en copa america FIFA wtf!!!
(they'll have spent the money on nothing because this guy is useless, same as all the colombians, they're full of hot air! Ranked 4th and they were hopeless at the FIFA america cup wtf!!!)

(30) *bora-bora; #221/08/2017 | 10:13*
Hierro leyenda de la seleccion española??? WTF jajaja tenia que escribirlo. Voy a seguir viendo el resto de jugadores.
(Hierro a legend of the Spanish national team??? WTF hahaha I had to write this. Let's look at the rest of the players.)

(31) *Llourinho4Ever; #126/05/2018 | 16:01*
Michael Amir Murillo en Panama WTF!!!! Pero que rayos jajajaja
(Michael Amir Murillo in Panama WTF!!!! What the heck hahaha)

The most immediate or close context is essential for the interpretation of *wtf* uses found in the corpus. Accordingly, not only the message itself (and the immediate context or utterance that precedes or follows *wtf*, as in (32) or (33)), but also the participant's nick or avatar (see example (34)) is crucial for the identification of meanings or effects in general, and particularly of ironic ones.

(32) *javix99; #105/01/2018 | 01:43*
Van a verlos y les roban en toda la cara, muy bien gente, muy bien. Wtf
(They go to watch them and they get robbed in broad daylight, well done, mates, well done. Wtf)

(33) *Beti_Errealaaaa; #1917/09/2017 | 12:30*
@vivaelbarca92 #13 Vendidos? WTF??? Are u fucking kidding me? Somos un equipo humilde de casta y pelotas mas que de millones como vosotros y el madrid, los cuales acaparais mas del 50% de los derechos televisivos de toda la liga cosa q en otras ligas de europa como alemania ni de koña es asi. Siempre e simpatizado mas con el barça y su juego ya que también me gusta el futbol, pero con todos mis respetos cada vez me dan mas asco el farsa y el mandril
(bribed? WTF??? Are u fucking kidding me? We are a modest team with bravery and balls, not loaded like you and madrid, who hoard more than 50% of the TV rights of the whole league, sth that would not bloody happen in other European leagues such as germany. I have always liked barça and its game because I also like football, but with due respect, I find barcelona and madrid more and more disgusting)

(34) *thortxu02; #10728/03/2017 | 21:04*
    WTF!?

At times, confusion may arise due to the absence of quotes or references to previous comments or posts indicating that a message is an answer to others and also the appearance of other posts in between. This may complicate or make the readers' interpretation of the message impossible, e.g.

(35) *Desdeahora; #401/03/2017 | 11:41*
    WTF?

It may be argued that at times there is a full degree of integration of *wtf* in Spanish football followers' comments in chats, as witnessed by the presence of initial and final question and exclamation marks (a distinguishing feature of Spanish), as in

(36) *Profeta Mequetrefe8Mundiales8; #819.nov.2015 | 14:22*
    ¿Nadie se ha fijado en el SonGoku con perilla de detrás? ¿WTF?
    (Hasn't anybody noticed the SonGoku with a goatee at the back? ¿WTF?)

These uses of question marks may also be interpreted as a sign of either the user's imperfect knowledge of the English language or the full integration of the word into the writer's Spanish; the latter reading seems more plausible.

Apart from that, it has also been observed that exclamation marks tend to accompany users' feelings of anger, irritability, disbelief or criticism, or are also preferred when these feelings are stronger than the surprise component (e.g. (37) and (38)). Conversely, question marks tend to appear with surprise uses of *wtf* or when this emotion is stronger than those of anger, irritability or criticism (e.g. (39)).

(37) *subcero; #225/02/2018 | 13:24*
    'mediocampista titular y ahora soy centro' … WTF !!! el que escribe sabe lo que teclea o simplemente no sabe de fútbol ?
    ('midfielder in initial line-up and now I am center' … WTF !!! does whoever's writing this know what they are writing or simply know nothing about football ?)

(38) *nikmak; #505.ene.2014 | 01:09*
    #2Toquero es Francés y lo calla??!!! Que yo sepa LAporte es central y lo dice tan alto que es capitan de la seleccion francesa sub 19??? WTF!!
    (#2Toquero is French and he keeps it secret??!!! As far as I know Laporte is a centre-back and he says it so loud that he's the skipper of the French under-19 national team??? WTF!!)

(39) *#5 duke_07; 20.Ago.2009 | 17:41*
'Van Gaal ha reiterado su intención de reposicionar a Ribery como medio centro' WTF?
('Van Gaal has repeated his intention to relocate Ribery as centre midfielder' WTF?)

Note also the combination of both question and exclamation marks in one single message, or in cases where the speaker expresses both surprise (see (40) and mockery (e.g. (41))).

(40) *chekrrk; #228.ago.2014 | 22:32*
calor en rusia??? WTF?! que sera lo siguiente, nieve en el sahara??
(hot in russia??? WTF?! what will come next, snow in the sahara??)

(41) *07Sheva; #4006/04/2017 | 19:26*
Noticia del Bayern, fans del Madrid y Barcelona peleando … WTF?!!
(News item about Bayern, Madrid and Barcelona fans fighting … WTF?!!)

Finally, it is worth commenting on the use of punctuation flooding, as shown in examples (42) to (44).

(42) *benze_marcelo; #213.jun.2013 | 18:16*
jajjajajjaj poneros en el video en el momento 0:30 pone: 3 goals in uefa 20154 qualifiers WTF???
(hahhahahhah play the video at 0:30 it reads: 3 goals in uefa 20154 qualifiers WTF???)

(43) *f_castro93; #126.oct.2015 | 16:41*
WTF??????????????

(44) *07Sheva; #1118/01/2018 | 13:09*
WTF!!!!! Ok 72 millones en salario. Supongamos que 40 millones al Arsenal (por poner una cifra) y que? 92 millones de prima para firme por tu club? jajajajajaja todo el mundo roba al United.
(WTF!!!!! Ok 72 millions in wages. Let's suppose 40 to Arsenal (just to say a number) and then what? 92 million in bonus so that he is signed by your team? Hahahahaha everybody swindles United.)

But the absence of punctuation marks is also not an exception:

(45) *MeRioDeLaFarsa; #11331/03/2017 | 03:22*

Pues viendo esto, me parece que la Conmebol deberia de 'fichar' a otras Federaciones de Concacaf aunque sea para que hagan lleno, porque por lo que se lee aqui ya no habran cupos de repechaje, me parece que es exagerado, creo que con 5 cupos era suficiente (actualmente son 4 directos y 1 de repechaje, no 5 directos ...) de 10 equipos pasan 6? wtf ...
(Well, seeing this, I think Conmebol should 'sign in' other Concacaf Federations, if only as fillers, because, from what I read here, there will not be any more repechage places, I think this is exaggerated, I think 5 places was enough (now it's four directly and 1 from repechage, not 5 directly ...) out of 10 teams 6 get through? wtf ...)

As seen, *wtf* is frequently used by Spanish football followers in chats to express feelings or emotions such as surprise, anger, irritability, disbelief, disappointment or even regret, but also to show downgrading attitudes, criticism and mockery towards either other chat participants, other chat participants' comments, journalists' news and opinions, general football events, etc.

5. Conclusions

This study shows that English swearwords, particularly *f*-words (but for *wtf*), used as code-switches by Spanish football followers in chats, have somehow undergone desemanticization or loss of their taboo, highly confrontational, rude, aggressive and offensive meaning(s). In fact, only two examples have been found where *fuck* in its idiomatic form, *fuck off*, has a provocative, disruptive and offensive meaning. Quite similarly, there is only one example where the speaker uses *wtf* to express a downgrading and humiliating attitude towards others.

F-words, in particular *fuck, fucking* and *wtf*, are primarily used to communicate the speakers' attitude and mainly their emotions. The most frequent swearword of these three is *wtf*, which is employed as an expletive interjection to express, on the one hand, emotions such as, in order of importance, surprise over something, anger and irritability, disappointment or disbelief and, on the other, attitudes such as criticism or mockery. Noteworthy is also its use in Spanish to mean 'fail'.

The second most frequently used swearword is *fuck*. In the corpus, this expletive occurs as a transitive verb, an interjection, in combination with other words to form idiomatic expressions, namely, *fuck off* and *fuck logic*, but also in nominal uses. The strongest chat users' emotions seem to be expressed by using these latter nominal uses but also *fuck off*, which are probably closer to disruptive and offensive meanings. Transitive uses of *fuck* tend to be used for both cursing at others and simultaneously expressing anger and dissatisfaction, while emotions such as anger, irritability or regret are expressed. *Fucking*, however, is used as either an adverbial emphatic intensifier or as an adjectival one to provide the word modified with additional emotional content and context, like in English.

In general, most of the functions, meanings, attitudes, emotions and feelings expressed as well as the distribution patterns of the *f*-words indicate that Spanish users replicate or imitate native uses of those words, probably motivated by context and/or chat (in-group) norms.

The findings of this study show that *f*-words, as pragmatic code-switches or borrowings in Spanish football chats, contribute to the sequentiality of discourse. In addition, they are also primarily used to express speakers' emotions and attitudes, and mostly negative, rather than positive, emotions.

Further complementary qualitative and quantitative research with larger corpora is called for in order to arrive at more definite and detailed conclusions and results. Studies focusing on face management and the use of swearwords as an impoliteness strategy are much in need and, hence, they would provide interesting insights into the language of football followers and/or online communities. Moreover, it would be interesting to carry out cross-linguistic comparisons of pragmatic force and/or connotative strength of these forms.

Notes

1 So-called pragmatic borrowing refers to both the process and the outcome of the incorporation of pragmatic and discursive elements (namely, interjections, discourse markers, expletives, general extenders, focus constructions, catch-phrases, greetings, politeness markers, quotatives, tags, vocatives and paralinguistic phenomena) from a source language into a recipient language (see Terkourafi 2011; Andersen 2014: 17; Beeching 2016; Andersen et al. 2017; Peterson 2017). As Andersen notes, these linguistic strategies 'carry signals about speaker attitudes, the speech act performed, discourse structure, information state, politeness, etc.' (2014: 17–18) and 'act as constraints on the interpretation process due to their subjective, textual, and interpersonal pragmatic functions' (Andersen et al. 2017: 73).

2 Swearing has often and historically been defined as a linguistic practice based on taboo or on anything that is forbidden, referring to (1) scatological elements which relate to bodily functions and are associated with body parts (e.g. *shit*); (2) sexual acts or genitalia (e.g. *fuck, prick*); or (3) profanity or religious issues (e.g. *goddamn, Christ*). Ljung (2011: 4), following Andersson and Trudgill (1990: 53),

suggests four criteria for what constitutes swearing: (1) swearing is the use of utterances containing taboo words or referring to something which is stigmatized; (2) the taboo words are used with a non-literal meaning; (3) many utterances that constitute swearing are subject to severe lexical, phrasal and syntactic constraints which suggest that most swearing qualifies as formulaic language; (4) swearing is emotive language: its main function is to reflect, or attempt to reflect, the speaker's feelings and attitudes.

References

Andersen, G. (2014), 'Pragmatic Borrowing', *Journal of Pragmatics*, 67: 17–33.
Andersen, G., C. Furiassi and B. Mišić Ilić (2017), 'The Pragmatic Turn in Studies of Linguistic Borrowing', *Journal of Pragmatics*, 113: 71–76.
Andersson, L.-G. and P. Trudgill (1990), *Bad Language*, Oxford: Blackwell.
Balteiro, I. (2018), '*Oh Wait*: English Pragmatic Markers in Spanish Football Chatspeak', *Journal of Pragmatics*, 133: 122–133.
Baruch, Y. and S. Jenkins (2006), 'Swearing at Work and Permissive Leadership Culture', *Leadership and Organization Development Journal*, 28: 492–507.
Beeching, K. (2016), *Pragmatic Markers in British English. Meaning in Social Interaction*, Cambridge: Cambridge University Press.
Beers Fägersten, K. A. (2000), 'A Descriptive Analysis of the Social Functions of Swearing in American English', PhD Dissertation, Florida: University of Florida.
Beers Fägersten, K. A. (2007), 'A Sociolinguistic Analysis of Swearword Offensiveness', *Saarland Working Papers in Linguistics*, 1: 14–37.
Bergh, G. and S. Ohlander (2012a), '*Free Kicks, Dribblers and WAGs*. Exploring the Language of "the People's Game"', *Moderna spark*, 106 (1): 11–46.
Bergh, G. and S. Ohlander (2012b), 'English Direct Loans in European Football Lexis', in C. Furiassi, V. Pulcini and F. Rodríguez González (eds), *The Anglicization of European Football Lexis*, 281–304, Amsterdam: Benjamins.
Bergh, G. and S. Ohlander (2017), 'Loan Translation versus Direct Loans: The Impact of English on European Football Lexis', *Nordic Journal of Linguistics*, 40 (1): 5–35.
Brown, P. and S. C. Levinson (1987), *Politeness: Some Universals in Language Usage*, Cambridge: Cambridge University Press.
Campos-Pardillos, M. Á. (2015), 'All Is Not English That Glitters: False Anglicisms in the Spanish Language of Sports', *Atlantis*, 37 (2): 155–174.
Christie, C. (2013), 'The Relevance of Taboo Language: An Analysis of the Indexical Values of Swearwords', *Journal of Pragmatics*, 58: 152–169.
Crystal, D. (2003), *English as a Global Language*, 2nd ed., Cambridge: Cambridge University Press.
Daly, N., J. Holmes, J. Newton and M. Stubbe (2004), 'Expletives as Solidarity Signals in FTAs on the Factory Floor', *Journal of Pragmatics*, 36 (5): 945–964.

de Klerk, V. (1991), 'Expletives: Men Only?', *Communication Monographs*, 58: 156–169.
Dewaele, J.-M. (2004), 'The Emotional Force of Swearwords and Taboo Words in the Speech of Multilinguals', *Journal of Multilingual and Multicultural Development*, 25: 204–222.
Fiedler, S. (2017), 'Phraseological Borrowing from English to German: Cultural and Pragmatic implications', *Journal of Pragmatics*, 113: 1–14.
Giera, I., E. Giorgianni, E. Lavric, G. Pisek, A. Skinner and W. Stadler (2008), 'The Globalized Football Team: A Research Project on Multilingual Communication', in E. Lavric, G. Pisek, A. Skinner and W. Stadler (eds), *The Linguistics of Football*, 375–389, Tübingen: Gunter Narr.
Jay, T. (2000), *Why We Curse: A Neuro-psycho-social Theory of Speech*, Amsterdam: Benjamins.
Jay, T. and K. Janschewitz (2008), 'The Pragmatics of Swearing', *Journal of Politeness Research*, 4: 267–288.
Johnson, D. I. (2012), 'Swearing by Peers in the Work Setting: Expectancy, Violation Valence, Perceptions of Message, and Perceptions of Speaker', *Communication Studies*, 63 (2): 136–151.
Johnson, D. I. and N. Lewis (2010), 'Perceptions of Swearing in the Work Setting: An Expectancy Violations Theory Perspective', *Communication Reports*, 23 (2): 106–118.
Krone, M. (2005), *The Language of Football: A Contrastative Study of Syntactic and Semantic Specifics in Verb Usage in English and German Match Commentaries*, Stuttgart: Verlag Haunschild.
Lantto, H. (2014), 'Code-switching, Swearing and Slang: The Colloquial Register of Basque in Greater Bilbao', *International Journal of Bilingualism*, 18 (6): 633–648.
Lavric, E. (2008), 'Introduction', in E. Lavric, G. Pisek, A. Skinner and W. Stadler (eds), *The Linguistics of Football*, 5–8, Tübingen: Gunter Narr.
Lavric, E., G. Pisek, A. Skinner and W. Stadler, eds (2008), *The Linguistics of Football*, Tübingen: Gunter Narr.
Leppänen, S. and S. Peuronen (2012), 'Multilingualism on the Internet', in M. Martin-Jones, A. Blackledge and A. Creese (eds), *The Routledge Handbook of Multilingualism*, 384–402, London and New York: Routledge.
Li, W. and L. Milroy (1995), 'Conversational Codeswitching in a Chinese Community in Britain: A Sequential Analysis', *Journal of Pragmatics*, 23: 281–299.
Ljung, M. (2011), *Swearing: A Cross-Cultural Linguistic Study*, Basingstoke: Palgrave Macmillan.
Matras, Y. (2009), *Language Contact*, Cambridge: Cambridge University Press.
McEnery, T. (2006), *Swearing in English: Bad Language, Purity and Power from 1586 to the Present*, Abingdon: Routledge.
McEnery, T. and Z. Xiao (2004), 'Swearing in Modern British English: The Case of *Fuck* in the BNC', *Language and Literature*, 13: 235–268.

McEnery, T., P. Baker and A. Hardie (2000), 'Swearing and Abuse in Modern British English', in B. Lewandowska-Tomaszczyk and P. J. Melia (eds), *PALC'99: Practical Applications in Language Corpora*, 37–48. Berlin: Peter Lang.

Medina Montero, J. F. (2007), 'La metáfora en el léxico futbolístico: el caso de los participantes en español, y sus posibles equivalentes en italiano', in L. L. Toro (ed.), *Léxico Español Actual. Actas del I Congreso Internacional de Léxico Español Actual*, 197–239, Venezia-Treviso: Libreria Editrice Cafoscarina.

Montagu, A. (1967/2001), *The Anatomy of Swearing*, Toronto: Collier-Machillan Canada Ltd.

Pennycook, A. (2007), *Global Englishes and Transcultural Flows*, London: Routledge.

Peterson, E. (2017), 'The Nativization of Pragmatic Borrowings in Remote Language Contact Situations', *Journal of Pragmatics*, 113: 116–126.

Pinker, S. (2007), *The Stuff of Thought*, London: Penguin Group.

Pintarić, A. P. (2008). 'English and German Loanwords in Croatian Football Language', in E. Lavric, G. Pisek, A. Skinner and W. Stadler (eds), *The Linguistics of Football*, Tübingen: Gunter Narr.

Pons, H. and J. L. Samaniego (1998), 'Marcadores pragmáticos de apoyo discursivo en el habla culta de Santiago de Chile', *Onomazein*, 3: 11–25.

Rieber, R. W., C. Wiedemann and J. D'Amato (1979), 'Obscenity: Its Frequency and Context of Usage as Compared in Males, Nonfeminist Females, and Feminist Females', *Journal of Psycholinguistic Research*, 8 (3): 201–223.

Rogerson-Revell, P. (2007), 'Humour in Business: A Double-edged Sword. A Study of Humour and Style Shifting in Intercultural Business Meetings', *Journal of Pragmatics*, 39: 4–28.

Ross, H. (1969), 'Patterns of Swearing', *Discovery: The Popular Journal of Knowledge*, November: 479–481.

Schneider, E. (2011), *English around the World*, Cambridge: Cambridge University Press.

Stapleton, K. (2003), 'Gender and Swearing: A Community Practice', *Women and Language*, 26: 22–33.

Stenström, A.-B. (1995), 'Taboos in Teenage Talk', in G. Melchers and B. Warren (eds), *Studies in Anglistics*, 71–79. Stockholm: Almqvist and Wiksell.

Stenström, A.-B. (2006), 'Taboo Words in Teenage Talk: London and Madrid Girls' Conversations Compared', *Spanish in Context*, 3: 115–138.

Terkourafi, M. (2011), '*Thank You, Sorry* and *Please* in Cypriot Greek: What Happens to Politeness Markers When They Are Borrowed across Languages?', *Journal of Pragmatics*, 43: 218–235.

8

Fighting for Integrity against a Corrupting Disease: The Legal Metaphors of Sports Fraud

Miguel Ángel Campos-Pardillos

1. Sport and fraud: The general framework

The history of corruption and fraud, in sports and in any human activity, is probably as old as mankind itself, from Greece, Rome or Byzantium, to present-day scandals. In the case of sport, there are documented instances of bribery in the Olympic Games in Ancient Greece (Maennig 2005: 187–188), fraud in cricket in the nineteenth century in Britain (Hill 2008: 142), and in modern times, there have been many high-profile stories, such as the Chicago White Sox Scandal in 1919, the British betting scandal in the 1960s or Totonero in Italian football in the 1980s. Quite recently, reports have listed numerous instances of corruption (e.g. as many as 2089 identified between 2000 and 2010 by Gorse and Chadwick 2011). A particularly critical year was 2011 in Europe, where, according to Bozkurt (2012: 2), most European football leagues were affected, even with the involvement of international criminal groups.

The first challenge, within the area of sports fraud, is delimiting the practice itself. For a start, there is the terminological problem of how to call it: the literature uses 'sports fraud', 'sports corruption', 'manipulation', 'cheating', 'manipulation in sports', 'rigging' or 'fixing', and such labels, apparently synonymous, do not completely coincide. For instance, corruption in sport has been defined as 'any illegal, immoral or unethical activity that attempts to deliberately distort the result of a sporting contest for the personal material gain of one or more parties involved in that activity' (Gorse and Chadwick 2011: 42). This definition presents a number of problems. First, the adjectives *immoral* and *unethical* are extremely relative and blurred, since ethics and morals are hardly universal (e.g. throwing the ball out in football when an opposite player has been injured is seen by some coaches as ethical, while others explicitly order their players not to do it). Second, not all things unethical or immoral are cases of corruption or fraud: to quote the same football situation, scoring a goal when the goalkeeper is unconscious is highly unethical, but can be hardly considered an instance of fraud. Another problem in the above definition would be the adjectives *personal* and *material* applied to gain, as fraud may be committed simply to prevail in any sports contest, even if there is no reward therefore (e.g. to win a title or a medal); as has been pointed out, corruption may involve what is known as 'status gain' (Nye 1967: 419), and also such gain may not be personal, but for a whole institution or even a country (e.g. allocation of hosting rights for international competitions, as mentioned by Masters [2015: 112]). Finally, one should also consider the issue of the parties involved in the activity, and whether gamblers are parties to the activity; this would include instances of sabotage, e.g. attacks attempting to injure a football player before a match, as confessed by a match-fixer himself in an autobiographical work (Perumal et al. 2014). Therefore, for the purposes of this study, I shall be using a working definition that leaves ethical/moral aspects aside, and includes any type of gain: 'any activity which deliberately attempts to distort the result of a sporting contest against the rules of such contest, for any type of gain' (on the problems on defining fraud and corruption in sport, see Brooks et al. 2013: 15ff).

Although the most common forms of sports fraud are doping and match-fixing (betting- or non-betting-related), there are other less commented forms, such as sabotage (causing rivals to lose or underperform in illicit ways) or fixed draws. In turn, the reasons for fraud are varied, and range from the non-financial (e.g. winning a title, avoiding relegation or gaining promotion, in football fixes) to the purely financial, usually related to betting. In fact, it has been said (Hill 2008: 10) that the defining factor leading to corruption in some sports is illegal gambling. This activity (legal or illegal) multiplies the possibilities of fraud *ad infinitum*, since the ultimate purpose might not be winning whichever contest is at stake, but simply securing the result on a bet, e.g. on how many fouls will be committed during a football match or whether a given player will score or not. This type of fix makes it possible to obtain the cooperation of the opponent, as they may allow a given situation to happen as long as the final result of the match is the one they need (e.g. the 'agreement' may be that a team loses 2–0 after the first half, and then makes a comeback and wins 2–3 at the end of the match).

In the face of these activities, governments, institutions and society at large have attempted to curb sports fraud. Of course, it may be argued that it is not an idea of cleanliness and honesty that lies beneath the fight against corruption, but a purely materialistic one, i.e. the fear of being 'tainted', which would lead to loss of interest by followers and the media, and, therefore, loss of sponsorship and revenue. This may affect individuals, either sportsmen or sportswomen whose contracts have been terminated because of alleged or proved fraud (Lance Armstrong, for instance, lost eight sponsors in one single day after the United States Anti-Doping Agency issued its report in 2012), or teams with decreased attendance after their involvement in match-fixing is exposed (e.g. after the 'Calciopoli' scandal; see Buraimo et al. 2015). What is worse, a whole championship or sport may be affected, such as the Chinese Super League (Hill 2008: 12) and the South Africa Football Association (Forrest and McHale 2015: 55). In fact, some economists have expressed the danger of fraud in purely financial terms, i.e. private, short-term gain vs. long-term general loss, when they euphemistically mention 'economic decisions that are privately optimal but not in the best interests of the sport' (Preston and Szymanski 2003: 621). It has even been suggested that the repercussions might affect the overall economy of a country if already fragile (a real danger for Greece and Ireland, according to Petropoulos and Maguire 2013: 89).

Whatever the reasons (at times ethical, at times materialistic), it cannot be denied that, over the last decades, the fight against fraud in sport has become more active. Strictly within the sports sphere, governing bodies have set up specific courts or agencies, either at a national level, such as the United States Anti-Doping Agency (2009) or at an international one, such as the Court of Arbitration for Sport (1984) and the World Anti-Doping Agency (1999). For their part, the ordinary courts have also heard cases related to sports fraud, especially where the violations committed exceed the games and involve civil or criminal offences (betting fraud, money laundering).

The legal framework varies from one country to another: even within the EU, which is supposed to share a more or less similar legal culture, some countries simply include sports fraud under the general category of corruption or fraud, whereas others have defined specific sport offences, either through direct mention in criminal codes (e.g. Spain) or through separate laws (e.g. Italy). In many common-law jurisdictions, if the episode is related to betting, it is prosecuted under the offence of gambling fraud. At an international level, it is worth mentioning that the Council of Europe opened for signature in 2014 the Convention on the Manipulation of Sports Competitions, which has not yet entered into force (for more detail on EU provisions, see KEA European Affairs 2012).

2. Metaphor, crime and fraud: The present study

Law is about abstract concepts: right and wrong, legal and illegal; it is about establishing categories in the human mind which enable us to make correct decisions before taking an action and to decide, once an action has taken place, whether it is correct or incorrect. This involves a great degree of abstractness, in such a way that the mind, as with all abstract concepts (e.g. love), requires objective, metaphorical images in order to try and grasp legal notions.

In other specialized areas, such as economics, there are countless expressions based on metaphorical extensions of everyday words, and concepts such as the solidness of a currency (Silaški and Kilyeni 2014) are purely metaphorical in nature. In the case of law, in spite of some detractors, who consider figurative language in principle undesirable (Tiersma 1999: 128) or warn that it may cause 'confusion, misunderstanding and frustration' (Anderson 1991: 1215), metaphor has been accepted as basic to legal reasoning (see, for instance, Murray 1984 or Winter 2008). In the field of criminal law, metaphor has also been used frequently, not only for exemplification purposes, but also with a strong ideological component (Duncan 1994; Butler 2012; Deignan 2015).

For this study, in order to illustrate the presence of metaphor in the description of sports fraud and the fight against it, I extracted manually all metaphors relating to sports fraud and fight measures from a selection of nine academic studies[3] (journal papers and book chapters, in both cases among the most quoted publications in the field) dealing with the topic from a legal or law enforcement perspective (see Appendix). I have followed a qualitative approach, focusing on the most salient metaphors and not on their specific density or the number of occurrences, although this analysis will also mention whether a metaphor is particularly frequent, as part of an intentional overall scenario. It is relevant to point out that some of the texts have been written by non-native speakers of English: far from being a problem, for the purposes of this study this is a bonus, since many of the metaphors are universal as they are grounded in basic human experience (Kövecses 2005), and in any case, English is a Lingua Franca (ELF) in the world of both sports and law enforcement. Therefore, it is only natural that an ELF corpus should be used for any linguistic analysis involving communication at an international level.

For the extraction of the metaphors from the corpus, the procedure put forward by the Pragglejaz Group (2007) was used, i.e. a metaphor is identified as such if its contextual meaning (be it a word or an expression) differs from the basic meaning, but a connection is still present between one and the other (on the advantages and limitations of this method, see Steen [2007: 91ff.]). As the purpose is to analyse metaphors appearing in the depiction of sports fraud, other metaphors will be disregarded, from both general areas (e.g. as in 'an example of the *deep-rooted* inequality in sports', EQUALITY IS A PLANT) and concerning non-fraud-related sports or legal matters (e.g. in 'High wages for players was a big *burden* on club finances', DEBTS ARE PHYSICAL WEIGHT). The result is a total of 203 metaphors related to sports fraud.

For the present analysis, my starting point has been the traditional classification by Lakoff and Johnson (1980: 14) between ontological metaphors, structural metaphors and orientational metaphors, as it provides deep insights into the way sports fraud and the fight against it are visualized. In the following section, I shall explore some of the most interesting subcategories found in the corpus.

3. Analysis

This section will analyse some of the most noteworthy metaphors used in the description and justification of the fight against sports corruption and fraud. Towards a better understanding of the metaphorical mappings and their effects in anti-fraud discourse, I have subdivided Lakoff's ontological category into 'living beings' and 'object' metaphors, and have grouped the structural and the orientational metaphors into one section.

In terms of numbers and domains, the breakdown of metaphors as shown in Table 8.1 is the following:

Table 8.1 Metaphorical domains in corpus

Type of metaphorical mapping	No. of metaphorical tokens
Buildings	16
Cleanliness	16
Disease	21
Human beings	12
Hunting/fishing	13
Instruments/tools	15
Light/seeing	13

Type of metaphorical mapping	No. of metaphorical tokens
Living beings	10
Journey/Movement	24
Physical properties	18
Vertical metaphors	14
War/fight	31
Others (e.g. clothing, religion)	9
Total metaphors	**203**
Total word count	**72,809**

3.1. Metaphors of living beings

As is the case in many other types of discourse, the consideration of anything as a living being makes it possible to attribute animated features to abstract objects. In this way, all the components of sports fraud (sports themselves, fraud/corruption and the fight against it) become 'alive' (SPORT IS A LIVING BEING, FRAUD/CORRUPTION IS A LIVING BEING, FRAUD PREVENTION IS A LIVING BEING). In each example, the metaphor is italicized, and the name of the author(s) of the paper is indicated between brackets.

(1) The article analyses the present anti-doping regime that is being *propagated* and sustained by WADA. (Dasgupta)
(2) WADA claims, since its early days, that the Code is a *living* document, subjected to a productive feedback chain. (Duval et al.)

The metaphor of the body itself is a frequent one, even if repeated usage has led to lexicalization (the *Oxford English Dictionary* [2009] shows examples of metaphorical uses of 'body' ever since the Renaissance) and loss of some expressive power. In spite of this, the identification is still present, whereby LAW IS A BODY and ORGANIZATIONS FIGHTING AGAINST FRAUD ARE BODIES. The conceptualization as bodies, in turn, leads to metaphorical tokens of body parts, both through general idioms (*under somebody's nose*) or specific legal ones (the expression *have teeth*, frequently applied to law, is used for codes and their power to punish offenders):

(3) This doping programme was being carried out right under *the nose* of UCI and the organizers of Tour de France. (Dasgupta)

(4) As the WADA does not dispose of any public (or private for that matter) authority to implement the Code, it must be transposed by the SGBs and governments at the national and international level to *gain some teeth*. (Duval et al.)

Probably the most expressive category within living beings is that of human metaphors, which allow us to conceptualize abstract concepts in the closest way possible (this is a 'peer-to-peer' approach to reality, i.e. we see things in the same way as we see ourselves). Such identification is especially useful for persuasive purposes, as '[a]nthropomorphized agents can act as powerful agents of social connection' (Epley et al. 2007). This is reflected in the corpus, where non-animated agents have human characteristics and attitudes:

(5) Another reason for the gulf between matches flagged and action taken stems from the *unwillingness* of sports to properly police themselves. (Kerr)

The view of sport as a living being is also present in the conception of fraud as a disease affecting a living body (SPORTS FRAUD IS A DISEASE) or as physical harm (SPORTS FRAUD IS A WOUND). This is greatly relevant from an ideological point of view, as the 'disease' conceptualization is a traditional one in the description of crime (see, for instance, Thibodeau and Boroditsky 2011). The disease mapping makes it possible to attribute to fraud the characteristics of a disease: fraud affects the human body (sport) by corrupting it, it can have epidemic proportions, and it can be cured. Hence the frequent use of metaphors of diseases and wounds:

(6) However, the magnitude of the latest doping scandal indicates a deeper *malaise* within the current anti-doping regime. (Dasgupta)
(7) [I]t would be foolish to state that the country is *immune* from this growing *epidemic* that threatens the integrity of football worldwide. (Petropoulos and Maguire)
(8) It [...] also reveals certain regulatory *vulnerabilities* within international sport. (Misra et al.)
(9) After all, as Hippocrates, the father of Western *medicine*, stated nearly twenty-five centuries ago '*prevention* is better than *cure*'. (Petropoulos and Maguire)

If prevention fails (note the previous reference to medicine, which is the concluding sentence in one of the chapters in the corpus), and the disease spreads, the result is death for sport as a living being:

(10) The regulatory corruption that has led to the *demise* of professional boxing as a mainstream sport is noteworthy. (Misra et al.)
(11) Continuous allegations of match-fixing in any of these leagues could lead to permanently damaging its reputation and ultimately to its *demise*. (Petropoulos and Maguire)

Logically, the fight against sports fraud is portrayed by means of various healing images (CORRUPTION IS A DISEASE, FIGHTING CORRUPTION IS CURING), also frequent in the discourse against crime (see, for instance, Allbritton 1995):

(12) Openness and transparency have long been considered *an antidote* to practices like corruption. (Kerr)
(13) It is necessary to have evidence gathering and prosecution when incidences of match fixing requiring a criminal justice *remedy* occur. (Abbott and Sheehan)

3.2. Object metaphors: The tangible presence of fraud against sports integrity

As seen in previous sections, the comprehension of abstract notions is hardly an easy process, unless they can be perceived by the senses, and become 'visible' (more on this below). However, 'seeing' sometimes is not enough: in John 20: 24–29, Thomas refuses to believe that Jesus has risen from the dead until he, literally, can 'put his finger' and 'his hand' into his wounds, and in most languages reality can be defined by means of the concept of physical, three-dimensional existence. It is no coincidence that, in English and in other languages, partial synonyms of *real* include *tangible* and *palpable*. Thus, one of the ways to portray the fight against fraud is to conceptualize both sport and fraud itself as 'tangible' elements (SPORT IS AN OBJECT WITH PHYSICAL PROPERTIES, FRAUD AND THE FIGHT AGAINST IT ARE OBJECTS WITH PHYSICAL PROPERTIES), i.e. to make them part of the 'world of objects' (Henly 1987: 82).

Once something has physical existence, it must remain 'unbroken' and 'undivided', which is the foundation for one of the most important metaphors of this corpus: the integrity of sport. This is a very powerful image that evokes physical characteristics, but also moral ones (the *OED* contains examples of *integrity* in the moral sense as early as the sixteenth century), and it constitutes one of the pillars of the discourse against sports fraud (it appears in all of the papers analysed). 'Integrity', therefore, although applicable to physical objects, points in the same direction as the disease metaphors commented on earlier:

(14) The INTERPOL–FIFA Initiative will continue to work with all stakeholders to better protect *integrity* in football. (Abbott and Sheehan)
(15) [W]e do in fact have a problem with match fixing, and not only in Asia, and [...] the *integrity* of football is at risk. (Feltes)

Another of the consequences of sport having physical entity is that it may be subject to physical actions: it can be 'manipulated', but it can also be 'protected', in order to preserve its integrity (note again that the images are also applicable to crime in general):

(16) Match fixing in football, particularly the *manipulation* by criminals often operating at a global level [...] is an increasing challenge. (Abbott and Sheehan)
(17) Specified, independent units within soccer associations like UEFA, DFL, DFB and security departments must *protect* and police the game. (Feltes)

A further ontological metaphor that provides strong connotations of physical (and moral) presence is that of buildings. Within human experience, construction metaphors are synonymous with progress ('constructive' criticism is always preferable to 'destructive' one), and institutional discourse is full of expressions relating to the domain of buildings and structures, which convey a sense of coordination and protection.[4] This is all the more important if the 'enemy' is also 'structured' (after all, Article 2(a) of the UN Convention against Transnational Organized Crime defines an organized group as a 'structured group'):

(18) For this purpose some average clubs use the illegal cash 'donated' by doubtful commercial *structures*. (Cheloukhine)
(19) [I]nvestigating such activities is very difficult and time consuming due to clandestine *structures*, very well (illegally and legally) connected actors. (Feltes)

Within this scenario, the threat of sports fraud is portrayed by describing sport as a structure whose foundations are endangered (SPORT IS A BUILDING), which evokes extremely powerful images of the whole building collapsing (parallel to the 'death' described when sport is compared to a living body):

(20) The money draws back from sports, which is shaken to the very *foundations* and suffer considerable image damage. (Feltes)
(21) Corruption and the manipulation of sport results jeopardize not only the ethical value and *structures* of sport; once the sport is ethically devaluated and the trust into sports is lost, the sources of finance will *collapse*. (Feltes)

Although also a container metaphor, closely related to the building metaphor is the 'house' domain, also very popular in politics (e.g. Chilton and Ilyin 1993; Musolff 2000). In the following example, the 'house' is used as a metaphor for sport, and 'order' belongs to the same figurative realm as 'cleanliness' (see below):

(22) Nevertheless, it is only when a country has its own *'house in order'* can it contribute materially and with due moral authority at the international level. (Misra et al.)

3.3. Structural and orientational metaphors: A visualization of procedures against fraud

Within the field of structural metaphors, I shall concentrate on three main framings: the light/darkness uncovering scenario, the journey scenario and the war scenario.

3.3.1. Light/darkness metaphors: Justice against the darkness of fraud

In many areas of law, and especially the fight against corruption, there is the underlying metaphor that crime lurks hidden in the darkness, and the fight against fraud consists in 'casting light', as is aptly summarized by this example from the corpus:

(23) *Openness and transparency* have long been considered an antidote to practices like corruption which thrive in *dark places*. (Kerr)

The general metaphorical mapping SEEING IS UNDERSTANDING has a number of ramifications in the description of criminal activities. Firstly, 'visibility' is treated as synonymous with 'existence' (for things to exist, they must be seen), and the danger is failing to 'see', and thus failing to perceive, especially if such failure is intentional:

(24) The authors analyse how sports corruption from being a *blind spot* of the law enforcement agencies [...] has become one of their top priorities. (Misra et al.)
(25) Most commonly, individual sports in individual countries appear underprepared, adopting an *ostrich-like* approach to the subject, hoping it just won't happen. (Abbott and Sheehan)
(26) And there will be more rigged matches in future if we *close our eyes*. (Feltes)

Therefore, fraud is 'covered' and all investigations consist in 'bringing light' or 'uncovering' (in the same way that, in criminal investigations, the truth and the culprit are 'discovered'):

(27) As a result of the investigation, a wide-spread match-fixing epidemic was *uncovered* affecting not only football, but volleyball, motorboat racing, and allegedly baseball. (Abbott and Sheehan)
(28) [T]he investigations *revealed* shocking details of doping by elite sports persons. (Dasgupta)

3.3.2. Journey and position metaphors

Human experience in general is defined as a journey (it is no coincidence that the most common preposition indicating purpose in English, *to*, also indicates direction), and so is sport. Note, for instance, that 'the road to Cardiff/Kiev, etc.' is one of the phrases used to describe the Union of European Football Associations (UEFA) Champions League. In the discourse on sports fraud, strategic efforts are also seen as a journey (THE FIGHT AGAINST SPORTS FRAUD IS A JOURNEY), the ultimate destination being 'integrity' or 'clean' sport (see the section on 'cleanliness' below).

(29) This chapter explores a number of *avenues* to combat match-fixing. Such *avenues* include reform of governance mechanisms. (Petropoulos and Maguire)
(30) The identification of 'Integrity Officers' within each UEFA member country is seen as a positive *step* on the part of member associations. (Abbott and Sheehan)

Within the journey scenario, forward movement is viewed as compulsory for legislation and any other procedure, while the great danger is not being able to keep abreast, or even to move backwards:

(31) The INTERPOL team follows up the workshops some 12 months after the event to ask whether *progress* in developing the response to match fixing has been continued. (Abbott and Sheehan)
(32) The *way forward* for WADA then is to change its pro-elitist approach. (Dasgupta)
(33) [T]he current legislation considerably *lags behind* the new and current complexities of match fixing. (Cheloukhine)
(34) [T]he aim of the 2015 Code is not to take 11 years' worth of *backward steps*. (Duval et al.)

But 'moving backwards' or 'falling behind' are not the only dangers: one must also beware of taking 'the wrong way', i.e. engaging in fraud. This is an interesting, positive metaphor, since those who commit fraud have simply taken the 'wrong path' and may be reinstated (i.e. go back to the 'correct path', which is consistent with viewing crime as 'deviation', 'being led astray', etc.):

(35) [L]ack of awareness programme and corrupt officials *misleads* the athletes to take substance which they are not supposed to. (Dasgupta)

Once the fight against sports fraud has been depicted as forward movement, anything preventing from reaching a destination is perceived as a barrier, i.e. PROBLEMS IN THE FIGHT AGAINST SPORTS FRAUD ARE PHYSICAL OBSTACLES:

(36) He anticipates the *stumbling blocks* ahead and identifies the key trends already under way. (Duval et al.)

In all these examples, the underlying scenario is (GOOD) RELATIONSHIPS ARE PHYSICAL CONTACT. Within this idea, the concept of 'liaison' creates both a physical relationship, also related to military jargon (and, therefore, connected to the war metaphors analysed below), and points of 'contact' indicate good relationships (these images are also used in international criminal cooperation, with 'contact points' and 'liaison magistrates'). This also establishes a powerful parallelism between the war against sports fraud and the war against international crime:

(37) [T]here are not even 'single *points of contact*' existing in the various organisations to discuss matters relating to match fixing. (Abbott and Sheehan)
(38) Such a unit could also *liaise* and be the conduit between Sports Controlling Bodies and Law Enforcement. (Misra et al.)

3.3.3. War metaphors: The battle against fraud

In the previous section, it has been seen how the fight against sports fraud shares many metaphorical scenarios with that of combatting crime. This becomes more visible when, in order to stress the importance of the prevention of fraud, it is portrayed as a battle, and the various types of fraud are depicted as the enemy (FRAUD IS THE ENEMY, FRAUD PREVENTION IS WAR). The 'war on crime' metaphor has been widely discussed by the academia, especially because of the possibilities it offers for extrapolation: once anything has been described as 'a crime', and therefore 'an enemy', a wide range of expenses, efforts and measures (even if unpopular) become justifiable. In the corpus studied, the participation of criminal organizations in sports corruption adds to the conception of sports fraud as a crime; once this has been established, it is possible to develop a powerful ideological discourse against sports fraud portrayed as an enemy, a danger to integrity. The war[5] is against both the criminal groups and the tricksters, seen as a threat and an enemy:

(39) WADA's key task was, and still is, to devise the global set of uniform rules applicable to the anti-doping *fight*: the WADC. (Duval et al.)

(40) Three of the men implicated, described by the prosecutor as *'enemies* of sport' were sentenced in April 2011 by the Bochum District Court for to up to 3 years. (Feltes)

(41) Doping also poses a *threat* to society outside the narrow confines of elite sports. (Kornbeck)

(42) *[C]ombating* gambling-led corruption should also focus on all parts of the corruption process and the enablers of the crime. (Misra et al.)

A special subdivision of the war metaphor is the hunting (or fishing) metaphor, also relying on the ontological conception of fraud as a prey, which can reach mythological proportions:

(43) Alerts are created for a third of all matches, which shows that *the net* is being cast very widely at this stage. (Kerr)

(44) Match-fixing is clearly a *many-headed dragon that we must slay* with a coordinated national and international effort. (Feltes)

The hunting metaphor works both ways: the concept of 'targeting' is used both for the activities of fraudsters and for those of law enforcement. On the one hand, the fraudsters are the hunters, the referees and players being the prey:

(45) [T]he players and referees [...] are so often the primary *targets* of the match fixers. (Abbott and Sheehan)

(46) Elite players in well-paid leagues [...] are unlikely to be *targeted* in this regard, unless they have a gambling problem or related debts. (Misra et al.)

Given this scenario, it is perfectly justified that the law enforcement agencies should become the hunters, so that the fraudsters become the prey (in other words, this is a shooting scenario, in which the only way to avoid victims is to shoot the shooters):

(47) [N]early 300 people have been arrested in police operations […], *targeting* illegal soccer gambling networks across Asia. (Feltes)

(48) [A] criminal offence of cheating at gambling, which would assist in *targeting* those involved in such conspiracies. (Misra et al.)

4. A multi-faceted metaphor: Cleanliness

In this section, I shall deal with a metaphor, that of cleanliness, which objectively speaking would pertain to the concept of physical properties (only tangible objects can be 'clean'), but it also possesses human connotations (because of the association between cleanliness, purity and morality) and is also a process metaphor, since the fight against fraud (and crime) can be equated to cleaning.

The metaphor identifying cleanliness with morality and dirt with immorality has been widely studied; Lakoff and Johnson mention the association between purity and morality (1980: 207), although some authors have suggested that the dirt metaphor is more related to the 'disorder' notion, i.e. things being out of place (Lizardo 2012). Whichever the conception, the link between 'clean' and 'pure' is so strong that one of the definitions of 'clean' in the *OED* is 'void of spiritual or moral stain or pollution (or what is so considered); pure; undefiled, chaste, innocent' (OED 2009). The *OED* even specifically lists as one of the meanings of 'clean', something or someone who is 'free from suspicion of criminal or treacherous intent or involvement; not carrying incriminating material (as drugs, weapons, etc.); not a security risk'.

In criminal law, words like *dirty, slimy* and *filth* have often been used, for instance, in order to justify criminal convictions (Duncan 1994), as part of a 'dehumanization strategy' (Haney 2005: 148ff.), whereby the fight against crime is not against people, but against something alien and undesirable. As regards sport, in its presentation of the 2015 version of the World Anti-Doping Code, the WADA describes the code as 'a stronger, more robust tool to protect the rights of the *clean* athlete worldwide' (World Anti-Doping Agency 2015, our italics). The opposition between 'clean sport' and 'dirty fraud' makes the image of 'cleanliness' a pervasive one in the fight against fraud (in our corpus, it appears in all but two of the papers):

(49) Athletes agree to disclose large parts of their privacy for the sake of *clean* sport. (Duval et al.)

Conversely, fraud is equated to various forms of 'uncleanliness':

(50) The follow up through underground bookmakers, or by bribing the rival club itself, results in an illegal profit and *tarnishes* the integrity of the game. (Cheloukhine)
(51) In all leagues, most trainers admitted involvement in some *dirty* tricks in relation to match fixing. (Cheloukhine)

If the goal is 'clean' sport, the fight against fraud is equated to 'cleaning up':

(52) The reputational difficulties that athletics and professional cycling have with regard to doping continue, despite recent progress in *cleaning up* the sports in question. (Misra et al.)
(53) A combined, aggressive approach […] is sending a clear signal that it wishes to *clean up* the game of soccer. (Cheloukhine)

Of course, there is a conceptual relationship between cleanliness/dirt and the lexicalized metaphor of money laundering, both in general organized crime activity and in sports fraud:

(54) Criminal organizations benefit from match-fixing […] in its ability to *launder* their ill-gotten gains from other criminal activities. (Feltes)

5. Conclusions

If it were true that sport is about participating and not about winning, there would be no fraud in sport, which probably would make it unique among human activities. However, this is not the case: more often than not, sport is – regrettably– about winning, at all costs if need be. The romantic idea of 'sportsmanship', based on fair play, as pointed out by Hanson and Savage (2012), is often replaced by that of 'gamesmanship', whereby winning is everything, cheating does not count if one does not get caught and the end justifies the means. This is why sports fraud exists: people and organizations try to make sure that they win, either at the games themselves, or betting on the outcome of the games.

In the face of such activities, society is constantly attempting to build a discourse that stresses that fraud is wrong, a crime in itself, and that it must be combatted as such. As with all discourses, institutional or not, figurative language plays a primary role, and the academic discourse against sports fraud makes frequent use of metaphors: the purpose is to shape the perception of concepts in such a way that the ideological component is accepted by audiences and users, often without discussion. Thus, the connotations and the message become part of the terminology itself (e.g. club owners might complain that their team is 'clean', but in doing so they are using the same metaphor). In this type of discourse, the role of metaphor is not illustrative, but ideological: the use of certain images is based on certain logical inferences, which justify actions. When describing sports fraud, the use of criminal imagery helps the audience to accept the suitability of the same measures that are wielded against crime; hence the specific metaphorical scenarios with such a highly intentional, persuasive nature. This is very forcefully illustrated, as we have seen, by the portrayal of fraud as a disease against which all 'remedial' measures are acceptable, however harsh (suspension, fines, imprisonment).

This analysis has shown that, while some of the metaphors have a clear, objective ontological basis, usually pertaining to the world of concrete objects, this basis has a number of connotations associated to human beings, such as integrity and cleanliness, and especially, the use of disease metaphors which portray fraud as something leading to the death of sport. In other cases, process and event scenarios, like war or journey images, are also employed to justify measures and actions that may at first sight seem strict or controversial, but are eventually accepted as inevitable within an all-out 'war against fraud'.

Metaphors are fundamental in creating a discourse where images become the self-evident component, the vocabulary which will frame any other discussion: one may discuss whether an athlete is 'clean', or whether a match has been fixed by criminals, but the issue of whether corruption equals dirtiness or crime is no longer under discussion. This is why it is important to be aware of the metaphors used, both in sports law contexts and in general discourse on sport (institutional, media, etc.) to know what is at stake, and of the role played by sport within the discourses of present-day society.

Appendix: Academic papers included in the corpus

Abbott, J. and D. Sheehan (2013), 'The INTERPOL Approach to Tackling Match-Fixing in Football', in M. R. Haberfeld and D. Sheehan (eds), *Match-Fixing in International Sport: Existing Processes, Law Enforcement, and Prevention Strategies*, 263–287, Heidelberg: Springer.

Cheloukhine, S. (2013), 'Match-Fixing in Soccer: Organization, Structure and Policing. A Russian Perspective', in M. R. Haberfeld and D. Sheehan (eds), *Match-Fixing in*

International Sport: Existing Processes, Law Enforcement, and Prevention Strategies, 113–132, Heidelberg: Springer.

Dasgupta, L. (2017), 'Russian Twister and the World Anti-Doping Code: Time to Shun the Elitist Paradigm of Anti-doping Regime', *International Sports Law Journal*, 17 (1–2): 4–14.

Duval, A., H. Ham, M. Viret, E. Wisnosky, H. L. Jakobs and M. Morgan (2016), 'The World Anti-Doping Code 2015: ASSER International Sports Law Blog Symposium', *International Sports Law Journal*, 16: 99–117.

Feltes, T. (2013), 'Match-Fixing in Western Europe', in M. R. Haberfeld and D. Sheehan (eds), *Match-Fixing in International Sport: Existing Processes, Law Enforcement, and Prevention Strategies*, 15–30, Heidelberg: Springer.

Kerr, J. (2017), 'How to Build an "Open" Match Fixing Alert System', *International Sports Law Journal*, 16: 118–122.

Kornbeck, J. (2016), 'Anti-doping Governance and Transparency: A European Perspective', *International Sports Law Journal*, 17 (1–2): 49–67.

Misra, A., J. Anderson and J. Saunders (2013), 'Safeguarding Sports Integrity against Crime and Corruption: An Australian Perspective', in M. R. Haberfeld and D. Sheehan (eds), *Match-Fixing in International Sport: Existing Processes, Law Enforcement, and Prevention Strategies*, 135–155, Heidelberg: Springer.

Petropoulos, N. and R. Maguire (2013), 'Match-Fixing: Case Studies from Greece and Ireland', in M. R. Haberfeld and D. Sheehan (eds), *Match-Fixing in International Sport: Existing Processes, Law Enforcement, and Prevention Strategies*, 89–99, Heidelberg: Springer.

References

Allbritton, D. W. (1995), 'When Metaphors Function as Schemas: Some Cognitive Effects of Conceptual Metaphors', *Metaphor and Symbolic Activity*, 10 (1): 33–46.

Anderson, D. A. (1991), 'Metaphorical Scholarship. A Review of the First Amendment, Democracy and Romance by Steven H. Shiffrin', *California Law Review*, 79: 1205–1220.

Bozkurt, E. (2012), *Match Fixing and Fraud in Sport: Putting the Pieces Together*. Available at: http://www.europarl.europa.eu/document/activities/cont/201209/20120925ATT52303/20120925ATT52303EN.pdf (accessed 7 August 2018).

Brooks, G., A. Azeem and M. Button (2013), *Fraud, Corruption and Sport*, Basingstoke: Palgrave Macmillan.

Buraimo, B., G. Migali and R. Simmons (2015), 'An Analysis of Consumer Response to Corruption: Italy's *Calciopoli* Scandal', *Oxford Bulletin of Economics and Statistics*, 78 (1): 22–41.

Butler, B. (2012), 'Capital Pretrial Publicity as a Symbolic Public Execution: A Case Report', *Journal of Forensic Psychology Practice*, 12 (3): 259–269.

Chilton, P. and M. Ilyin (1993), 'Metaphor in Political Discourse: The Case of the "Common European House"', *Discourse & Society*, 4 (1): 7–31.

Deignan, A. (2015), 'Payback and Punishment: Metaphors in Scottish Penal Policy', in J. B. Herrmann and T. Berber Sardinha (eds), *Metaphor in Specialist Discourse*, 79–100, Amsterdam: Benjamins.

Duncan, M. G. (1994), 'In Slime and Darkness: The Metaphor of Filth in Criminal Justice', *Tulane Law Review*, 68 (4): 725–757.

Epley, N., A. Waytz and J. T. Cacioppo (2007), 'On Seeing Human: A Three-Factor Theory of Anthropomorphism', *Psychological Review*, 11 (4): 864–886.

Forrest, D. and I. G. McHale (2015), *An Evaluation of Sportradar's Fraud Detection System*. Available at: https://fds.integrity.sportradar.com/wp-content/uploads/sites/18/2016/03/Sportradar-Security-Services_Univsersity-of-Liverpool_An-Evaluation-of-the-FDS.pdf (accessed 7 August 2018).

Gorse, S. and S. Chadwick (2011), *The Prevalence of Corruption in International Sport. A Statistical Analysis*. Centre for the International Business of Sport, Coventry University Business School.

Haney, C. (2005), *Death by Design: Capital Punishment as a Social Psychological System*, Oxford: Oxford University Press.

Hanson, K. O. and M. Savage (2012), *What Role Does Ethics Play in Sports?* Available at: http://www.scu.edu/ethics/publications/submitted/sports-ethics.html (accessed 7 August 2018).

Henly, B. (1987), 'Penumbra: Roots of Legal Metaphor', *Hastings Constitutional Law Quarterly*, 15: 81–100.

Hill, D. (2008), *The Fix: Soccer and Organized Crime*, Toronto: McClelland & Stewart.

KEA European Affairs (2012), *Match-Fixing in Sport. A Mapping of Criminal Law Provisions in EU 27*. Available at: http://ec.europa.eu/assets/eac/sport/library/studies/study-sports-fraud-final-version_en.pdf (accessed 7 August 2018).

Kövecses, Z. (2005), *Metaphor in Culture. Universality and Variation*, Cambridge: Cambridge University Press.

Lakoff, G. and M. Johnson (1980), *Metaphors We Live By*, Chicago: University of Chicago Press.

Lizardo, O. (2012), 'The Conceptual Bases of Metaphors of Dirt and Cleanliness in Moral and Non-moral Reasoning', *Cognitive Linguistics*, 23 (2): 367–393.

Maennig, W. (2005), 'Corruption in International Sports and Sport Management: Forms, Tendencies, Extent and Countermeasures', *European Sport Management Quarterly*, 5 (3): 187–225.

Masters, A. (2015), 'Corruption in Sport: From the Playing Field to the Field of Policy', *Policy and Society*, 34: 111–123.

Murray, J. E. (1984), 'Understanding Law as Metaphor', *Journal of Legal Education*, 34: 714–730.

Musolff, A. (2000), 'Political Imagery of Europe: A House without Exit Doors?', *Journal of Multilingual and Multicultural Development*, 21 (3): 216–229.

Nye, J. S. (1967), 'Corruption and Political Development: A Cost-Benefit Analysis', *The American Political Science Review*, 61 (2): 417–427.
Oxford English Dictionary (2009), CD-ROM, 2nd ed., Oxford: Oxford University Press.
Perumal, W. R., A. Righi and E. Piano (2014), *Kelong Kings: Confessions of the World's Most Prolific Match Fixer*, London: Invisible Dog Classics.
Pragglejaz Group (2007), 'MIP: A Method for Identifying Metaphorically Used Words in Discourse', *Metaphor and Symbol*, 22 (1): 1–39.
Preston, I. and S. Szymanski (2003), 'Cheating in Contests', *Oxford Review of Economic Policy*, 19 (4): 612–624.
Silaški, N. and A. Kilyeni (2014), 'The MONEY IS SOLID Metaphor in Economic and Business Terminology in English', *Professional Communication and Translation Studies*, 7 (1–2): 73–80.
Steen, G. J. (2007), *Finding Metaphor in Grammar and Usage. A Methodological Analysis of Theory and Research*, Amsterdam: Benjamins.
Thibodeau, P. H. and L. Boroditsky (2011), 'Metaphors We Think With: The Role of Metaphor in Reasoning', *PLoS ONE* 6 (2): e16782.
Tiersma, P. M. (1999), *Legal Language*, Chicago: University of Chicago Press.
Winter, S. L. (2008), 'What Is the "Color" of Law?', in R. W. Gibbs (ed.), *The Cambridge Handbook of Metaphor and Thought*, 363–379, Cambridge: Cambridge University Press.
World Anti-Doping Agency (2015), 'The Code'. Available at: https://www.wada-ama.org/en/what-we-do/the-code (accessed 7 August 2018).

Part Three

Modalities. Multimodal Studies

A Multimodal Analysis of Football Live Text Commentary

Valentin Werner

1. Introduction

While traditional forms like TV and radio broadcasting increasingly seem to struggle to attract audiences (He and Abboud 2017), with the rise of provision of online content, live text (LT) has emerged as a popular web-based alternative for live sports reporting. LT has been termed an 'immediate form of journalism' (Werner 2016: 300; see also Thurman and Walters 2013: 95), particularly apt for the coverage of football matches as pre-scheduled events with a limited duration. Stylistically, it has been described as a 'mash-up […] of different journalistic styles (reporting, commenting, glossing)' (Werner 2016: 279). Structurally, it is characterized by a combination of textual (e.g. short commentary, statistics) and visual elements (e.g. images, maps), whose exact organization and representation often can be modified by the user (cf. Jucker 2010: 59). A further characteristic feature is the regular update of content, so that from a textlinguistic perspective the terms 'text-in-motion' (Hauser 2008: 5) or 'text-in-process' (Chovanec 2018: 511) have been coined. In sum, then, the audience deals with a dynamic, interactive and multimodal environment that serves a dedicated 'infotainment' function, that is, the simultaneous provision of factual information and entertainment (Fairclough 1995: 10; McEnnis 2016: 969).[1]

There is a comparatively long (of more than fifty years) and productive history of linguistic enquiries relating to football language (Meier 2017a: 345) and to the discourse of sports and sports reporting more generally (e.g. Reaser 2003). Analyses of sports-related LT, which has been published since the late 1990s (McEnnis 2016: 967), are naturally much scarcer (see Werner 2016; Meier 2017a for broader summaries). Even rarer are analyses of the multimodal properties of LT and football live text (FLT) in particular. The multimodal nature of FLT has repeatedly been acknowledged (e.g. Hauser 2008; Jucker 2010), but researchers to date have largely sidelined this aspect in their analyses and have merely focused on the language used in the actual play-by-play commentary. This is not to say that purely linguistic (i.e. monomodal) analyses of FLT are not worthwhile. They provide important insights into issues such as the use and function of formulaic language (see, e.g., Levin 2008; Meier, this volume), the hybridity of electronic media regarding the speech-writing dichotomy (see, e.g., Jucker 2006; Chovanec 2008, 2010) or how time and space are cognitively and linguistically conceptualized (see, e.g., Meier 2017a; Meier and Thiering 2017), among others. However, taking into account the multimodal nature of FLT arguably will do more justice to the format and overall communicative situation. Going away from the strong 'bias towards the verbal mode' (Pauwels 2012: 250) identified as a general constraint of analyses of electronic communication also ties in with a recent broader trend towards recognizing the importance of formal layout (Werner 2016: 294) and co-occurring textual and non-textual material. In other words, 'ever more phenomena that would previously have been termed paralinguistic, in the sense of accompanying but only weakly influencing linguistic form and expression, are now being moved into the center of concern' (Bateman 2012: 3990).

A related aspect is the issue of audience participation and its potential effects on FLT reporting. A previous study (Werner 2016: 299–302) has identified different degrees of interactivity across various FLT manifestations and has hypothesized that technological advancement in connection with increasing demands for audience participation may lead to a change in reporting style. It remains to be tested whether and how this has actually materialized.

The present study thus considers the multimodal nature of FLT and revisits the role of audience participation in the electronic medium. It specifically aims at expanding the description of sports/football discourse, which is intrinsically relevant in terms of football language potentially having a bearing on general language use and change (e.g. Wyatt and Hadikin 2015 on how the football-related 'park the bus' expression has entered general discourse), and can be situated at the intersection of media linguistics (LT as an online register) and multimodal analysis (LT as a multimodal artefact). While calls for further studies of (F)LT as an underresearched form of journalism have repeatedly been voiced from different angles (e.g. Hauser 2008 from a linguistic; McEnnis 2016 from a media studies perspective), a multimodal framework for the analysis of this type of communication appears as an obvious choice due to the very multimodal nature of the artefact (see above and Section 2), simultaneously facilitating the exploration of issues such as media convergence (Bateman et al. 2017: 67).

The contribution is structured as follows: Section 2 comprises an outline of the multimodal approach for the analysis of webpages employed. The data for the present study is introduced in Section 3, followed by an exploration of the material from a multimodal perspective in Section 4. Section 5 contains the discussion and conclusion part that provides an overall summary and contextualization of results, and indicates avenues for further research.

2. Multimodal analysis and webpages

Whenever multimodal research is carried out, decisions to determine the scope and limits of the analysis have to be made. In the following, some central concepts are introduced to pave the way for the actual application to webpages as the medium where FLT is found. Note that representations of webpages on mobile devices (which may or already have become the default way for FLT consumption)[2] may slightly differ in their layout from the original version (in practical terms involving more vertical scrolling), while general structure and content usually remain the same. The analysis of FLT as one specific multimodal representation is to follow in Section 4.1.

Within the widely used framework developed by Bateman and colleagues (e.g. Bateman 2012, 2017; Bateman et al. 2017), multimodality has been defined as a 'way of characterising communicative situations [...] which rely upon combinations of different "forms" of communication to be effective' (Bateman et al. 2017: 7). Any multimodal analysis and interpretation has to take account of the four broad factors 'materiality, language, semiotics and society' (Bateman et al. 2017: 26), and it will subsequently be described how these can be operationalized.

To start with the issue of materiality, an important distinction is to be drawn between the specific medium (a newspaper, a webpage, etc.) and the various modes (e.g. textual, iconographic)[3] that occur within the medium and serve to create meaning (Bateman et al. 2017: 71). An axiom underlying multimodal analysis is that communication is by default multimodal, so that multimodal analysis commonly deals with 'complex artefacts' or composite 'ensembles' that combine at least two different modes (Bateman et al. 2017: 7–9). A related point is that distinct modes operating in an artefact should only be established through an assessment of the artefact itself and not be presumed *a priori*, so a thorough description (see below and Section 4.1) always constitutes the first step of analysis (Bateman 2017: 240–241). Another layer of complexity is introduced through the general layout of the material studied, where linear and non-linear data are distinguished. The former is represented by speech and writing, for instance, which both 'unfold along a single dimension of actualization' (Bateman 2012: 3984). By contrast, whenever we have to deal with spatial and/or logical organization of information, for instance as represented on webpages, data can be described as non-linear, that is, going beyond a single dimension of actualization (Bateman 2017: 243).

A central concern of multimodal analysis is the exploration of how modes interact to create synergies in communicating effectively (Pauwels 2012: 250; Bateman 2017: 251). Therefore, it is self-evident that multimodal analysis may have to rely on the methodologies of various fields (Bateman et al. 2017: 8–9). Despite this interdisciplinary approach toward the co-occurrence of different modes it is usually necessary to separate the layers of analysis or 'subcanvases' (in terms of slightly different communicative situations) that exist within the medium to be able to better structure the investigation. How exactly this is done very much depends on the focus of the actual research and the medium (Bateman et al. 2017: 223), but in any case it is necessary to consider extant descriptive frameworks (e.g. from linguistics, art history) that may help to decide which levels of analysis are sensible to discern (Bateman et al. 2017: 218).[4]

FLT is transmitted through webpages, which have been labelled 'one of the most obvious manifestations of the growth of multimodal communication and the co-deployment of information' (Bateman et al. 2017: 347). From a broader perspective, webpages have been considered highly relevant instruments for the delivery of content in present-day societies (Herring 2010: 233), with some shares of these societies even exclusively relying on information available online to satisfy their informational (and entertainment-related) needs. Thus, it appears helpful to consider some more specific (multimodal) properties of this type of medium, relating back to the issues of materiality and semiotics (see above).

From a methodological point of view, webpages have been viewed as some kind of naturally occurring and preservable multimodal artefact, as they can be stored as they are (i.e. preserving text, image and layout) and thus 'directly reflect [...] the experience of the digital reader' (Caple 2017: 209). More specifically, communication through webpages has been described as less restricted than other communicative types as it is multimodal, non-linear, hypertextual (i.e., it possesses a logical link structure), interactive and digital (Meier 2017b: 410). While all aspects are important, multimodality and non-linearity appear to represent the central properties as they are constitutional for the modularity (as yet another feature) of the webpage as artefact (Meier 2017b: 411). The co-occurrence of multiple semiotic resources or modes (e.g. text and image; Djonov and Knox 2015: 172)[5] results in some kind of 'multimodal orchestration' (Meier 2017b: 415; cf. the term 'ensemble' as explained above). In terms of communicative practice this implies a deliberate and conscious design process involving language/text, pictures, figures, typography as well as screen layout (Meier 2017b: 415, 425). A related issue is the topic of media convergence (Hauser 2010). Media convergence is facilitated by the fact that the electronic medium allows a combination and display of various communicative forms, and that new types of media may consciously 'rely on such combinations in order to make their points, have their emotional impacts, raise interest and so on' (Bateman et al. 2017: 14).

Closely related to the last aspect, others have emphasized the importance of spatial organization (i.e. non-linearity) and how iconographic means can be used to support the (as a rule) two-dimensional display. Non-linearity apparently occurs on many layers and a common distinction drawn for the analysis of webpages is between content and functional sections as well as navigation zones (cf. the issue of hypertextuality above) of webpages (Djonov and Knox 2015: 176). A generic layout principle that emerges is a two- or three-column structure, with blogs (of which LT arguably is a subcategory) displaying the content (i.e. the textual blog entries) in the central column, again in segmented/modularized form (i.e. shorter entries, combined with or interrupted by pictures and figures; Meier 2017b: 415–416), and usually in reverse chronological order (Herring 2010: 240).

By way of summary, it is important to note, however, that despite the modular nature of webpages, they can be seen as one larger semiotic unit (or 'super sign') coherent both at the surface level and as regards content (Meier 2017b: 418). Prototypically, this unit serves an overall communicative function, such as entertainment, education and persuasion (Meier 2017b: 428).

3. Data

The present study is based on a corpus of FLT reports (all English Premier League and German Bundesliga matches where FLT was available) from

The Guardian (GUAR; www.theguardian.com) and *Spiegel Online* (SPON; www.spiegel.de) media outlets. The material analysed was collected from December 2017 to February 2018 and comprises sixty-eight FLT reports (*c.* 160,000 words). As it sometimes offers two types of textual commentary, SPON had to be split up (see Section 4.1) into the so-called SPON 'Liveticker' (SPON L), which is always offered, and the SPON 'High-Liveticker' (SPON H), available only for selected matches. A breakdown of the data is shown in Table 9.1.

Table 9.1 Corpus frequency information.

	N match reports	N tokens	Average/min/max text length (tokens) per report	SD of text length (tokens) per report
GUAR	19	58,996	3,105/1,960/3,739	404
SPON L	41	72,466	1,725/843/3,072	1,137
SPON H	8	29,424	3,678/2,102/5,728	482

GUAR and SPON are prototypical news webpages (see Meier 2017b: 429 for detailed description) and their FLTs were chosen as they fulfil the properties of (i) being socially relevant as they (as popular manifestations of FLT) 'achieve particular communicative purposes in society' (Bateman et al. 2017: 348; see also Section 2) and of (ii) 'exhibit[ing] a useful degree of homogeneity with respect to their formal properties and internal organization' (Bateman et al. 2017: 348) due to their communicative purpose – reporting on a football match. A secondary motivation for choosing data from these media outlets is that they were shown to be characterized by different degrees of interactivity in an earlier study (Werner 2016: 299–300), and it will be interesting to see how the situation has developed with the increasing importance of social media.

Data were stored in two formats. First, the webpages were saved in their entirety to be able to assess them as multimodal super signs or ensembles (cf. Section 2). Second, the textual data from the main commentary was saved separately as plain text to allow its analysis with standard corpus software (*AntConc* 3.4.4; Anthony 2016). This necessitated some pre-processing with the help of a custom-built Regex-based script in Notepad++[6] to remove boilerplate material (e.g. links to Facebook and other social media appearing with each post in GUAR), time stamps, photograph captions.

4. Results

4.1. Describing the communicative situation

Against the background of the principles and categories for multimodal analysis in general and for the investigation of webpages as one multimodal artefact in particular (presented in Section 2), we may now turn to a more detailed description of the communicative situation in FLT as the first important step of our analysis proper.

Basic issues to consider are the production and consumption circumstances, as these may determine the style of FLT and are motivated by its communicative function. A general point to note is that technological change has a huge bearing on the actual production. Thus, while widely used commercial content management platforms for FLT like *Engage* ('the world's leading audience engagement platform'; see www.scribblelive.com/products/content-curation-live-blog/broadcast-media/) facilitate the production of online content, commentators are constrained by the affordances of the platforms used (Meier 2017b: 412). Previous research on sports-related LT has indicated that input commonly is created in an office by individual freelance journalists or interns that rely on TV coverage[7] and other sources of information, and act as commentator voice (McEnnis 2016: 973; Werner 2016: 276).[8] At least for the subgenre of FLT, there seems to be a shift in this practice in two important respects: first, the analysis of GUAR and SPON suggests that the share of regular sports editors has been increasing; second, in SPON we regularly find two commentator roles (see further Section 4.2), one providing play-by-play commentary, the other one colour commentary and evaluation (e.g. by relating to statistics, strategies of teams, adding anecdotes), which mirrors distributions of commentator roles also found in traditional types of live sports coverage, such as TV and radio reporting (cf. Reaser 2003: 317; Clarke 2017: 37). Both developments can be seen in the light of an increased recognition of FLT as another 'serious' (and revenue-bearing) form of sports journalism, while practitioners seem to value the relative autonomy as regards content and style of the format compared to other types of reporting (McEnnis 2016: 977).

From the perspective of the user, FLT typically is consumed in a quick and cursory manner during the game, but may be read afterwards as well (Werner 2016: 275; Meier and Thiering 2017: 46).[9] For our data, both GUAR and SPON offer the opportunity to access the FLT after the end of the actual coverage. Another factor identified as increasing audience appeal of FLT, and arguably connected to the entertainment function of FLT, is the affordance of flexible and individualized consumption (determined by the digital medium), as users may have various options to manipulate the actual display on their screen (Hauser 2008: 5). While this seems to hold true for SPON, where users have access to different display modes through links and tabs, the structure of GUAR is comparatively rigid (see also below). A potential motivation for the latter fact is that GUAR intends to follow a recent trend where FLT is consumed on mobile devices as some kind of by-medium in addition to the TV coverage. The small screen necessitates simplified modes of display and structure to keep the content accessible (McEnnis 2016: 971; Werner 2016: 284).

When we turn more closely to actual examples of FLT, it can be described as a combination of linear and non-linear data (cf. Section 2). While the linear data (i.e. textual material in the main commentary) will be analysed separately in Section 4.2, an analysis of the non-linear structure of FLT has to refer to various issues of visual design. As can be seen in Figure 9.1 from GUAR and Figure 9.2 from SPON, both FLTs follow a traditional pattern in using squared ordered pages and black (and blue) text on white background in the textual parts. A potential function assigned to this is to convey an image of factuality (Djonov and Knox 2015: 183–184). Both GUAR and SPON follow the two-column layout structure associated with blogs (see Section 2), and the display can be subdivided into three (GUAR) or four (SPON) content zones.[10]

In zone 1, GUAR presents the basic information of the match (teams and their emblem, current score, scorers, time when goals were scored, league, name of the stadium), supposedly for those users that merely want to obtain an overview of the current state of affairs or the final score. Zone 2 presents the names of the commentators, their Twitter ID (if available), buttons that prompt a shared link of the FLT page on the default mail program or on different types of social media (Facebook, Twitter, LinkedIn, Pinterest, the now discontinued Google+).[11] Its second subsection comprises a vertical timeline with key moments of the match in reverse chronological order (final score, goals and scorers, red cards, penalties, presentation of team lineup). A click on the circle symbol or the accompanying text entry leads to the relevant section of the main commentary (zone 3). This supposedly serves as a means of orientation and information for users that want to have a more detailed description of the key moments. In addition, basic statistics (percentage of ball possession as well as number of attempts on goal, corners, fouls and offsides) updated in real time during the match are presented at the bottom of zone 2. Zone 3 contains the main textual commentary in reverse chronological order (with time stamps), which is interspersed with photographs

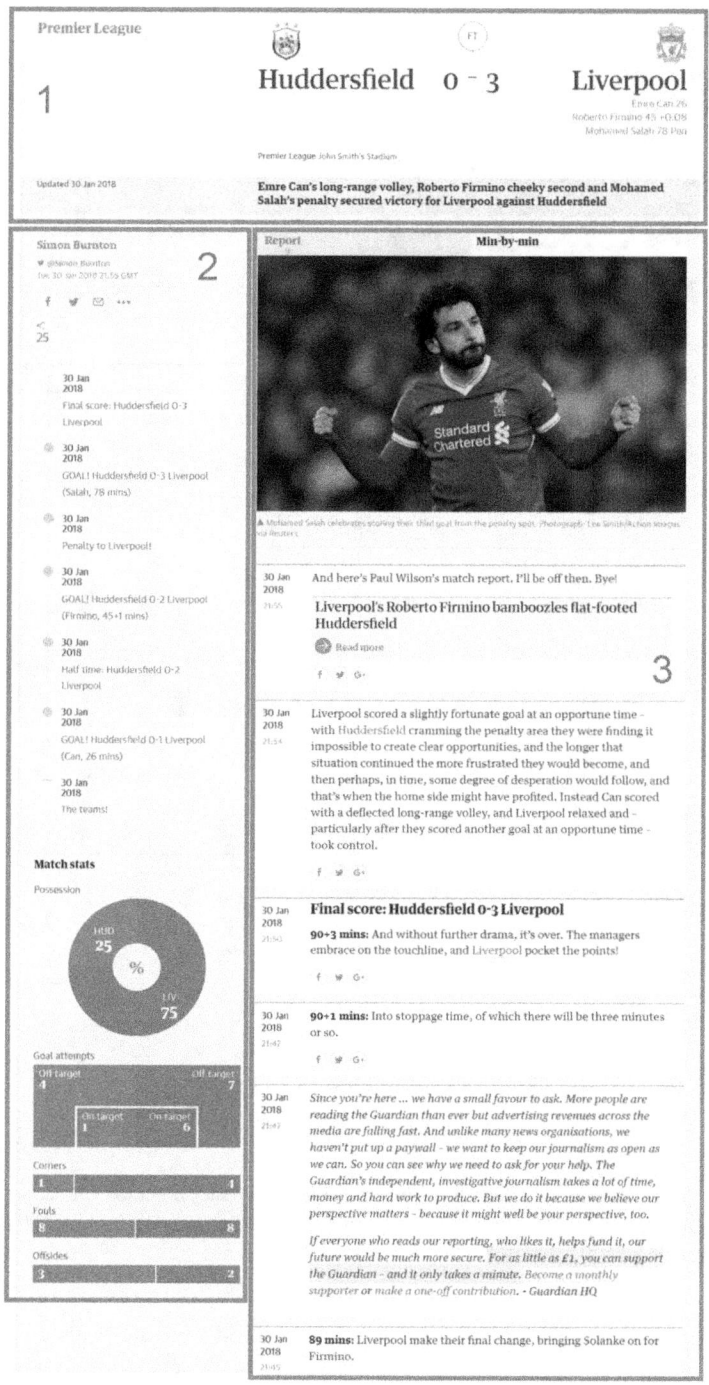

Figure 9.1 Screenshot from GUAR. Source: https://www.theguardian.com/football/live/2018/jan/30/huddersfield-town-v-liverpool-premier-league-live.

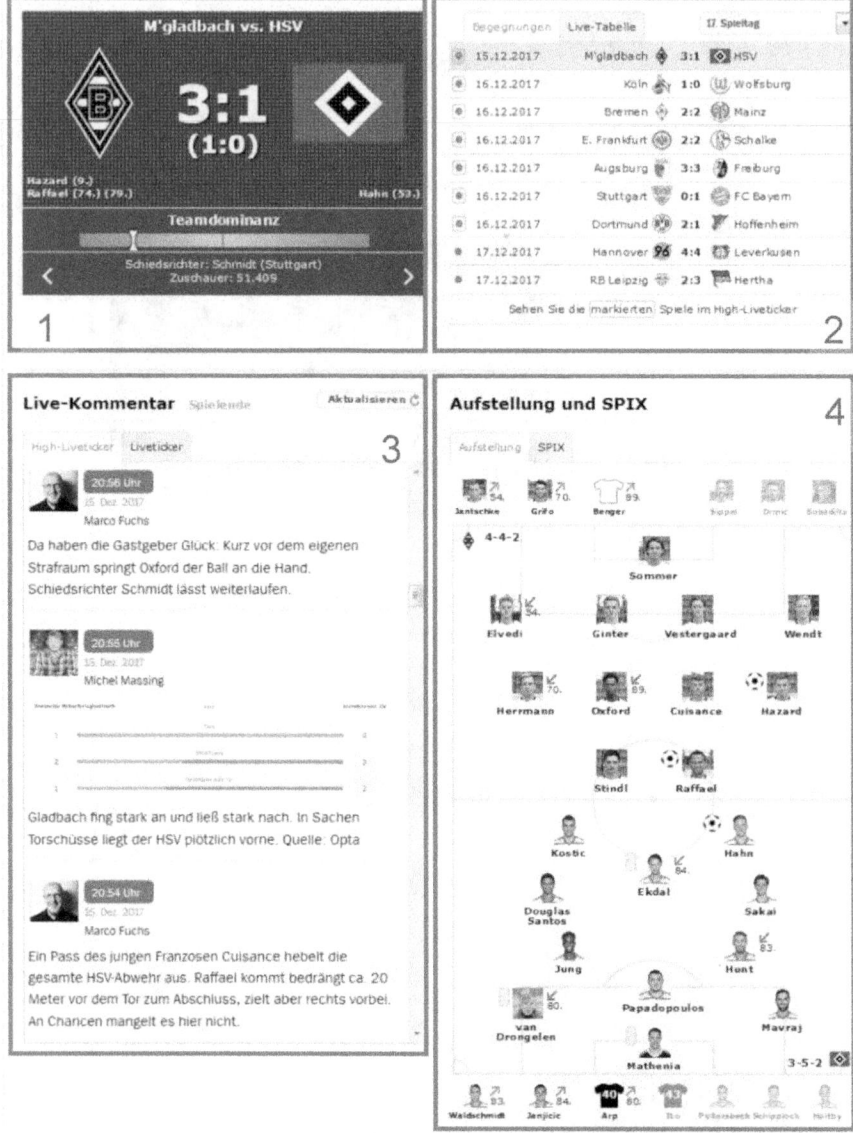

Figure 9.2 Screenshot from SPON. Source: http://www.spiegel.de/sport/fussball/
bundesliga-live-ticker-tabelle-ergebnisse-spielplan-statistik-a-842988.html#contest=
bl1&matchday=17.

and advertisements. Team names are clickable and automatically linked to a separate page where all news items relating to the respective team are listed, and, similarly to the element in zone 2, each post underneath the text offers buttons to automatically create a shared link of the individual post on social media. Note that the commentary zone also includes various items of pre-match reporting posted before kick-off, such as reviews, relevant quotes from the team managers involved as well as internal links to longer interviews and analytical pieces related to the match. After the match has ended, there is the opportunity to directly access the overall match report (in prose) by clicking the 'report' navigational tab at the top of zone 2, and a short subheading is added to the bottom of zone 1.

Zone 1 in SPON (see Figure 9.2) can be compared to zone 1 in GUAR, even though it contains some additional information, such as the half-time score. At the bottom the user can click on the arrow symbols to view various pieces of information, such as the name of the main referee, attendance numbers, some basic statistics (percentage of ball possession, number of attempts on goal, percentage of successful passes, percentage of successful one-on-ones, number of touches on the ball, and number of fouls) as well as a visualization of overall team dominance (in German 'Teamdominanz') calculated from the basic statistics measures. Zone 2 is specific to SPON and can be considered a combined content and navigational zone. Users can see the current (and final) scores of all matches of the respective match day. By clicking on a line, the relevant information for the match selected will appear in zones 1, 3 and 4. In addition, users can see whether a match is still on or has ended (green or red button at the left-hand side of the zone) and can access a dynamic league table (German 'Live-Tabelle') through clicking on the eponymous tab. Another navigational element is a drop-down list in the upper-right-hand corner, where users can navigate to different match days. Zone 3 of SPON (German 'Live-Kommentar') can be compared to zone 3 of GUAR again, as it contains the (scrollable) main textual commentary. However, the audience here can switch between the 'High-Liveticker' (SPON H) and the 'Liveticker' (SPON L) through clicking on the respective tabs at the top.

The crucial difference between the two types is that the latter (see Figure 9.3) concentrates on the reporting of play-by-play action and only rarely provides background information (in textual form as parts of the time-stamped posts). Users have the opportunity to use a filter function, clickable through the symbols at the bottom, to reduce the display to key moments of the match (cards, goals and substitutions). Note that SPON L contains some pre-match reporting as one larger post, including information on the referee, team lineups, results of their last matches, shorter statements by the team managers, and some basic background statistics with the function to contextualize the match. Apparently, SPON L content is integrated from an external source, Germany's main sports

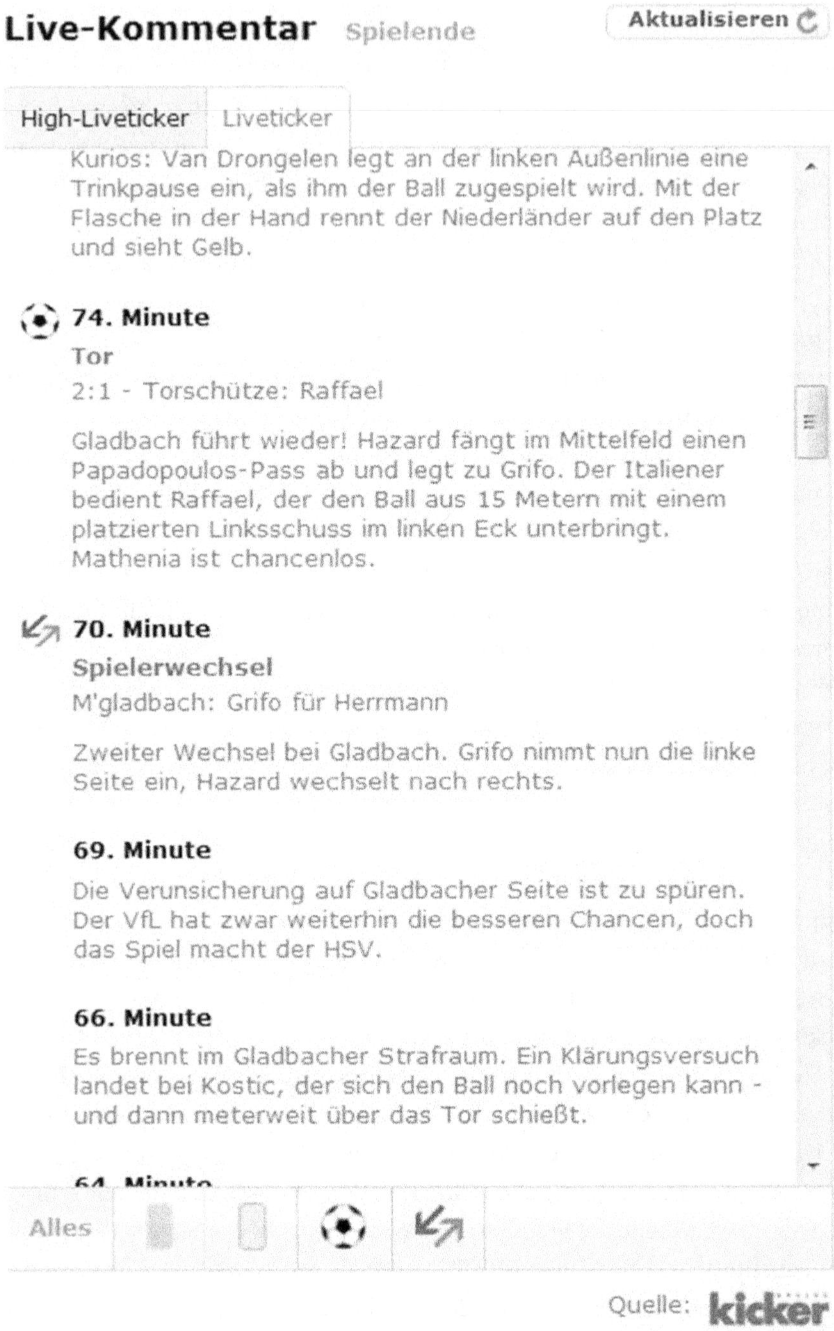

Live-Kommentar Spielende   Aktualisieren

High-Liveticker   Liveticker

Kurios: Van Drongelen legt an der linken Außenlinie eine Trinkpause ein, als ihm der Ball zugespielt wird. Mit der Flasche in der Hand rennt der Niederländer auf den Platz und sieht Gelb.

74. Minute
Tor

2:1 - Torschütze: Raffael

Gladbach führt wieder! Hazard fängt im Mittelfeld einen Papadopoulos-Pass ab und legt zu Grifo. Der Italiener bedient Raffael, der den Ball aus 15 Metern mit einem platzierten Linksschuss im linken Eck unterbringt. Mathenia ist chancenlos.

70. Minute
Spielerwechsel

M'gladbach: Grifo für Herrmann

Zweiter Wechsel bei Gladbach. Grifo nimmt nun die linke Seite ein, Hazard wechselt nach rechts.

69. Minute

Die Verunsicherung auf Gladbacher Seite ist zu spüren. Der VfL hat zwar weiterhin die besseren Chancen, doch das Spiel macht der HSV.

66. Minute

Es brennt im Gladbacher Strafraum. Ein Klärungsversuch landet bei Kostic, der sich den Ball noch vorlegen kann - und dann meterweit über das Tor schießt.

64. Minute

Alles

Quelle: **kicker**

Figure 9.3 SPON – alternative display (SPON L) of zone 3. Source: http://www.spiegel.de/sport/fussball/bundesliga-live-ticker-tabelle-ergebnisse-spielplan-statistik-a-842988.html#contest=bl1&matchday=17.

magazine focused primarily on football (online version available at www. kicker.de), and no commentator voice is identified.

By contrast, the pair of commentators explicitly introduces themselves in SPON H, where all time-stamped posts are assigned to one of them (as shown in Figure 9.2, zone 3). As stated above, one of the commentator voices takes the role as play-by-play commentator, and provides a narrative of match-related action, while the other one mainly acts as provider of statistical background information and evaluation. This may be read as increasingly professionalized work routines in SPON H. The statistics-based posts are often supported by figures of various kinds (from OPTA, a commercial provider of sports statistics; cf. Meier and Thiering 2017: 46). Commentator posts are interspersed with photographs from the match, tweets from OPTA,[12] the official channels of the clubs involved, and from users, as well as with links to relevant articles form SPON. Note in addition that the reporting finishes shortly after the end of the match and a few posts with overall match analysis, and that SPON H may also report on multiple simultaneous matches.

Zone 4 (German 'Aufstellung und SPIX') is reserved for a real-time display of team line-ups, including player images, information on substitutions, cards and goal scorers as well as on the tactical system of the two teams. A click on the 'SPIX' (an acronym for German 'Spieler-Index', i.e. player index) tab leads to a tabular player list with a star-shaped symbol assigned to each player's name (see Figure 9.4). A click on the symbol opens another display with real-time information on the player's overall performance on the current match day based on various statistics, also in comparison to other players that are fielded on the same position.[13]

The description of the general layout and communicative situation represented in the content sections of GUAR and SPON suggests that the textual commentary (zones 3 in both GUAR and SPON) constitutes the core part of the FLT (Hauser 2008: 3–4). Yet, we find a range of additional structural features, some of which are shared (provision of basic statistics, links to relevant articles form the respective media outlet, etc.). This converges with previous statements on the modularity and multimodality of FLT in terms of different carriers of information united in a larger semiotic unit representing an overall action – in our case, a football match (Hauser 2008: 3). However, two caveats apply. First, SPON appears to exploit the affordances of the electronic medium more than GUAR (cf. Werner 2016: 279, 295), as it provides more options for manipulating the FLT display and offers a more diversified range of information types. It remains to be tested whether this has linguistic consequences as well. Second,

Aufstellung und SPIX

Aufstellung	SPIX			
♣ **M'gladbach**			♦ **HSV**	
T	Sommer	☆	T Mathenia	★
A	Vestergaard	☆	A van Drongelen	★
A	Ginter	★	A Mavraj	☆
A	Elvedi	☆	A Papadopoulos	★
A	Wendt	☆	M Ekdal	★
M	Herrmann	☆	M Sakai	★
M	Hazard	☆	M Douglas Santos	★
M	Oxford	☆	M Jung	☆
M	Cuisance	★	M Hunt	★
S	Raffael	★	S Hahn	☆
S	Stindl	☆	S Kostic	☆
	Jantschke	★	Arp	-
	Grifo	-	Waldschmidt	-
	Benger	-	Janjicic	-

Figure 9.4 SPON – alternative display (SPIX) of zone 4. Source: http://www.spiegel.de/sport/fussball/bundesliga-live-ticker-tabelle-ergebnisse-spielplan-statistik-a-842988.html#contest=bl1&matchday=17.

it is important to note that despite its intricate structure, only two modes – text and image – are employed in the various parts of the two FLT types described.

In sum, following the typology developed in Bateman et al. (2017: 226–229), FLT squarely falls within the category of spatiotemporal interactive medium. FLT fulfils the properties of being spatial (set in a two-dimensional space on a webpage), dynamic (content is updated regularly), unscripted (the unfolding of events cannot be preplanned, with the concession that there are repetitive situations leading to the use of pre-constructed phrasing) and interactive (there is exchange between the commentator(s) and audience, with the concession that commentators may control the frequency and content of audience contributions (see Section 4.3); and users have the opportunity to set individualized display options depending on their preferences; cf. Hauser 2008: 4).[14] A qualification that needs to be added to the 'dynamic' nature of FLT is that even though FLT – as its name implies – is supposedly 'live', it is rather to be seen as quasi-synchronous, as there is a slight delay between the actual action and its mediated representation (Hauser 2008: 2; Meier 2017a: 347; cf. Jucker 2010: 64).

Based on the above descriptions, FLT can also conveniently be located within the (more specific) model of potentials of sports reporting developed in Caple (2017: 212–213), as shown in Figure 9.5. It considers the dimensions of time (horizontal axis) and voice (vertical axis) as a way of categorizing sports reporting around a specific event (inner layer). In simplified terms, time signifies when the publication in relation to the sports event takes place. Voice represents a continuum from 'reporter voice', mainly providing factual description, to 'writer voice', providing opinion and evaluation. The model further considers text-image

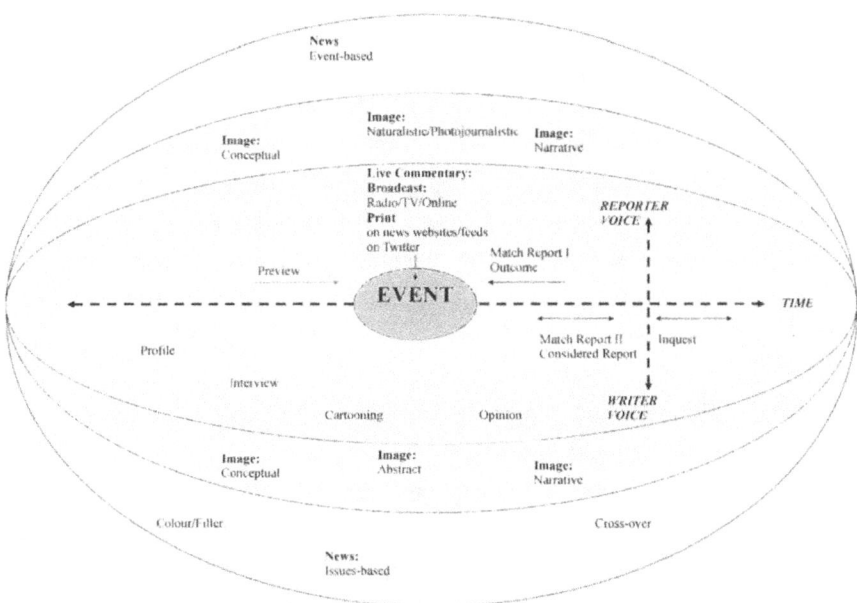

Figure 9.5 The potentials of sports reporting (Caple 2017: 213).

interaction (intermediate layer): the former is associated with naturalistic/photojournalistic images (e.g. player photos taken during the match), while the latter more often uses abstract images (e.g. diagrams). The outer layer contains reporting 'more loosely associated with a particular sporting event or which may only occur on special or one-off occasions – e.g. if there is an accident' (Caple 2017: 212).

According to Caple's (2017) model, FLT emerges as form of reporting that focuses on reporting during the event, while it includes almost the full scope of the time axis as it provides preview (e.g. team manager interviews) and an overall match report (if viewed after the actual event has finished or through a linked match report) as well as reporting located in the outer layer of the model (through links) (cf. Werner 2016: 280). As to voice, in GUAR, which operates with one commentator only, we find a mixture of reporter and writer voice. In SPON, almost exclusively reporter voice appears in SPON L, while clearly separate voices (and associated imagery) are featured by the two commentators in SPON H (see Sections 4.2 and 4.3).

4.2. Linguistic analysis

As the textual commentary represents the core part of every FLT (cf. Section 4.1), its narrative merits closer linguistic scrutiny. Previous research has suggested that specialized vocabulary and spatial/temporal location and movement feature prominently in sports reporting and in FLT specifically (Reaser 2003: 304–305; Werner 2016: 285–287; Clarke 2017: 37, 46; Meier and Thiering 2017: 45–46). Furthermore, a number of recurring lexical patterns have been identified (Kuiper 1996; Levin 2008). This use of formulaic language has also been mainly associated with the reporting of space and time. For the FLT audience to be able to follow the coverage this means that they have to be familiar with specialized jargon and conventions in addition to the layout of a football pitch as a mental image (Werner 2016: 287–288). Indeed, the corpus data confirm previous research in that game-related vocabulary (Table 9.2) as well as items (Table 9.2) and bundles (Table 9.3) relating to spatial and temporal location are highly frequent in the FLT data.

Note further that there is considerable cross-linguistic overlap between GUAR and SPON, so that FLT in this respect emerges as a cross-cultural register (cf. Werner 2016). While these quantitative aspects are relevant, arguably larger databases are more suitable for fine-grained analyses (see Meier and Thiering 2017; Meier, this volume).

Table 9.2 Content word categories from the top 100 *AntConc* wordlists

	GUAR	SPON L	SPON H
Team names	Liverpool, (Manchester) City/United, Chelsea, Spurs, Everton, Arsenal	Bayern, Schalke	Bayern, BVB, Schalke, Köln, Dortmund, Hannover
Temporal location	time, half	Minuten ('minutes')	Minute(n) ('minute(s)'), Hälfte ('half')
Sports vocabulary	ball, goal, corner, shot, pass, area, game, kick, cross, box, league, post	Ball ('ball'), Tor ('goal'), Strafraum ('penalty area'), Spielerwechsel ('substitution'), Ecke ('corner'), gelbe Karte ('yellow card'), Spiel ('match'), Partie ('fixture'), Freistoß ('free kick'), Torschütze ('scorer'), Kugel ('ball'), Abschluss ('finish'), Flanke ('cross'), Schuss ('shot')	Ball ('ball'), Tor ('goal'), Spiel ('match'), Strafraum ('penalty area'), Ecke ('corner'), Pfosten ('post')

Table 9.3 Five most frequent 4-Grams

GUAR		SPON L		SPON H	
Freq.	4-gram	Freq.	4-gram	Freq.	4-gram
46	the edge of the	43	von der rechten Seite ('from the right-hand side')	14	auf der anderen Seite ('at the other side')
29	on the edge of the	36	von der linken Seite ('from the left-hand side')	10	auf den zweiten Pfosten ('to the far post')
21	down the left and	23	auf der linken Seite ('on the left-hand side')	8	in den ersten Minuten ('in the first minutes')

GUAR		SPON L		SPON H	
Freq.	4-gram	Freq.	4-gram	Freq.	4-gram
21	edge of the area	19	Blick auf die Live-Daten ('look at the live data')	8	in der zweiten Hälfte ('in the second half')
18	from the edge of	18	über die linke Seite ('over the left-hand side')	7	von der rechten Seite ('from the right-hand side')

From a broader (textlinguistic/stylistic) perspective, FLT has been described as an 'amalgamation of different journalistic, or [...] discursive styles (narration, description, opinion, quasi-conversation)' (Werner 2016: 300). Particularly the last type has been connected to the topic of staged orality and the concomitant phenomenon of pseudo-intimacy, that is, a pretence, mainly on part of the commentator, but also the audience, that their 'relationship is not mediated and is carried on as though it were face-to-face' (O'Keeffe 2006: 92). Linguistic means to achieve this in FLT are the use of slang items and informalisms, puns and ad-hoc formations, and the representation of features of speech within the restrictions of the (written) electronic medium (Werner 2016: 288–293), referred to as 'parlando prosodics' (Jucker 2006: 128) or 'emulated speech' (Hauser 2008: 6). Such findings have been interpreted along the lines of FLT as a new communicative type being characterized by stylistic lag (Hauser 2008: 2). This lag is due to the fact that whenever new media types are introduced, they will rely on conventions and practices used in established formats, for instance radio and TV coverage in the case of FLT, so that older and newer formats interweave (O'Keeffe 2006: 27; Werner 2016: 300).

It is the first aim of this section to trace linguistically whether this stylistic lag persists or whether FLT has developed its specific communicative practices in the meantime, so that the impact of structure (LT as a multimodal form of electronic communication) on activity (the style of reporting) has increased (cf. O'Keeffe 2006: 31; Werner 2016: 278).

The data yield a differentiated picture. As to the issue of parlando prosodics, the use of expressive punctuation (example 1) and capitalization (examples 1, 3 and 4) as well as typographic indications of vowel lengthening (examples 2 and 3) and syllable emphasis (example 4) is absent from SPON L, and appears to a restricted degree in GUAR and SPON H.

(1) WEST BROM HAVE A SHOT!!!!!!!!!!! (GUAR)
(2) Ooooh! Ireland, in the centre circle, passes to the right and starts running (GUAR)
(3) TOOOOOOOOOOOR in Frankfurt! (SPON H)
   'GOOOOOOOOOOAL in Frankfurt'
(4) UN-GLAUB-LICH! (SPON H)
   'UN-BELIEV-ABLE'

Interjections seem to constitute a regular feature of GUAR and SPON H (see examples 5 and 6), but again are absent from SPON L commentary.

(5) Wowee. The celebrations behind Mignolet's goal are inevitably wild. (GUAR)
(6) Der HSV und der VfL Wolfsburg trennen sich 0:0. Puh! (SPON H)
   'HSV and VfL Wolfsburg draw 0:0. Phew!'

Closely related to parlando prosodics is the use of informalisms (cf. Werner 2016: 288), as exemplified in (7) to (9). This occurs in all FLT types.[15]

(7) Bournemouth payers are hugging and stuff (GUAR)
(8) More like snowin' Hargreaves, amirite? (GUAR)
(9) Der BVB kriegt gerade nichts auf die Reihe (SPON H)
   'The BVB doesn't get its act together'

What further differentiates the different FLT types is the amount of commentator presence. SPON L follows a traditional pattern as first-person pronouns are absent from the commentary posts. In addition, the commentator stays anonymous. In contrast, commentators introduce themselves in both GUAR and SPON H (see also Section 4.1), and we find strongly personalized commentator voices, even though realized differently in the two FLTs. In the former, the single commentator uses exophoric reference and expressions of stance (cf. Meier 2019), as shown in (10) and (11).

(10) I'd like to see that again. (GUAR)
(11) Alonso is booked for fouling the keeper Adrian. That's a bit harsh I think. (GUAR)

In SPON H, all posts are supplied with the commentator name and a photograph (see Figure 9.2). However, commentator presence most strikingly materializes through dialogue between the pair of commentators created through directly adjacent posts. This may be realized in various ways: In the data there are, first, exophoric references and vocatives, as in (12); second, explicit prompts by the one fulfilling the role of play-by-play commentator (reporter voice) directed at the one fulfilling the role of providing colour commentary and (statistics-backed) evaluation (writer voice), as in (13).[16] Further, longer exchanges, as in (14), occur, sometimes with a humorous slant.

(12) Du spielst auf meine Verbundenheit zu den 96ern an, Michel. (SPON H)
'You're alluding to my connection to the 96ers, Michel'

(13) A: Um ehrlich zu sein, hatten wir uns von diesem Spieltag ein bisschen mehr versprochen. Nur nicht vom BVB, der hat genau das gemacht, was wir erwartet hatten: Gegen den Tabellenvorletzten verloren. Aber warum nur, Michel, warum? Die Blitzanalyse, bitte!
B: Der BVB hatte mehr Ballbesitz, klar. Bezeichnend aber, wie schnell die Dortmunder nach gutem Start in Hälfte zwei wieder nachließen. Die ersten 15 Minuten nach Wiederanpfiff waren es 74,9 Prozent Ballbesitz, die nächsten nur noch 68,5 Prozent und die letzten 62,4 Prozent. Ein Aufbäumen, das sieht anders aus.[17] (SPON H)

A: To be honest, we had expected a bit more from this match day. Not only from the BVB, which did exactly what we assumed: Losing against the team one position above the bottom. But why, Michel, why? A quick analysis, please!
B: The BVB had more possession, sure. But is characteristic how fast the Dortmunders weakened again after a good start in the second half. In the first 15 minutes after the second half commenced they had 74.9 percent possession, in the following 15 only 68.5 percent and in the last 15 only 62.4 percent. Rearing up is something different.'

(14) A: Bislang haben wir sechs Schüsse aufs Tor gesehen, davon waren vier drin. Hashtag Effizienz.
B: Wer # ausschreibt, hat # nicht verstanden, Kollege Fuchs.
A: Das nennt man „Meta-Ebene". (SPON H)
'A: So far, we've witnessed six shots on target, and four hit the net. Hashtag efficiency.
B: Who spells # hasn't understood #, colleague Fuchs.
A: This is called "meta-level".'

It remains an open question whether this type of mediated exchange should be subsumed under pseudo-conversation or can rather be interpreted as a move towards resembling the distribution of commentator roles in traditional media (cf. Section 4.1). In any case, it is testimony to the higher acceptance of subjectivity established for sports coverage in contrast to other news types (McEnnis 2016: 968; Meier 2019; see also examples 10 and 11).

The fact that GUAR and SPON L have only one commentator voice and SPON H two naturally also has repercussions on the nature of the individual commentary posts. While the roles are more clearly compartmentalized in SPON H, where posts with evaluation and statistics often appear directly adjacent to the play-by-play commentary (cf. example 13 and Figure 9.2), the single commentator voice in GUAR in the posts provides both play-by-play commentary and evaluation and analysis, as in (15) or (16). Note in addition that statistics to support the analysis in contrast to SPON H are less important in GUAR, and are often only mentioned at the beginning of a match or subtly as part of a post rather than explicitly, as illustrated in (17) and (18).

(15) Fabregas stoops to head Zappacosta's cross towards goal, and Ogbonna makes another vital block. Chelsea are all over West Ham like a cheap cliche. (GUAR)

(16) Kenny's long ball downfield is hit and hope and Klavan soon snuffs that out. That's all Everton have mustered in truth and that's not good enough really. It's been totally one-way traffic. (GUAR)

(17) A gentle reminder that this fixture has seen a record 21 red cards issued across the 50 Premier League meetings, with 14 for Everton and seven for Liverpool. (GUAR)

(18) Sergio Agüero, who has scored in his last nine away games and has so often been United's nemesis, will be watching Gabriel Jesus' penalty area efforts with interest. (GUAR)

Similarly to GUAR, we find combinations of play-by-play commentary and evaluation in SPON L, as in (19), and posts with statistical background information merely in textual form, as exemplified by (20).

(19) Heller steckt auf Finnbgosan [sic] durch, der ins Dribbling gegen Hummels geht, aber hängenbleibt. Immerhin ein kleiner Nadelstich der Baum-Elf. (SPON L)
'Heller passes to Finnbogason, who attempts a dribble against Hummels, but gets stuck. At least a small pinprick by the Baum-eleven.'

(20) Am Rande notiert: Die Eintracht traf im 10. Bundesliga-Spiel in Folge – die längste Serie für Frankfurt seit 2014/15 (16 Spiele). (SPON L)

'Just a side note: Eintracht has scored 10 Bundesliga matches in a row – the longest series for Frankfurt since 2014/15 (16 matches).'

4.3. Beyond text

Even though the textual commentary represents the core part, we have to consider further modes and elements within this part of FLT to establish a complete picture of the artefact (also beyond the multimodal aspects discussed in Section 4.1).[18] This may happen on two planes. First, we may describe the use of images and its potential interaction with the text. This pays tribute to the fact 'the image now takes centre stage in digital journalism' (Caple 2017: 210)[19] as well as to the increased availability and use of match-related statistics (Clarke 2017: 46). Second, we may focus on the issue of audience participation and interactivity, as it has repeatedly been identified as one of the growing mass media trends (Pauwels 2012: 258; McEnnis 2016: 975; Werner 2016: 284; Chovanec 2018: 516)[20] with the potential to shape the content and style of FLT reporting.

Figure 9.6 provides a quantitative perspective of additional material (i.e. material other than textual commentary produced by the main commentators)

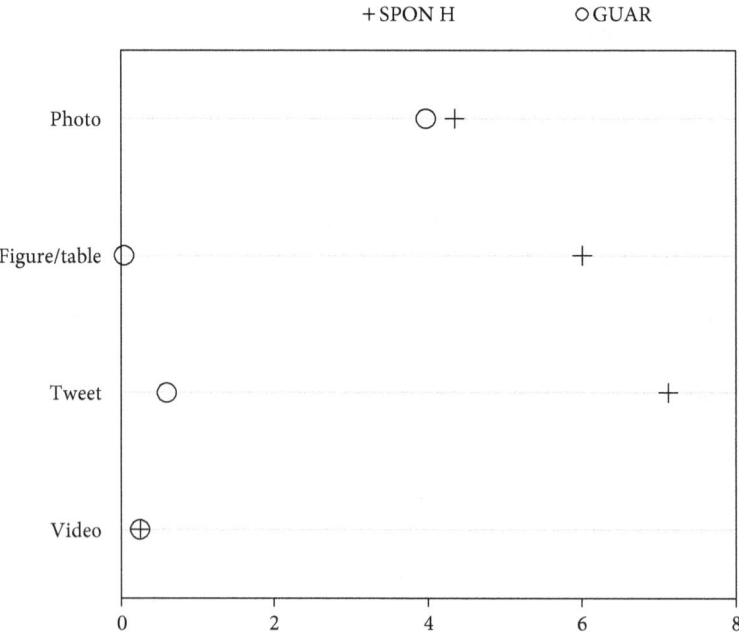

Figure 9.6 Frequencies of occurrence of additional material in FLT (normalized per 1,000 words of commentary).

present in GUAR and SPON H (SPON L is not included as it does not contain any such material). It emerges that both FLT types almost to the same extent rely on photorealistic images, while other imagery (figures and tables) is almost absent from GUAR. A similar picture occurs for tweets, where frequencies are considerably higher for SPON H.[21] Videos appear to play only a minor role in both FLT types.

This quantitative analysis suggests that, overall, SPON H can be considered to exploit the affordances of the electronic medium to a higher degree as it has higher frequencies for all categories, and particularly higher frequencies for abstract imagery and tweets. In journalistic terms, this may be read as more elaborated routines for collecting information present in SPON H. However, a few qualitative differences are salient.

A first noteworthy point is that the inclusion of imagery is only a recent development that was not present in earlier FLT (cf. Werner 2016: 295). As shown in Figure 9.7, photos in GUAR (taken from commercial press and picture

Figure 9.7 GUAR – post with photorealistic image. Source: https://www.theguardian.com/football/live/2018/jan/30/huddersfield-town-v-liverpool-premier-league-live.

agencies) are either used as a head photograph displayed permanently at the top of the page (Caple 2017: 211) or are directly associated with a post, usually displaying moments of heightened competition (*sensu* Ferguson 1983: 156–157) described in that post (e.g. shots on goal, players and/or managers celebrating, fouls, fans cheering; cf. Caple 2017: 222).

In contrast, photos in SPON H more rarely display match action, but rather players warming up, close-ups of managers, etc., commonly supplied with a humorous or sarcastic comment by one of the commentators. As stated above, SPON H employs a variety of abstract imagery visualizing statistics (heatmaps, touchmaps, passing maps) in the evaluative posts. These visualizations are taken from a commercial statistics provider (OPTA) and accompanied by evaluative comment, as shown in Figure 9.8. It is evident that image and text in these

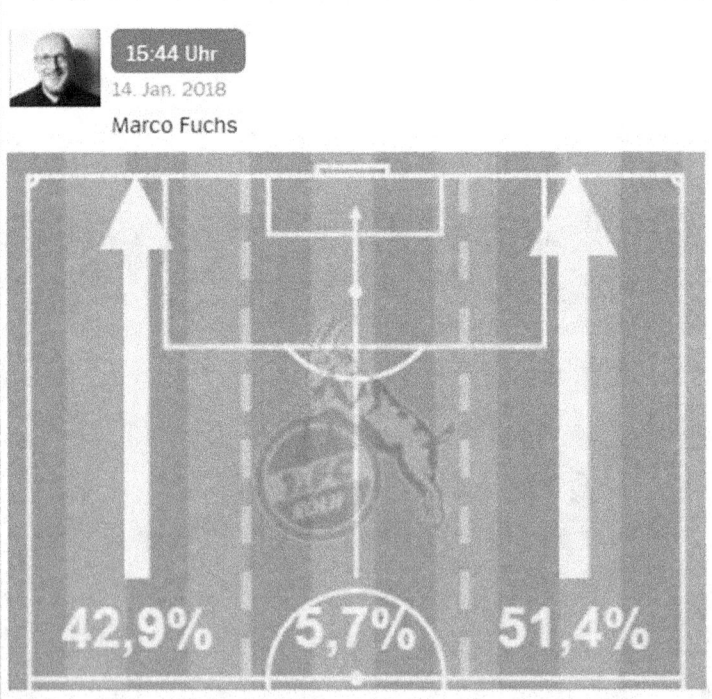

Figure 9.8 SPON H – abstract image with statistical information and comment. Source: http://www.spiegel.de/sport/fussball/bundesliga-live-ticker-tabelle-ergebnisse-spielplan-statistik-a-842988.html#contest=bl1&matchday=16.

instances are mutually dependent and would be of restricted communicative value if appearing on their own (cf. Bateman 2017: 251).

In SPON H, combinations of statistics and evaluation occasionally are also present through (uncommented) tweets from OPTA, chosen by the colour commentator, illustrated in Figure 9.9. In GUAR, in the present data this happens only once at all.

Other types of tweets appearing in SPON H are those from users, sometimes with photos (usually from outside or inside the stadium) or official tweets from the league or the clubs involved in the match (see also Meier 2019). These are apparently also selected by the colour commentator and usually posted without further comment or editing (cf. Chovanec 2018: 514). As shown in Figure 9.6, direct tweets are rare in the GUAR commentary, but may derive from the same sources as for SPON H.

As to the types of videos integrated into the commentary, GUAR and SPON H converge in that these are not football-, but rather pop-culture-related (e.g. a music video clip or a scene from a movie), and used for entertainment purposes.

Figure 9.9 SPON H – tweet with statistics from external source. Source: https://twitter.com/OptaFranz/status/967773893300715521.

Previous research has established that different types of FLT offer different degrees of interactivity on a continuum from no opportunity for the audience to get involved to unfiltered contribution, for instance through another content zone exclusively reserved for audience tweets (Werner 2016: 283–284). For the current data, SPON L does not offer any interactive features. GUAR commentators invite the audience to contribute via e-mails and tweets (cf. Chovanec 2018: 515), as in (21), and include selected mailings in the main commentary posts (Werner 2016: 282), as in (22) or (23), or indirectly, as in (24).

(21) Thoughts? Predictions? Hopes? Fears? Send them my way. (GUAR)
(22) 'Thoughts? I think United need to make a statement tonight. It's all for City to lose,' says Ahmed Aly. 'Predictions? 3–2 to United. Hopes? I hope it's not a drab nil-nil draw after all those column inches about "the game of the season." Fears? Spiders.' (GUAR)
(23) 'Allardyce fiddling with his earpiece is the new Wenger struggling with his coat zip,' emails Marie. I like it, I like it. (GUAR)
(24) This, as Tom Jordan points out, is the kind of dirty, tough game Diego Costa would have loved. Chelsea have lacked a bit of mongrel. (GUAR)
(25) That's all from me. Thanks a lot for your company, emails, tweets. That was jolly good fun (GUAR)

As can be seen in (21) and (22), commentator and audience seem to engage in direct conversation, or the commentator may at least comment on a user post, as in (23). In addition, thank you notes may occur at the end of the live reporting, as in (25). Further interactive features, such as informal online polls, as shown in Figure 9.10, only occur very rarely.

The function of the presence of these audience participation features is worth discussing. The relationship between (expert) commentator and (lay) audience in traditional mass mediated sports events characteristically has been distant and without any affective dimension (Clarke 2017: 37), as communication is largely uni-directional. By contrast, even though it would not be apt to speak of a 'cozy relationship' (McEnnis 2016: 976) between commentators and audience, a clear dividing line between the two (and a corresponding affective distance) does not seem to be as much the case in FLT. Media analysts have claimed that user-generated content is part and parcel of modern journalistic (particularly online) practices, that it is valued by journalists, and that users want to get involved not for financial compensation but for being part of an online community (McEnnis 2016: 975–977). The communicative practices in FLT, supported by the affordances of the multimodal electronic medium, arguably achieve this

Wie geht das Spiel aus?

- Der HSV gewinnt. (317)
- Köln gewinnt. (896)
- Können nicht beide verlieren? (221)
- Egal wer gewinnt, die Zuschauer verlieren. (151)

Figure 9.10 SPON H – audience poll during live match coverage. Source: http://www.spiegel.de/sport/fussball/bundesliga-live-ticker-tabelle-ergebnisse-spielplan-statistik-a-842988.html#contest=bl1&matchday=19.

through making the audience part of the mediated representation of a sporting event, while FLT commentators still fulfil the 'expert' role (cf. Chovanec 2018: 519).

Linguistically, this aspect of community building (and representation of commentators as experts) can be supported through subtly relating to insider knowledge (Werner 2016: 291), as exemplified in (26) and (27).

(26) Ndidi curls a long pass down the right to Vardy, who tries to repeat his famous goal against Liverpool from the right edge of the box. He doesn't. (GUAR)

(27) Kleiner Blick auf die Live-Tabelle: Die Eintracht ist aktuell Dritter. Vorrunde 2016/2017 repeating. (SPON H)
'A quick look at the live table: Eintracht is currently third. First half-series 2016/2017 repeating.'

On a related note, it has been suggested that an extended use of images in multimodal representations is only possible if 'knowledgeable recipients' (Bateman et al. 2017: 33) able to interpret the imagery in the respective context are present. For FLT this requirement appears to be fulfilled in that the genre uses topic-specific text (see Section 4.2; cf. Werner 2016: 291) and images, especially abstract visualizations as in SPON H (see above), directed at an online community of football enthusiasts.

A few caveats apply, however. It could be argued that in GUAR, we still find 'quasi-conversational interactions' (Chovanec 2010: 252; cf. Chovanec 2008), as the commentator decides which user comments to post and to which user contributions to react. Note also that the frequency of user mailings (including tweets) mentioned is comparatively low (0.84 user postings per 1,000 words of commentary; cf. Figure 9.6). By contrast, in SPON H user contributions appear much more often (see Figure 9.6) and as they originally did (on Twitter), but are selected by the colour commentator and posted alongside the main commentary without any further comment. Overall, commentators thus fulfil, somewhat comparably to traditional roles of journalists, a gatekeeping role in creating a multi-authored and multi-layered text, as the audience has the opportunity to contribute to FLT reporting, even though subject to the restrictions outlined in the foregoing. This scenario is also found in other digital environments (Bateman et al. 2017: 350).

5. Discussion and conclusion

The present contribution took a multimodal approach towards FLT as an artefact connecting offline and online practices (cf. Pauwels 2012: 260). It considered linguistic features represented in the textual commentary as the core part of FLT, but went beyond a mere linguistic description to provide a more comprehensive description and analysis of FLT as a multimodal format representing sports discourse.

FLT emerged as a multimodal ensemble sharing similarities across the different realizations studied, mainly relying on text and image as communicative means. It was shown that FLT as a spatiotemporal interactive medium represents a complex artefact necessitating the analysis of linear and non-linear data. The FLT types assessed are also characterized by different options for manipulating the display, which is testimony to their interactive nature. Following Caple's (2017) model, SPON H features two types of voice within FLT that fulfil different functions (reporter voice: play-by-play commentary vs. writer voice: analysis/evaluation/statistics) and that are associated with different types of imagery (photorealistic pictures vs. abstract images; see Sections 4.2 and 4.3). As Caple (2017: 212) rightly notes, the model (Figure 9.5) could be extended. For FLT in particular, the issue of audience participation (Section 4.3) as well as the entertainment function of FLT (see below) could be added as labels/categories to the central (e.g. audience participation through tweets), intermediate (e.g.

images provided by the audience and clubs) or outer layer (e.g. links to articles/ webpages only loosely related to the actual match added for entertainment).

The linguistic analysis focused on the issue of stylistic lag in terms of FLT emulating patterns commonly found in spoken live sports coverage. Overall, features associated with stylistic lag persist, but to a much more restricted degree compared to what analyses of older FLT datasets have suggested (cf. Jucker 2006; Hauser 2008; Werner 2016). Conveying a 'live' atmosphere though employing expressive devices and features associated with involved language still plays a part in FLT, but appears to be receding. Therefore, claims of an overemphasis on spoken features, and more specifically those found in traditional live sports reporting (i.e. the stylistic lag referred to above; cf. Hauser 2008: 7), have to be partly revised. This can also be interpreted as an indication for FLT overcoming the stylistic lag present in older manifestations and developing into a format of its own guided by the attempt on part of the FLT producers to strike 'a balance between making it informal and fun and chatty and the core journalistic values' (McEnnis 2016: 973).

From a multimodal perspective, factuality as one of these values is supported by the general layout (Section 4.1) and the reliance on statistical information, often displayed in iconographic form (Section 4.3). Note that a dialogic structure occurs in SPON H that maps commentator roles found in traditional sports reporting (reporter vs. writer voice), which strongly exploits the affordances of the electronic medium, however, and thus is qualitatively different from traditional formats.

In terms of the function of FLT, a differentiated picture emerged. While the commentary in SPON L is mainly information-related (also reflected by its reduced length per match report; see Section 3), GUAR and SPON H can be assigned the additional functions of entertainment and community building (see also Chovanec 2010: 242; Werner 2016: 301; Meier 2017b: 418). GUAR and SPON H break the uni-directionality of communication and create another layer of interactivity (beyond the opportunity to merely manipulate the display), interpretable in the light of a loosening of hierarchies (producer vs. consumer) in online sports journalism (McEnnis 2016: 975). This is facilitated by the affordances of new media, particularly social media. User-generated content features especially in SPON H and can be related to the broader issues of remediation and media convergence (see also Hauser 2010); that is, FLT as a complex type of web-based artefact combines and integrates content from various sources (textual commentary, photorealistic and abstract imagery, tweets, videos, etc.) and different producers (commentator(s), users, sports clubs, etc.)[22] to create a multi-layered and multi-authored discourse that is communicatively effective. The content of the genre is still is very much filtered by the media outlets, however, so that the alleged development towards less prioritizing of information by the commentators in electronic communication (cf. Jucker 2005: 17) or towards 'participatory journalism' (Chovanec 2018: 510)[23] is not fully borne out.

From a methodological perspective, the present study aimed at showing the additional gains of going beyond a purely textual towards a multimodal analysis of FLT, arguably doing more justice to this – in multiple respects hybrid and non-linear – web-based artefact than linguistic analysis alone. This study of how 'communicative practices work together' (Bateman et al. 2017: 7) has been achieved through relying on an eclectic set of principles (from media studies, linguistics, etc.) and a comparatively small dataset. This leaves room for individual aspects to be elaborated on in future work, for instance in terms of a closer analysis of image types used in FLT, as to how participant roles are realized (cf. Chovanec 2015), as to how emotionality is expressed (Meier 2019) or as to whether FLT reporting can be considered conventionalized cross-culturally, of which there are some indications in the present and other studies (Werner 2016; cf. Caple 2017: 209). Another aspect merely touched upon was the receptive dimension (which could possibly be assessed through eye-tracking experiments, for example). Even though (F)LT has become an established form of online reporting, technological advances will continue to shape its general and linguistic form, so that it is likely that future analyses will have to take account of still other aspects and elements that are not yet foreseeable.

Acknowledgement

I would like to thank Hendrik Michael, an anonymous reviewer, and the editors for suggestions and comments on earlier versions of this contribution.

Notes

1   For a general overview, see Baym (2008).
2   The 2017 data for *Spiegel Online* overall yield a usage rate of *c.* 70% on mobile devices (see www.spiegel.de/video/spiegel-online-in-zahlen-daten-fakten-statistiken-video-1784116.html). The 2018 numbers for *The Guardian* (63%) are only slightly lower (see www.newsworks.org.uk/the-guardian). See further Sections 3 and 4.1.

3   See Bateman et al. (2017: 18–19) for an overview of various definitions of mode.
4   For the case of (F)LT, fortunately it is possible to rely on schemes developed for linguistic analysis and for the analysis of webpages (as the form of electronic medium used) as well as on previous descriptions that have explicitly considered the co-occurrence and interaction of text and image, in general and in sports/football discourse (see Section 4.1). Thus, it is possible to triangulate the current findings with results from previous research on related topics, another central (though by no means exclusive) principle of multimodal analysis (Bateman et al. 2017: 230).
5   However, even though multimodality (text-image-audio combinations) may be prevalent, as a rule only two of the five senses (sight and hearing) are addressed through webpages. It is evident that multimodality thus is to be conceived of as a 'wide variety of expressive systems' (i.e. text, image, typography, layout, etc.) rather than multiple sensory channels that are activated (Pauwels 2012: 250).
6   Thanks are due to Fabian Vetter for support.
7   That this is still common practice is shown by comments such as *Nobody really appeals for a penalty – apart from Steve McManaman, the BT Sport co-commentator, who instinctively shouts 'handball'* (GUAR).
8   On occasion, the actual commentary may be taken from external sources and be merely embedded into the visual layout of the FLT (Simon Meier, p.c.).
9   FLT, somewhat counterintuitively, has even been published in printed form (e.g. Smyth and Murray 2014) to obtain an *ex post* perspective.
10 Figures 9.1 and 9.2 do not display certain navigational and functional zones located at the top or bottom of the pages, which are of indirect concern for the present analysis only. They may either lead to other general sections of the media outlet (politics, film news, etc.) or contain additional sports-related information, such as upcoming matches, league tables, and further statistics (e.g. on top goal scorers, team fairness). Recall that the display on mobile devices may slightly differ.
11 It has been suggested that such features 'provide for the remediation and sharing of media content in the direction away from the media itself toward user-to-user interaction' (Chovanec 2018: 515) and thus introduce another layer of interactivity (cf. Section 4.3).
12 For information on how OPTA creates their data, see www.optasports.de/de/%C3%BCber-uns/so-arbeiten-wir/the-data-collection-process.aspx. An interesting side note is that OPTA has created a multitude of culturally adapted Twitter channels with football-related information (*optajoe* for the UK, *optafranz* for Germany, *optajose* in Spain, *optaivan* in Russia, etc.).
13 For details on how the SPIX measure is calculated, see www.spiegel.de/sport/fussball/bundesliga-spielernoten-spix-und-spon11-die-vermessung-der-bundesliga-a-1160253.html.

14 The second type of interactivity is further restricted, of course, as 'the data selected for the visualisation is typically immutable, that is, the producer has chosen the data for the consumer' (Bateman et al. 2017: 350).
15 In the English data, as a rule contracted forms (*it's, they're, should've*, etc.) are used, which may serve as another indicator of more informal usage. Note, however, that forms such as *gonna* or *gotta* are absent.
16 For ease of readability, the consecutive posts are represented in chronological order.
17 This post is accompanied by a figure (see further Section 4.3).
18 Minor issues, such as the affordance of the electronic medium to represent alternative (seemingly deleted) text to express the commentators' opinion, as in the following example, are not considered in detail: *Fabian Delph is asked if City have won hand on the trophy. He says* ~~more like two hands Geoff, we'll walk it~~ *that City will take it game by game* (GUAR).
19 On the basis of eye-tracking research, others have suggested that 'readers' gaze is typically attracted to writing first' (Leckner 2012; cited in Djonov and Knox 2015: 187).
20 If we consider the longer history of mass media, the apparent recent increase in audience participation in fact represents the reversal of a trend. Chovanec (2017: 183) explores the practice of early English newspapers to merely reprint letters from members of the public, so that they became authors (and recipients at the same time if they read the newspaper). Restrictions on external content were imposed only in the nineteenth century.
21 The data only yield one example each from a Facebook and Instagram post displayed in the commentary, which indicates that Twitter is the social medium of choice for FLT.
22 From the user perspective, the simultaneous consumption and production of content, facilitated by various social media, has also been labelled with the blend 'prosumption' (Beer and Burrows 2013: 49).
23 Cf. also Glaser's (2009: 578) concept of 'citizen journalism'.

References

Anthony, L. (2016), *AntConc (3.4.4)*, Tokyo: Waseda University. Available at: www.laurenceanthony.net/software.

Bateman, J. (2012), 'Multimodal Corpus-based Approaches', in C. A. Chapelle (ed.), *The Encyclopedia of Applied Linguistics*, 3983–3992, Malden, MA: Wiley-Blackwell.

Bateman, J. (2017), 'Using Multimodal Corpora for Empirical Research', in C. Jewitt (ed.), *The Routledge Handbook of Multimodal Analysis*, 238–252, London: Routledge.

Bateman, J., J. Wildfeuer and T. Hiippala (2017), *Multimodality: Foundations, Research and Analysis*, Berlin: Mouton de Gruyter.

Baym, G. (2008), 'Infotainment', in W. Donsbach (ed.), *The International Encyclopedia of Communication*, Malden, MA: Wiley-Blackwell.
Beer, D. and R. Burrows (2013), 'Popular Culture, Digital Archives and the New Social Life of Data', *Theory, Culture & Society*, 30 (4): 47–71.
Caple, H. (2017), 'Results, Resolve, Reaction: Words, Images and the Functional Structure of Online Match Reports', in D. Caldwell, J. Walsh, E. W. Vine and J. Jureidini (eds), *The Discourse of Sport*, 209–227, London: Routledge.
Chovanec, J. (2008), 'Enacting an Imaginary Community: Infotainment in On-line Minute-by-minute Sports Commentaries', in E. Lavric, G. Pisek, A. Skinner and W. Stadler (eds), *The Linguistics of Football*, 255–268, Tübingen: Narr.
Chovanec, J. (2010), 'Online Discussion and Interaction: The Case of Live Text Commentary', in L. Shedletsky and J. E. Aitken (eds), *Cases on Online Discussion and Interaction*, 234–251, Hershey: IGI.
Chovanec, J. (2015), 'Participant Roles and Embedded Interactions in Online Sports Broadcasts', in M. Dynel and J. Chovanec (eds), *Participation in Public and Social Media Interactions*, 67–95, Amsterdam: Benjamins.
Chovanec, J. (2017), 'From Adverts to Letters to the Editor', in M. Palander-Collin, M. Ratia and I. Taavitsainen (eds), *Diachronic Developments in English News Discourse*, 175–197, Amsterdam: Benjamins.
Chovanec, J. (2018), 'Participating with Media: Exploring Online Media Activity', in C. Cotter and D. Perrin (eds), *The Routledge Handbook of Language and Media*, 505–522, London: Routledge.
Clarke, B. (2017), 'Representations of Experience in the Language of Televised and Radio Football Commentaries', in D. Caldwell, J. Walsh, E. W. Vine and Jon Jureidini (eds), *The Discourse of Sport*, 34–55, London: Routledge.
Djonov, E. and J. S. Knox (2015), 'How-to-analyze Webpages', in S. Norris and C. D. Maier (eds), *Interactions, Images and Texts*, 171–193, Berlin: Mouton de Gruyter.
Fairclough, N. (1995), *Media Discourse*, London: Arnold.
Ferguson, C. A. (1983), 'Sports Announcer Talk. Syntactic Aspects of Register Variation', *Language in Society*, 12: 153–172.
Glaser, M. (2009), 'Citizen Journalism: Widening World Views, Extending Democracy', in St. Allan (ed.), *The Routledge Companion to News and Journalism*, 578–590, London: Routledge.
Hauser, St. (2008), 'Live-Ticker: Ein Neues Medienangebot zwischen Medienspezifischen Innovationen und Stilistischem Trägheitsprinzip', *kommunikation@gesellschaft*, 9 (1): 1–10.
Hauser, St. (2010), 'Der Live-Ticker in der Online-Berichterstattung: Zur Entstehung einer Neuen Mediengattung', in H.-J. Bucher, Th. Gloning and K. Lehnen (eds), *Neue Medien – neue Formate: Ausdifferenzierung und Konvergenz in der Medienkommunikation*, 207–225, Frankfurt: Campus.
He, E. and L. Abboud (2017), 'Soccer Is Losing Its Grip on TV: English Football's Ratings Problem Is More Than a Blip', *Bloomberg*, Available at www.bloomberg.com/gadfly/articles/2017-01-16/football-is-losing-its-grip-on-tv.

Herring, S. C. (2010), 'Web Content Analysis: Expanding the Paradigm', in J. Hunsinger, L. Klastrup and M. Allen (eds), *International Handbook of Internet Research*, 233–249, Dordrecht: Springer.
Jucker, A. (2005), 'News Discourse: Mass Media Communication from the Seventeenth to the Twenty-first Century', in J. Skaffari, M. Peikola, R. Carroll, R. Hiltunen and B. Warvik (eds), *Opening Windows on Texts and Discourses of the Past*, 7–21, Amsterdam: Benjamins.
Jucker, A. (2006), 'Live Text Commentaries: Read about It While It Happens', in J. K. Androutsopoulos, J. Runkel, P. Schlobinski and T. Siever (eds), *Neuere Entwicklungen in der Linguistischen Internetforschung*, 113–131, Hildesheim: Olms.
Jucker, A. (2010),'"Audacious, Brilliant!! What a Strike!" Live Text Commentaries on the Internet as Real-time Narratives', in Ch. R. Hoffmann (ed.), *Narrative Revisited: Telling a Story in the Age of New Media*, 57–77, Amsterdam: Benjamins.
Kuiper, K. (1996), *Smooth Talkers: The Linguistic Performance of Auctioneers and Sportscasters*, Mahwah: Erlbaum.
Leckner, S. (2012), 'Presentation factors affecting reading behaviour in readers of newspaper media: An eye-tracking perspective', *Visual Communication*, 11(2): 163–184.
Levin, M. (2008), '"Hitting the Back of the Net Just before the Final Whistle": High-frequency Phrases in Football Reporting', in E. Lavric, G. Pisek, A. Skinner and W. Stadler (eds), *The Linguistics of Football*, 143–155, Tübingen: Narr.
McEnnis, S. (2016), 'Following the Action: How Live Bloggers Are Reimagining the Professional Ideology of Sports Journalism', *Journalism Practice*, 10 (8): 967–982.
Meier, S. (2017a), 'Corpora for Football Linguistics: A Multilingual Research Resource on the Language of Football Reports', *Zeitschrift für germanistische Linguistik*, 45 (2): 345–349.
Meier, St. (2017b), 'Websites als Multimodale Digitale Texte', in N.-M. Klug and H. Stöckl (eds), *Handbuch Sprache im Multimodalen Kontext*, 410–436, Berlin: Mouton de Gruyter.
Meier, S. (2019), '*Mitfiebern* – Mediatisierte Emotionale Kommunikationspraktiken in Fußball-Livetickern und Livetweets', in St. Hauser, M. Luginbühl and S. Tienken (eds), *Mediale Emotionskulturen*, Frankfurt: Lang.
Meier, S. and M. Thiering (2017), 'The Encoding of Motion Events in Football and Cycling Live Text Commentary: A Corpus Linguistic Analysis', *Yearbook of the German Cognitive Linguistics Association*, 5 (1): 43–56.
O'Keeffe, A. (2006), *Investigating Media Discourse*, London: Routledge.
Pauwels, L. (2012), 'A Multimodal Framework for Analyzing Websites as Cultural Expressions', *Journal of Computer-Mediated Communication*, 17 (3): 247–265.
Reaser, J. (2003), 'A Quantitative Approach to (Sub)registers: The Case of "Sports Announcer Talk"'. *Discourse Studies*, 5 (3): 303–321.
Smyth, R. and S. Murray (2014), *And Gazza Misses the Final: Epic World Cup Clashes Minute-by-minute as They Really Happened*, London: Constable.

Thurman, N. and A. Walters (2013), 'Live Blogging: Digital Journalism's Pivotal Platform', *Digital Journalism*, 1 (1): 82–101.

Werner, V. (2016), 'Real-time Online Text Commentaries: A Cross-cultural Perspective', in Ch. Schubert and Ch. Sanchez-Stockhammer (eds), *Variational Text Linguistics: Revisiting Register in English*, 271–305, Berlin: Mouton de Gruyter.

Wyatt, M. and G. Hadikin (2015), '"They Parked Two Buses": A Corpus Study of a Football Expression', *English Today*, 31 (4): 34–41.

10

'Fear and Disgust' – A Corpus Study of Sentiment towards Sporting Events as Expressed Multimodally on 4chan's/sp/board

Peter Crosthwaite and Joyce Cheung

1. Introduction

4chan (www.4chan.org) is an online community message/chat forum that allows for anonymous posting of images and text on a wide variety of topics. With an average 22 million monthly visitors worldwide, it is widely known for being a hotbed of internet culture and memes alongside frequent off-site real-world activism. Most research conducted on 4chan focuses on its negative reputation for trolling (Phillips 2015; Nissenbaum and Shifman 2017) as well as racism (Potts and Harrison 2013). The anonymity afforded by 4chan is both its main advantage and its main source of controversy, with its largely white, male and right-wing audience able to engage in frequently misogynistic, racist and anti-Semitic discourse without fear of censure.

Other research has focused on the multimodal discursive practices on 4chan boards, particularly in terms of how images or memes can be used to establish online communities and to consolidate one's membership in them (Blommaert and Varis 2015; Katz and Shifman 2017). Memes, originally coined by Dawkins (1976), describe the genetic nature of imitating and transforming cultural genes, in this case via the sharing of images in 4chan posts. In modern digital social practice, memes are, according to Shifman (2014), a set of resources carrying characteristics, forms and/or stances known to Internet users, and can be circulated among and transformed by those communities. Memes have been extensively used and blended in online forums, and are known for their virality – quickly disseminated in a large scope which establishes a temporal, yet influential, online community (Blommaert 2015) and also brings about social impacts in a short time. Research on 4chan meme culture has focused on how group identity and individual status can be created anonymously through images and memes (Bernstein et al. 2011), how memes can be used to express subcultural knowledge, present unstable equilibriums and act as discursive weapons (Nissenbaum and Shifman 2017), and how memes can be used as coping mechanisms arising from fear of disasters such as Ebola (Marcus and Singer 2017). Due to 4chan's tight word limits on posts, accompanying images can be said to have more 'reality' than a written description of the same image (Norris 2004: 2), 'expanding, exemplifying or modifying' (Bezemer and Jewitt 2009: 181) the meanings carried in text postings. Making sense of memes is never easy due to their 'non-sense' content to sustain phatic communion (Senft 2009) and their openness causes difficulty in determining their meaning and functionality (Blommaert 2015), making it all the more difficult to capture the usage of memes in forums. However, by scrutinizing both text and memes together, we can try to make sense of memes' temporal meaning and functionality with reference to the verbal cues in a specific post, and to enrich the 'missing content' in text as informed by memes.

Increasingly, linguistic corpora are being used for this kind of analysis. For example, Milner (2013) conducted a corpus-based multimodal critical discourse analysis on studying the deployment and development of memes on the Occupy Wall Street Movement, in which intertextuality between memes and text was considered as crucial. Bayerl and Stoynov (2016) used Google as a corpus to discuss the distribution of the 'pepper spray cop' meme outside of its original pictorial context. Corpus studies on 4chan are now increasingly popular, with Gordeev (2016) using a neural network approach to characterize the sentiment of 4chan posts that mention Cable News Network (CNN), and Wagener (2017) applying a corpus-based critical discourse analysis approach to look at misogynistic representation of women by 4chan posters.

Despite its moniker as the 'internet hate machine' (Shuman 2007), 4chan hosts a variety of boards devoted to (seemingly harmless) special interests including anime (/a/), origami (po), and, the focus of this study, sports (/sp/)./sp/covers a range of global sports, in 4chan's typically unrestrained, anonymous, and multimodal format. To date, there has been very little to no research covering 4chan's discursive practices on sporting events, yet 4chan arguably represents one of the largest anonymous multimodal communities for discussing such events, with the sheer number of posts during a popular event (almost as many as one post every three seconds) allowing for a (semi-) real-time archive of multimodal exchange.

With this in mind, the present chapter involves the construction and analysis of a corpus of threads and multimodal posts collected during the preliminary and main fight cards of the Ultimate Fighting Championship's (UFC) 2017–2018 New Year's Eve flagship event UFC 219 – Cyborg vs. Holm. We apply sentiment analysis to the text and images, focusing on positive and negative appraisals of action from the sports event itself as it occurs in real time, as well as 'reaction' images of the poster's personal response to the event or reactions to other user's reactions. We aim to quantify and characterize the intermodality regarding 4chan posters' juxtaposition of text, images and videos while communicating their reactions to the event itself, and to other posters, as the event unfolds, showing how the meanings made in one mode are interwoven with the other modes to co-present and co-operate during the event. We also show how hyperlinks serve to direct the sentiment of text and images to other specific posters on an anonymous message board. The results shed light on the discourse practices within a typically shady corner of the internet population (as occupied by 4chan users), as well as contribute to a greater understanding of online sports discourse as mediated by thousands of users in (semi-) real-time.

2. 4chan's multimodal communication infrastructure: An overview

While 4chan is not a synchronous chat medium, the large number of users online at any given time allow for an almost real-time multimodal documentation of a given sports event. Posts are organized by threads, or individual webpages within a topic board, of which the/sp/board is one among others including/v/- video games or/b/- random. There are approximately fifteen threads on a given board page, and a board has a maximum of ten pages. A thread moves to the top of the first page of a board any time a new post is made, pushing other threads further down the page. A thread holds 500 text posts or 100 images before new posts cannot be made in a thread, and the thread slowly drops out of the board's maximum ten pages. Particularly popular or important threads may be archived on an external site but this is the exception rather than the rule, leaving most threads to be deleted automatically once they drop below page ten of the board.

A given post within a thread can include text-only comments, text with static images, text with animated images (.gif) or text with video (.webm).

Figure 10.1 Hyperlinked response to a specific poster.

These are available as thumbnail images with the text post, and clicking on the thumbnail opens up the file-size version of the image or runs the video. Posts can either be written as monologue, in dialogue to the thread followers, or to specific posters. Dialogue between specific posters is handled via hyperlinks. Each post is numbered (which can lead to interesting use of images for 'dubs' posting, where a meme is used to signal double/triple/quad recurring digit post numbers, with accompanying reaction images), and posters have the ability to click on a post number of a previous post to link their post to the previous post. This results in the post itself to be preceded by a red hyperlink within a post with the symbols ≫ followed by the post number, as shown in Figure 10.1.

Reading dialogue as the thread unfolds is then a matter of following the train of hyperlinks, and one can hover the mouse above the hyperlink to obtain a pop-up image of the post the hyperlink directs to. Often users (glibly) summarize the original post before making their point via green-text (which is intended to represent the internal thought processes of posters, also shown in the line 'Khabib is confirmed non-meme fighter' Figure 10.1) and can include an image to increase the sentiment of any post or to characterize the self-image of the poster. Replies can be made to support or challenge a preceding post; alternatively, posters can also make a request or just supplement their own thoughts.

3. Corpus construction

Threads involving discussion of live sports events are not typically archived on 4chan repositories as they span multiple threads. To collect the data during the event, we used the BASC 4chan archiver software Version 0.9.7 (https://

pypi.python.org/pypi/BASC-Archiver/; Wu and Oakes 2014) to download the threads as the event unfolded. This software is a Python library with a command-line interface that allows for all images and/or thumbnails in given threads to be downloaded, along with a complete HTML version of the page so that hyperlinks connecting posts or images within posts can be restored to their original functionality even after the thread has been removed from 4chan's servers. 4chan posters on /sp/ use an unwritten rule of keeping up only a single thread on a given sports event, so as to consolidate posts into one location. Each thread is given a unique code number upon creation, and users of the BASC archiver input the thread's code number at the command line interface. The software then checks for any new posts or images within that thread every twenty seconds, downloading any new posts, and keeps downloading until the thread is removed from the board. It can sometimes be the case that two threads are created simultaneously by different users as an old thread meets its post limit. The first author watched the full event in real time while checking to ensure which thread was currently the agreed upon 'main' thread for any posts relating to the event.

In total, eleven full threads relating to UFC 219 were collected for this study. Table 10.1 describes the sequencing of the threads according to the actual events on the fight card, the number of posts, and number of image posts, and word count of each thread.

Table 10.1 Corpus thread, word and image counts

Thread number	Timing of event	Number of posts	Number of image posts	Word count of thread[1]
1 (80599754)	Pre-event discussion, 1 hour prior to 1st undercard fight	4,231	133	10,657
2 (80603248)	30 mins prior to 1st fight then into first preliminary bout (Lewis Smolka vs. Matheus Nicolau)	2,362	114	8,981
3 (80604502)	Smolka vs. Nicolau continued into Omari Akhmedov vs. Marvin Vettori	5,185	95	8,030

Thread number	Timing of event	Number of posts	Number of image posts	Word count of thread[1]
4 (80605560)	Myles Jury vs. Rick Glenn into Khalil Rountree Jr. vs. Michał Oleksiejczuk	2,606	105	8,512
5 (80606498)	Rountree Jr. vs. Oleksiejczuk continued into Main UFC card introduction	3,834	112	9,585
6 (80607414)	Main UFC card pre-fight talk into Neil Magny vs. Carlos Condit	6,371	123	10,042
7 (80608457)	Magny vs. Condit continued into Carla Esparza vs. Cynthia Calvillo	1,552	113	8,562
8 (80608495)	Esparza vs. Calvillo continued into Dan Hooker vs. Marc Diakiese	2,684	102	9,583
9 (80618346)	Hooker vs. Diakiese continued into Khabib Nurmagomedov vs. Edson Barboza	2,952	108	9,295
10 (80610617)	Nurmagomedov vs. Barboza continued into Christiane 'Cyborg' Justino vs. Holly Holm	2,247	79	8,178
11 (80612778)	Cyborg vs. Holm continued	1,826	85	10,967
Total (11 threads)		35,850	1,169	102,392

4. Analysis

Instead of fine-categorizing posts' speech acts (e.g. Grundlingh 2018) or limiting the scope to similes (e.g. Lou 2017), this chapter adopts a broader analytical approach via sentiment analysis. In this case, a sentiment analysis involves the use of Natural Language Processing procedures in determining the attitude, polarity and emotional reaction of 4chan posts and posters with respect to the event and interaction at hand. For this analysis, we utilized the Sentiment Analysis and Cognition Engine (SEANCE; Crossley, Kyle and McNamara 2017) on the 4chan corpus. The eleven 'threads' from the 4chan corpus were converted into plain text files and cleaned for header and footer information, symbols, and numbers, leaving only the text from posts. The files were then analysed via the SEANCE software.

SEANCE employs a 'knowledge-based' method of sentiment analysis, classifying text by first POS tagging the data, then compiling affect categories (e.g. fear, anger) based on the frequency of particular affect words such as *happy, sad, afraid*, and *bored* and other words with a probable affinity to particular emotions. These target words are contained in multiple wordlists such as The General Inquirer (Stone et al. 1966), the Lasswell dictionary lists (Lasswell and Namewirth 1969; Namenwirth and Weber 1987) and the Hu and Liu (2004) polarity word lists (a complete list of these is provided in the SEANCE manual). SEANCE then analyses the corpus texts for the presence of words on these lists. Due to the large number of potential indices arising from this analysis (almost 3,000), SEANCE conducts a principle component analysis (PCA) on the dataset to reduce the number of indices selected from SEANCE to a smaller set of just twenty individual components, with resulting scores standardized across these components to facilitate comparison.

In order to determine the sentiment of posts in the 4chan corpus, we selected the CROWN corpus (Xu and Liang 2013) as a potential reference corpus. Ordinarily, we would have used regression analysis to determine the main predictor component within the 4chan data itself, but as the 4chan corpus is comprised of only eleven 'threads' this proved impossible. CROWN is based on the 1 million word BROWN corpus (Francis and Kučera 1964) using the same sampling frame, but with much more recent data taken between 2008 and 2010, making it more suitable as a reference corpus. The CROWN corpus was also selected as it is a controlled corpus of general American English. According to Alexa.com, 53.3 per cent of visits to 4chan.com come from the United States, with fewer than 10 per cent coming from other countries (Germany, Italy, Australia, Romania round out the top 5; see https://www.alexa.com/siteinfo/4chan.com). Another reason for selecting CROWN is that it is a relatively general corpus, spanning only 1,000,000 words, which makes it more suitable for comparison with our small 4chan corpus than the use of a larger general reference corpus.

For the analysis and annotation of image/video content, we used the qualitative analysis software Atlas.Ti (version 7, Friese 2014 and Scientific Software Development GmbH 2013). Using Atlas Ti, we assigned codes directly to the pictures in-situ, using a coding scheme adapted from the SEANCE coding scheme in part (for coding of sentiment), with a number of additions dealing with the specific pictorial nature of the data. The three main branches of coding involve:

- *Content*: Codes describing the object shown in the picture, and the sentiment of the post. The sentiment coding scheme is built based on six macro categories of emotive parameters adapted from its text analytical counterpart in SEANCE, namely, joy, desire, contentment, tension, power and virtue, while the object scheme is developed with a grounded approach taking foreground characters/objects into consideration alone.
- *Function*: Borrowing the idea of directionality (Wiggins 2016), function consists of codes describing the addressee focus of a picture in terms of whether the picture is intended to be directed at other 4chan users, others, or the UFC fighters, polarity in terms of whether images are intended to challenge, criticize, or support, and the positioning of the picture, i.e. whether the object in the image is pointing up (at previous posters), or at the reader, etc.
- *Structure*: The way that the image has been constructed, i.e. a drawing, animation, screenshot, image macro, etc. Our structure scheme extended Milner's (2012) Taxonomy of Memes with new hybrids found in our corpus, namely, cover 3D and selfie. The whole list includes annotated stills, demotivationals, image macros, quotes, photoshops, text, comics, stacked stills' drawings, memes in real life, graphs, photographs, screenshots, selfie, 3D and covers.

Images were annotated with multiple codes according to these three factors by both authors together, with the authors conferring where the nature of the image was unclear or where disagreement in coding occurred. In total, 576 images were annotated from the six threads involved in the commentary on the main fight card only. UFC events are divided into the undercard and main card fights, with the undercard fights involving less famous fighters and which are not shown during the Pay-Per-View broadcast. Atlas.Ti was also used to track hyperlinked multimodal communication, with the first author performing a close reading of the text to extract multi-user discussions, then marking hyperlink sources, targets and functional relations using Atlas.Ti's quotation linking function.

5. Results

5.1. Multi-user hyperlinked image and text discussion

As mentioned previously, multi-party communication in 4chan is facilitated for specific users and the general audience via multimodal, hyperlinked chains of posts. In Figure 10.2, we visualize how a general post directed at the audience was reacted and replied to by numerous other posts as the thread unfolded.

Figure 10.2 outlines the functional relations between the original post [80607445, at the top] and other posts linked to the original or to subsequent posts. Posts in this diagram are organized chronologically from top to bottom, evidenced by the timestamps in the top right of the post. Arrows between posts show the direction of the reply in terms of direct hyperlink. They also show how the sentiment of a post means one can reasonably infer its impact on the posters of adjoining posts even though these may not be directly hyperlinked to the post in question. In this instance, the original poster (OP) claims to the general

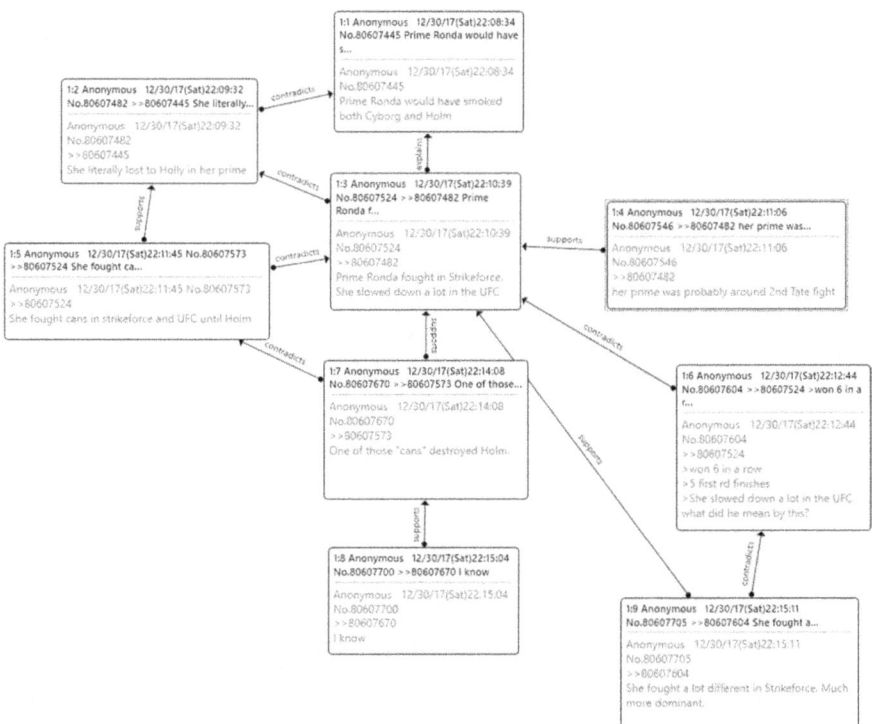

Figure 10.2 Hyperlinked text discussion of Ronda Rousey.

audience that the former UFC champion Ronda Rousey, in her prime, would have beaten ('smoked') both Cyborg and Holm, the two main event contenders for UFC 219. This results in a contradictory post from another user [80607482], which is supported by another (later) post either by the same user or a different user [80607573] (note, a 'can' is a derogatory term to refer to a fighter that does not represent a real challenge and is there just to take punishment). The third post [80607524] is presumably the OP contradicting post [80607482], as well as explaining his reasoning for the OP. This post receives support from another poster [80607546]. That third post is directly contradicted twice, once presumably from the poster who contradicted the OP [80607573], and another user [80607604], who also makes use of the green-text function (by preceding a string in a post with a single '>' character[2]) in the post to strengthen his critique. The remaining posts serve to support or contradict the other posts.

This next example of a hyperlinked discussion (Figure 10.3) is taken from the first thread, which began one hour prior to the first fight on the UFC undercard matches, which are fights not shown on Pay-Per-View but which are shown on streaming websites. Here, a poster lists the fights on the card, summoning other posters to make their preferred 'picks' for fighters who will win their fights on the main card. This post is responded to via direct hyperlink twenty-four times (the

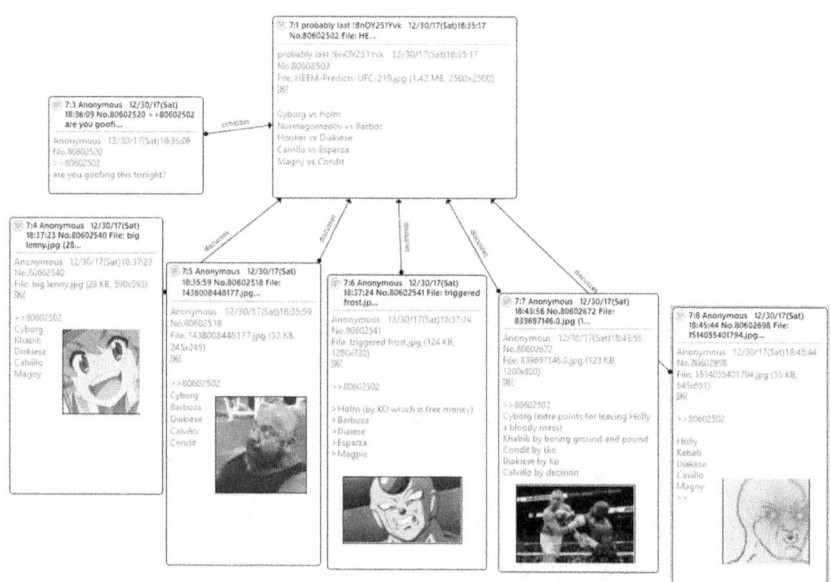

Figure 10.3 4chan posters predicting the night's winners.

highest frequency of hyperlinked posts for a single post in the entire corpus), and the diagram represents some of those twenty-four posts with accompanying still reaction images that serve to boost the sentiment of the poster towards their picks:

In this way, 4chan users are able to both communicate their chosen picks to the global audience as well as specific posters via hyperlinking, and use images and memes to both express the sentiment of their posts and to construct a personal identity, even when posting anonymously to other anonymous users.

5.2. Sentiment analysis of text

The next procedure in determining 4chan's overall discursive approach to this sporting event was to use SEANCE to perform a sentiment analysis on the dataset. Once the SEANCE analysis was completed on both the 4chan and CROWN corpora, we compared the twenty component scores SEANCE produces across both corpora (Figure 10.4).

We then used SPSS to determine any significant difference across these component scores via Mann-Whitney U tests, using a corrected alpha value of 0.0025 for the twenty tests to avoid 'p-fishing' or 'data-dredging' from too

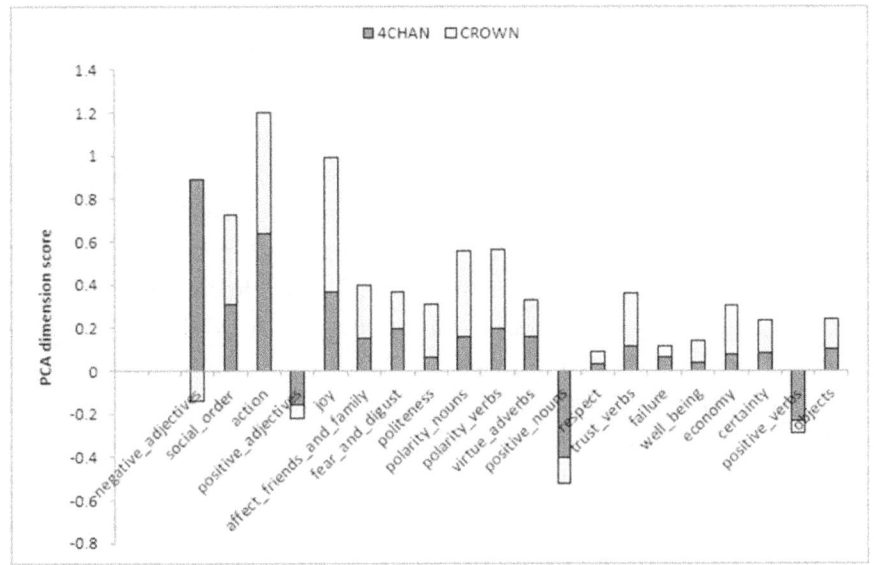

Figure 10.4 Component score comparison across 4chan and CROWN corpora.

many multiple pairwise tests (Young and Karr 2011). The results of this analysis showed that the 4chan corpus had significantly higher component scores with small effect sizes for the sentiment categories 'negative adjectives' (U=1241, $z=-3.860$, $p<.001$, $r=-.145$) and 'fear and disgust' (U=2295, $z=-2.883$, $p=.002$, $r=-.105$). The small effect sizes are likely due to the low number of texts in the 4chan corpus. Significantly lower component scores were found for 'social order', 'joy', 'friends and family', 'politeness', 'polarity nouns/verbs', 'positive nouns', 'respect', 'trust verbs', 'well-being', 'economy' and 'certainty' (all $p<.001$ with increased PCA scores in the CROWN corpus). It is therefore these two sentiments (negative adjectives, fear and disgust) that appear to typify 4chan sports posts as compared with general American English. By implication, the sentiment of 4chan posts on this sporting event contain little in the way of joy, positivity, respect or politeness towards the event, the fighters, the UFC or each other.

As SEANCE does not yet output data as to which individual words are involved with a sentiment component within a dataset, Kristopher Kyle gratefully provided the relevant wordlists via personal correspondence. Due to the massive number of words involved, we used the corpus analysis software *Coquery* (version 0.10, Kunter 2017) and loaded both the 4chan and CROWN corpora into the software. *Coquery* allows a user to search a corpus for the frequencies of search terms as embedded in a text file, allowing us to search for the frequencies of the thousands of terms in the wordlists related to negative adjectives and fear and disgust in less than a minute. We then used the Log-Likelihood Calculator (Rayson and Garside 2000) to compare the keyness of individual terms from the wordlists across the 4chan and CROWN corpora.

For words related to fear and disgust, the following terms (Table 10.2) appear at least ten times in the 4chan corpus and were considered after analysis as specific to the 4chan corpus. We have removed certain terms specific to fighting (e.g. *fight, punch*) from this list, as these terms are directly related to the event at hand and not necessarily constitutive of the posters' sentiment. These terms all have a log-likelihood value of over 15.13 ($p<.0001$) and are ordered here by the Bayes Factor (BIC, Wilson 2013).[3]

The use of *shit* is by far the most prevalent term from the fear and disgust sentiment component in the 4chan corpus (with twenty-eight hits in the CROWN corpus). We used *Antconc* (version 3.4.4., Anthony 2014) to determine potential collocates for *shit* in the corpus, with *looked* (MI=6.2) ranked as the strongest collocate – as in a fighter *looked like shit*:

Table 10.2 Fear and disgust sentiment in 4chan Text Posts

Word	Freq. 4chan	Freq. CROWN	Log-Likelihood	Bayes Factor BIC
shit	227	28	907.87	893.93
suicide	70	26	225.62	211.71
hate	42	41	136.27	122.35
retard	21	0	99.81	85.90
damn	39	29	98.22	84.31
bitch	26	24	59.02	45.11
trash	23	13	64.76	45.11
war	87	308	57.04	43.12
weird	16	22	46.11	32.20
disgusting	14	5	45.61	31.70
garbage	19	18	42.55	28.63
awful	15	13	35.15	21.24
horrible	13	10	32.24	18.33
ugly	15	19	28.33	14.42
lose	29	83	25.9	11.99
beast	10	7	25.86	11.95
filthy	10	8	24.36	10.44
opponent	11	11	23.93	10.01
terrible	19	41	23.38	9.47
bad	43	201	16.33	2.42

(1) Cyborg is a can crusher among can crushers. *Looked like shit* against Evinger. Fought flyweights at 145

Another strong collocate of 'shit' was that of [the UFC fight] 'card' (MI=5.39):

(2) Man, this *card is shit*
(3) I had 1 [Jager]bomber and realized *this card was shit* so I stopped drinking. Looking forward to getting up early tomorrow and lifting

The term *suicide* also features strongly in the 4chan corpus. In terms of collocates, the UFC president Dana White (MI=5.67) and the term *watch* (MI=9.49) often features in the phrase *on suicide watch*, a term commonly used in 4chan to describe someone or a group/team who may be experiencing a negative effect:

(4) Last ppv worst ppv. Dana *on suicide watch.*

This is exemplified in the following post with an image of Dana White looking upset accompanying the same expression (Figure 10.5).

As for *hate*, the strongest collocate was that of *women*. Information on the gender of 4chan posters is unknown, yet it is thought to be overwhelmingly male-dominated – a distribution almost certainly to be skewed towards men on the UFC general threads of the/sp/board:

(5) Does anyone else just *hate women*? It is definitely the result of some bad relationships, but I just fucking HATE them

This trend extends to the use of the terms 'bitch', 'ugly' and 'fat':

(6) That ring girl has an *ugly* ass
(7) Why are South American women so goddamned *ugly*? Are they even human?
(8) She's a mouthbreather and *ugly* AF
(9) Holly is so fucking *ugly* and annoying.

For negative adjectives, Table 10.3 describes those with a significant likelihood to be specific to the 4chan corpus (that were not already present in Table 10.2). As with Table 10.2, each term has a log-likelihood value of over 15.13 ($p<.0001$) and these are ordered by Bayes Factor BIC.

The words *decision* (MI=7.08), *fight* (MI=6.02) and *card* (MI=5.24) were strong collocates of the negative adjective *boring* for this UFC event, where almost all of the fights (including the main event) went the distance. This is exemplified in this example green-text post (Figure 10.6), where the green text reflects the internal thought process of the poster, before the final sentence (*Oh well*) which is intended to be said out loud to the general audience.

The use of the term *garbage* (in Table 10.2, but also featured in the analysis for 'negative adjectives') has a strong collocate in *WMMA* (MI=6.99), short for

Anonymous   12/30/17(Sat)23:12:20 No.80609714
File: 1512273120348.png (750 KB, 810x860)

HAHAHAHAHAHAHAHAHAHAHHAHAAHHAHAHAHAHAHAHA
DANA ON SUICIDE WATCH

>>

Figure 10.5 Image meme used to express negative sentiment.

Table 10.3 Negative adjectives used in 4chan text posts

Word	Freq. 4chan	Freq. CROWN	Log-Likelihood	Bayes Factor BIC
bullshit	38	8	139.6609	125.7479
boring	38	13	125.2422	111.3292
retarded	20	3	77.83029	63.91729
overrated	11	0	52.28144	38.36845
sucks	14	4	48.25045	34.33746
fake	16	9	45.1295	31.21651
dumb	13	6	39.25806	25.34507
scary	15	13	35.15415	21.24116
sad	24	43	35.03306	21.12007
stupid	21	33	34.07302	20.16003
freak	14	12	32.98994	19.07694
worst	27	69	27.70677	13.79378
annoying	11	11	23.92758	10.01458
fat	22	73	15.97164	2.058648
wrong	22	140	15.42583	1.512841

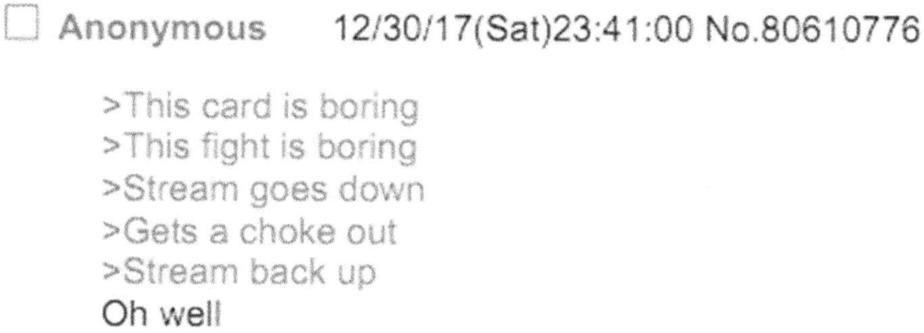

☐ Anonymous   12/30/17(Sat)23:41:00 No.80610776

>This card is boring
>This fight is boring
>Stream goes down
>Gets a choke out
>Stream back up
Oh well

Figure 10.6 Green text as internal thought processes.

Women's Mixed Martial Arts, continuing the misogynistic tone of the/sp/board in that women's MMA is seen as inferior to the men's divisions. *Retarded*, on the other hand, appears to be mostly directed at other posters, e.g.:

(10) Are you guys actually this *retarded*?'
(11) … and someone from Los Angeles totally isn't from America? What kinda *retarded* logic is that?

Most of the use of *scary* was reserved for a single fighter – Khabib Nurmagedov – and his dominant three-round performance over Edson Barbosa

(12) Khabib is a *scary* looking guy. He looks like you could hit him in the face with a 2x4 and he just wouldn't stop coming at you
(13) My god. Is there anyone more *scary* on the ground than Khabib?
(14) Khabib is a legitimately *scary* human being. He takes killing machines like Barboza and breaks them mentally and physically.

Sentiment of image posts

Given the findings above for the sentiment of textual posts, the final analysis of this corpus involves the coding of pictorial/video posts. Focusing first on structure and memes, 4chan images are structured according to a wide variety of categories. We identified sixteen main structural types for images posted by users shown in Table 10.4.

4chan users are often the creators of the pictorial content they post, as evidenced in the large number of photoshops or self-made drawings. Since

Table 10.4 Structure of images and memes

Structure and memes	Freq. in corpus
Remixed images	
Photoshops	43
Comics	33
Image macros	27
Stacked stills	12
Annotated stills	3
Quotes	3
Demotivationals	2
Single image	
Photographs	281
Drawings	93
Screenshots	83
Graphs	21
Memes in real life	3
3D	2
Selfie	1
Text	1
Cover	1

samples are taken from the UFC thread, foreground characters found in many images are UFC fighters themselves, very often photoshopped with peculiar features such as a big nose or a different face to both misrepresent the identity of the fighter and to increase the sentiment of the text post, as with this example of the fighter Dominick Cruz (Figure 10.7).

Another popular photoshop meme source is that of the UFC President Dana White, whose face here was transposed to a female fighter's body (Figure 10.8).

4chan posters also create their own hand-drawn images, with a number of these becoming 4chan-specific memes. Pepe the frog and Feels Guy (also known as Wojak) are the two most frequent hand-drawn memes found in our corpus, and such memes are usually used to represent posters' emotion or reaction to a particular post, event or poster while maintaining a personal image centred around 4chan culture. Wojak/Feels Guy (Figure 10.9) carries a puzzled, confused gaze that acts as the sentiment of the post and the self-image of the poster.

The basic image template of these memes can be easily modified to carry particular sentiments, making them particularly flexible memes for 4chan posters

Figure 10.7 Dominick Cruz photoshop meme.

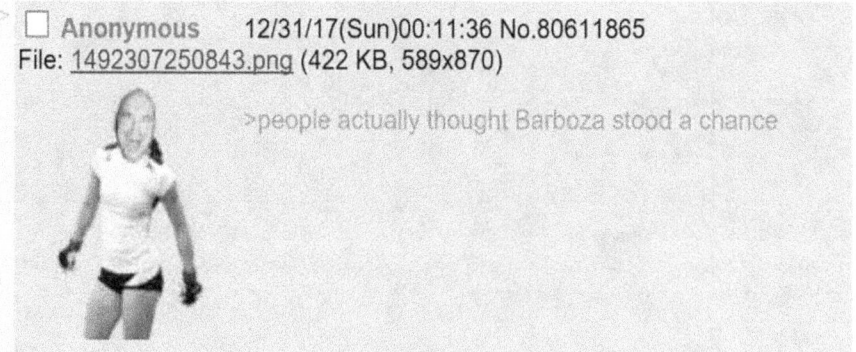

Figure 10.8 UFC president Dana White photoshop meme.

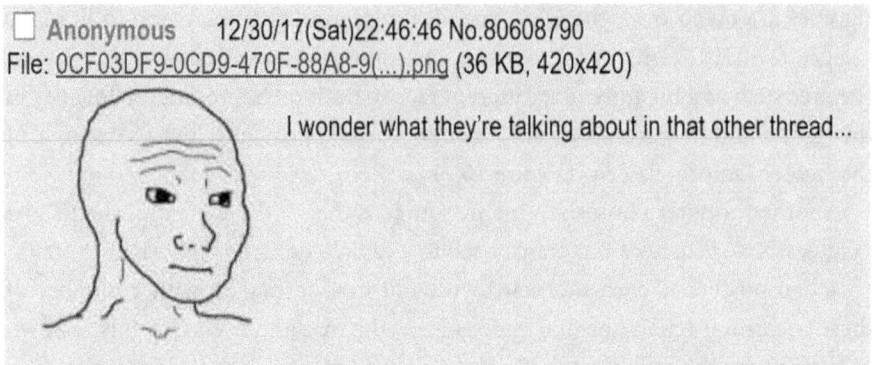

Figure 10.9 Wojak/Feels Guy meme as representative of 4chan posters' identity.

to express or even intensify their emotion while acting as a channel of interpersonal communication. Figure 10.10 shows the same Feels Guy character, but heavily modified to look physically and intellectually disabled so as to mock the producer of the text expression in green text (relating to a grappling move). We can see that through meme production, circulation, use and reproduction (Nowak 2016) a chain of memes can serve the purpose of creating a temporal subcommunity sharing similar taste in humour and 'meme knowledge' within a thread.

The blending effect is also well observed in the Pepe meme. Similarly to Feels Guy, Pepe is now a major target of meme adoption, in which it functions like an emotive icon in posts. In Figure 10.11, Pepe is used to express positive sentiment for the act of finding an illegal stream of the UFC event online.

Figure 10.10 Manipulation of Wojak/Feels Guy.

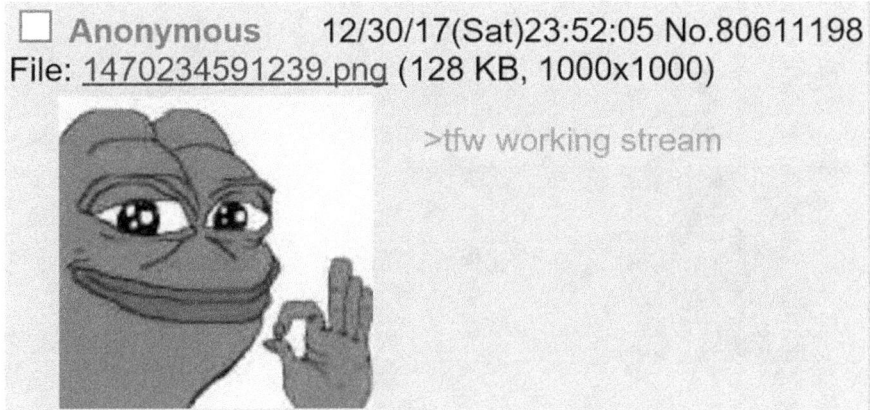

Figure 10.11 Pepe the Frog expressing positive sentiment.

Figures 10.12 and 10.13, on the other hand, show how easily Pepe can be modified to express negative sentiment.

Apart from blending memes from the same domain (as in the example of the Feels Guy chain and the Pepe chain above), borrowing memes from one domain to another target is also well-attested in our data. Such recontextualization of memes across different groups allows for numerous complex and creative emotive signifiers. Figures 10.14 and 10.15 are examples of recontextualizing Pepe into Feels Guy and vice versa.

Figure 10.12 Pepe used to express racist sentiment.

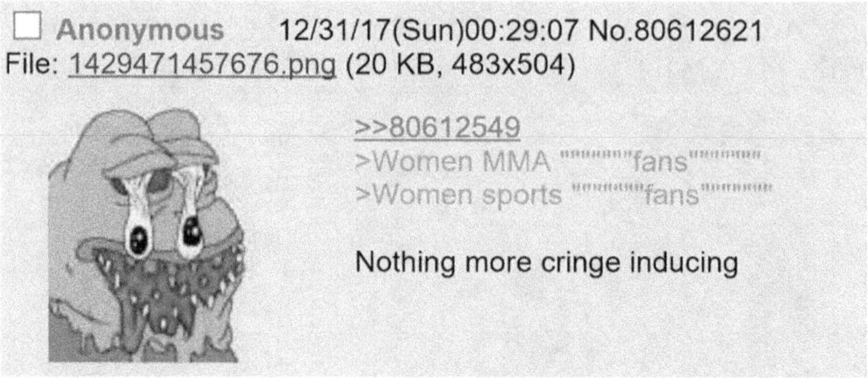

☐ Anonymous   12/31/17(Sun)00:29:07 No.80612621
File: 1429471457676.png (20 KB, 483x504)

>>80612549
>Women MMA """"""fans""""""
>Women sports """"""fans""""""

Nothing more cringe inducing

Figure 10.13 Pepe used to express misogynistic sentiment.

☐ Anonymous   12/30/17(Sat)22:47:15 No.80608811
File: 1496117730699.png (323 KB, 576x467)

>>80608682
i believe you anon

Figure 10.14 Feels guy recontextualized as Pepe the Fong.

☐ Anonymous   12/30/17(Sat)23:18:00 No.80609915
File: 1425190201761.png (407 KB, 4500x4334)

What's the FBI stream they were talking about?

Figure 10.15 Pepe the Frog recontextualized as Feels Guy.

5.3. Reaction

4chan posters in general, as illustrated above, may bring up new issues as OPs, challenge or support existing posts, or request information/help. We differentiate different types of reactions with a focus on the interpersonal relation negotiated by means of memes and text. The example below shows a typical argument over posters' favourite fighters, in which the poster 'challenged' a preceding post praising Conor McGregor as a mighty fighter and a family-man by counterarguing his credibility with the image in Figure 10.16, which shows the fighter 'fooling round' with a woman who is apparently not his wife.

Posts replying to preceding ones, as signified by the red hyperlink >>xxx citing a previous post number, also (very rarely) 'support' and encourage other posters, so as to maintain the veneer of a positive, harmonious community. A cool-looking image of dog framed in Figure 10.17 forms an image macro with

Figure 10.16 Negative reaction image post.

Figure 10.17 Positive reaction image post.

>> ☐ Anonymous   12/30/17(Sat)22:40:10 No.80608542
File: 100433.jpg (26 KB, 200x200)

post a stream for gosh sake

Figure 10.18 Request image.

the words *very nice*. This appreciative, chilled look adds a second layer to the verbal content *aww*. We can by no means decide whether the expression *aww* was intended to deliver contempt or anticipation by reading the text alone; however, as informed by this additional layer of meaning, we have better reason to believe the post is intended to convey a supportive sentiment.

On top of 'challenge' and 'support', 'requests' are another frequent inter-post reaction as observed in Figure 10.18. Typical requests range from inviting fellow posters to share their picks of who will win the fights, to asking for information on a fighters' previous performance. Seeking sources for illegal livestreaming sports events (as illustrated in the example above) is also not uncommon in 4chan/sp/. Figure 10.18 made use of a pray gesture (i.e. palms together) and the image text 'high praise' to reach out for posters who provide illegal streaming links.

5.4. Sentiment of image posts

Table 10.5 describes the frequency of images used and annotated by sentiment. Due to difficulty with agreeing on the exact subcategory when coding an image for each of the main six superordinate categories (e.g. choosing between either *strength, pride or dominance* under the main *power* sentiment), we did not make a distinction between these subcategories during coding, and coded these subcategories under one joint heading.

As with the textual sentiment outlined above, the sentiment carried in 4chan image posts tends to be on the negative cline of each of the main superordinate

Table 10.5 Sentiment of image posts

Sentiment	Freq. in corpus
Contentment	
Feeling loved/Satisfaction	25
Dissatisfaction/Disappointment/Desperation/Jealousy	33
Desire	
Anticipation/Admiration/Attention/Arousal/Lust/Longing/Hope/Interest	50
Boredom/Hatred/Irritation/Disgust/Contempt	46
Joy	
Enjoyment/Amusement	63
Anger/Sadness/Pain	75
Power	
Strength/Pride/Dominance	66
Weakness/Fear/Shame	13
Tension	
Relief/Relaxation/Serenity	56
Surprise/Stress/Sensitivity/Anxiety	74
Virtue	
Trust/Gratitude/Being Touched/Compassion	9
Humiliation/Guilt	45

categories. Dissatisfaction is found more often than satisfaction, anger features more prominently than enjoyment, serenity gives way to stress and humiliation is dominant over trust and compassion. The manipulated Feels Guy image in Figure 10.19 has been used alongside green-text to express the posters' frustration at the quality of the internet stream they are using to watch the event. The image of Pepe in Figure 10.20 was manipulated with a red overlay to express anger about female fighters' underperformance. Stress and anxiety can be seen from the image character's choking face as he held onto his mic, see Figure 10.21.

Humiliation is also commonly seen in memes such as Figure 10.22. The late actor Orson Welles' appearances in movies have been adapted to memes, here shown laughing along with other cropped images also laughing so as

>> ☐ Anonymous   12/31/17(Sun)00:01:29 No.80611500
File: 1513640270211.png (384 KB, 808x805)

>stream crapping out

Figure 10.19 Feels Guy as sentiment of frustration.

>> ☐ Anonymous   12/30/17(Sat)23:04:19 No.80609427
File: 1512580095710.jpg (68 KB, 900x900)

I'm actually pissed off at how shit this card has been so far
I fucking hate wmma!!!! REE!!!!!!!!

Figure 10.20 Pepe as sentiment of anger.

>> ☐ Anonymous   12/30/17(Sat)22:47:39 No.80608835
File: fightandwin4.png (210 KB, 286x266)

LET THE BODIES HIT THE FLOOR

AHHHHHHHHHHH

Figure 10.21 Human image as sentiment of anxiety.

to convey a humiliating sentiment to those who are supporters of the fighter Khabib Nurmagomedov.

The inverse appears to be the case where a power sentiment is shared via image, with images conveying strength, pride or dominance much more frequent than images displaying fear or weakness, in what is a male-dominated,

Figure 10.22 Orson Welles as sentiment of humiliation.

Figure 10.23 Carlos Condit as sentiment of power.

testosterone-filled environment of communication. Even the first post of the thread (see Figure 10.23) contains an image of a male fighter to initiate the discussion, regardless of the fact that female fighters were on the main card. Women in the background were, however, framed applauding the male fighter's power.

5.5. White, male dominant? – Object of image posts containing humans

Continuing the discussion on white, male images, Table 10.6 describes the human objects featured in image posts.

Focusing particularly on the sentiment of power shown above, one of the code categories we included was that of the ethnicity of images if an image of a human was posted, either as a photograph or as animation. Given 4chan's predominately white user base and generally right-wing political leanings (as evidenced in a number of 4chan boards such as/pol/, which is continually featured in media

Table 10.6 Object of human image posts

Object	Freq. in corpus
Character	
Athletes	229
Unidentified	107
Actor/Actress	47
Programme host	27
Politician	19
Businessman	8
Musician	6
Sports judge	4
Model	3
Age	
Young	270
Middle aged	104
Old	14
Kid	8
Baby	5
Race	
White	305
Black	41
Hispanic	29
East Asian	25
Middle East Asian	6
Gender	
Male	318
Female	115
Unidentified	0

coverage on the alt-right or white supremacist organizations), we find that picture posts featuring white people appear to dominate ($n=305$), compared with that of images featuring those coded as black ($n=41$), Hispanic ($n=29$), East Asian ($n=25$) and with Arabic features ($n=6$). Males ($n=318$) are also preferably depicted over females ($n=115$), with young ($n=270$) and athletic characters ($n=229$) the most frequent objects for images. This is indicative of the perceived self-identity of 4chan posts, exemplified in images of whiteness, youth and masculinity, although this goes against the stereotypical image of 4chan posters as a whole as derived from boards such as/r9k/, where the standard image is that of the physically unimposing 'geek' or 'neckbeard'. White UFC fighters present the ideal foil to that version of 4chan's self-image. In the following examples, images of fighters either clenching their fists or extending their arms to show off their muscles are used to both signify the fighters' strength and power, as well as the self-image of the poster themselves (Figures 10.24 and 10.25).

On the contrary, black fighters framed in the memes in our corpus are generally emasculated or shown as defeated. One shot of the British-Dutch black fighter Alistair Overeem was screen captured and spread as he was pinned on the ground, carrying a painful look, and this image was used in a variety of positions as a common 4chan meme (Figures 10.26–10.28). The image is used mostly to comment on a fighter's suffering, as a visual representation of their internal

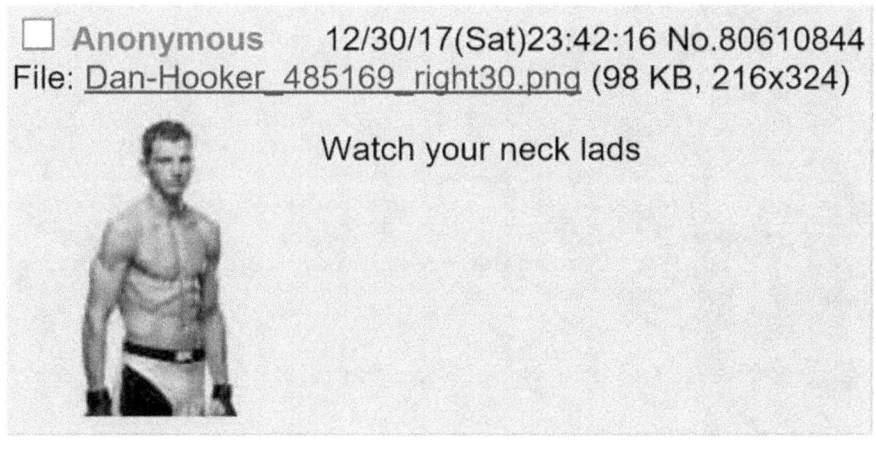

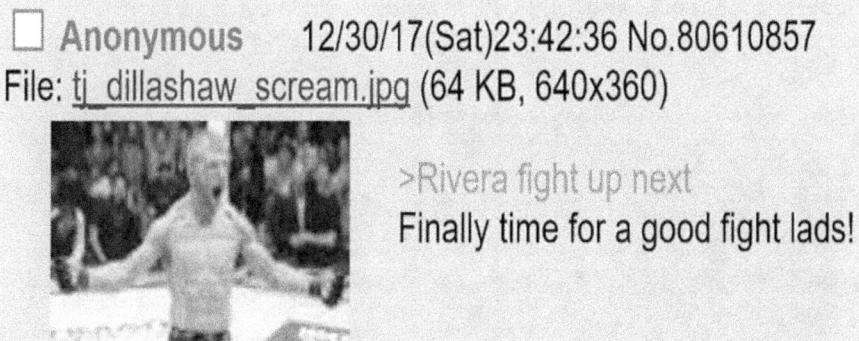

Figures 10.24 and 10.25 White male fighters as powerful figures.

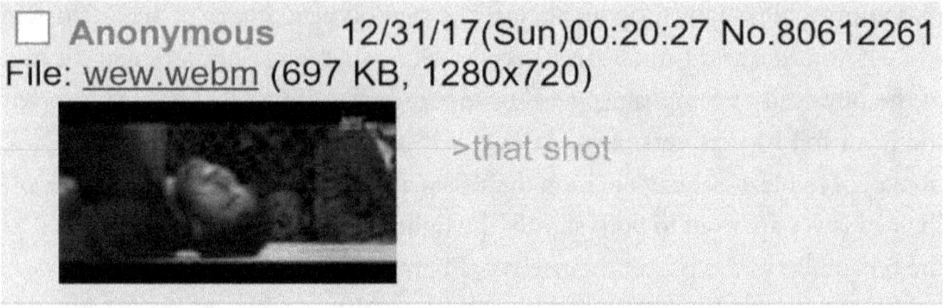

☐ Anonymous   12/31/17(Sun)00:20:27 No.80612261
File: wew.webm (697 KB, 1280x720)

>that shot

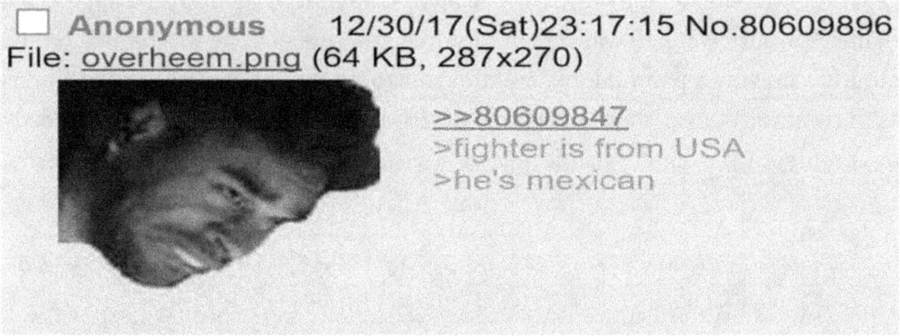

☐ Anonymous   12/30/17(Sat)23:17:15 No.80609896
File: overheem.png (64 KB, 287x270)

>>80609847
>fighter is from USA
>he's mexican

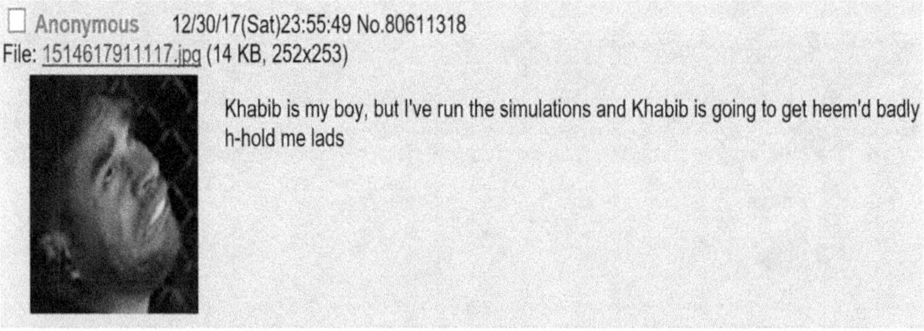

☐ Anonymous   12/30/17(Sat)23:55:49 No.80611318
File: 1514617911117.jpg (14 KB, 252x253)

Khabib is my boy, but I've run the simulations and Khabib is going to get heem'd badly h-hold me lads

Figures 10.26, 10.27 and 10.28 Black fighter as sentiment of derision.

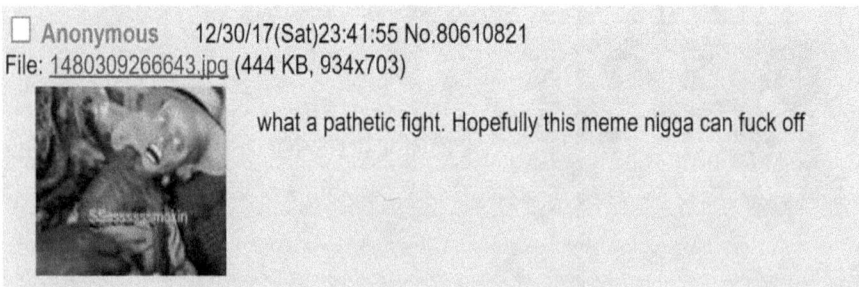

☐ Anonymous   12/30/17(Sat)23:41:55 No.80610821
File: 1480309266643.jpg (444 KB, 934x703)

what a pathetic fight. Hopefully this meme nigga can fuck off

Figure 10.29 Black starving child manipulated for intended racist comic effect.

thought processes, or to mock people race/ethnicity. The preference of 'black faces' over 'white faces' in derogatory memes is an obvious choice based on racism.

Outside of athletes, black characters in images are often the sources of mockery in memes, appear less frequently than their white counterparts, and are more prone to image manipulation for further humiliation. This is exemplified in Figure 10.29 in which the green face of the 1990s movie character *The Mask* is morphed onto an image of a starving black child, accompanied by the derogatory term *nigga* in the text content.

While men, particularly male fighters, often show their broad chest and strong biceps in the images, shots of female fighters are often captured with a focus on their buttocks. Exposure of body parts is well presented in images of both genders, but exposure of male buttocks is not found in our corpus. Such disparity in gender representation and sexist focus on particular body parts are a common theme of 4chan image posts, even when discussing sports. Figures 10.30 and 10.31 below illustrate how images of female fighters are

Figures 10.30 and 10.31 Images of female fighters used to expresses sexist/misogynistic sentiment.

framed to connotate a sexual innuendo, which is rarely suggested in our samples featuring male fighters. The sexist content of the image posts is also in keeping with the above results for the sentiment analysis of 4chan text post content (e.g. *bitch*).

6. Conclusion

In this chapter, we have sought to characterize the multimodal discursive practices of 4chan's discussion of a live sporting event, using corpus-based analysis of form and function. The general sentiment conveyed in 4chan's discussion of sporting events as evidenced via text and image and facilitated by computer-mediated communication is almost entirely negative, with a strong sense of both fear and disgust expressed multimodally in images and words. This negativity is directed at the fighters, at other posters, and even to the self-identity of the posters involved, and is accompanied by fantasies of white male dominance over other races and genders. While this is perhaps obvious to anyone who has visited 4chan for more than five minutes, the present study represents one of the very few principled multimodal corpus-based analyses of 4chan data. Other studies have typically dealt with either images or text separately, but have not explored how the juxtaposition of modalities present in 4chan posts co-construct the often harmful and offensive sentiments of anonymous internet postings. We have shown how these 'intermodal' patternings as evidenced in our corpus analysis can be used make sense of how anonymity prompts a completely different type of sports discourse to that of mediums where a user's ID is public knowledge, such as Facebook or Twitter.

In terms of the limitations of the study, the ambiguous nature of posting means that one is not able to tell exactly if more than two people are engaged in dialogue, but this may often be inferable by an image of a country's flag contained in each post, which serves to reveal the location of the poster via their IP address. For our analysis, the 4chan downloader software does not store these flag images in saved threads, so we are unable to know for sure if a poster might be referring to a single post at any one time. It is also often unclear as to when a single dialogue ends, as due to the almost real-time nature of 4chan posts, replies can often span a considerable amount of other unrelated posts before conversations eventually fizzle out. In addition, as with any natural language processing tool, there is also likely to be some degree of error in terms of the SEANCE sentiment coding on the text data, although as SEANCE does not (at the time of writing) give access to the coded files, we are unable to make any modifications. This means that while we could be selective in the vocabulary used for the keyword lists, we were unable to do this for the regression analysis or the results shown in Figure 10.4.

That said, the present study has presented a corpus-based, multimodal insight into the discursive practices of one of the world's most popular – and controversial – online message boards. Future research should attempt to take into account the myriad of other 4chan boards when considering the sentiment and identity of 4chan users – does fear and disgust find its way onto the origami board, for example? Given what we have found here for sports discussion, it would not surprise us in the slightest.

Notes

1 After cleaning boilerplate of 4chan thread layout.
2 We cannot reproduce the green text colour in this image.
3 Bayes Factor can be interpreted as degrees of evidence against the null hypothesis (i.e. prevalence of terms is not different across corpora) as follows:
 0–2: not worth more than a bare mention
 2–6: positive evidence against H0
 6–10: strong evidence against H0
 > 10: very strong evidence against H0.

References

Anthony, L. (2014), *AntConc (Version 3.4.4)* [Computer Software], Tokyo, Japan: Waseda University. Available online: http://www.laurenceanthony.net/software.
Bayerl, P. S. and L. Stoynov (2016), 'Revenge by Photoshop: Memefying Police Acts in the Public Dialogue Bout Injustice', *New Media & Society*, 18 (6): 1006–1026.
Bernstein, M. S., A. Monroy-Hernández, D. Harry, P. André, K. Panovich and G. G. Vargas (2011), '4chan and/b: An Analysis of Anonymity and Ephemerality in a Large Online Community', in *5th International AAAI Conference on Weblogs and Social Media Proceedings*, 50–57, California, CA: AAAI Press.
Bezemer, J. and C. Jewitt (2009), 'Multimodal Analysis: Key Issues', in C. Jewitt (ed.), *The Routledge Handbook of Multimodal Analysis*, 28–39, London: Routledge.
Blommaert, J. (2015), 'Meaning as a Nonlinear Effect: The Birth of Cool', *AILA Review*, 28 (1): 7–27.

Blommaert, J. and P. Varis (2015), 'Conviviality and Collectives on Social Media: Virality, Memes, and New Social Structures', *Multilingual Margins*, 2 (1): 31–45.

Crossley, S. A., K. Kyle and D. S. McNamara (2017), 'Sentiment Analysis and Social Cognition Engine (SEANCE): An Automatic Tool for Sentiment, Social Cognition, and Social Order Analysis', *Behavior Research Methods*, 49 (3): 803–821.

Dawkins, R. (1976), *The Selfish Gene*, Oxford: Oxford University Press.

Francis, W. N. and H. Kučera (1964), *Manual of Information to Accompany a Standard Corpus of Present-day Edited American English, for Use with Digital Computers*, Providence, Rhode Island: Department of Linguistics, Brown University.

Friese, S. (2014), *Qualitative Data Analysis with ATLAS.ti*, London, UK: Sage.

Gordeev, D. (2016), 'Detecting State of Aggression in Sentences Using CNN', in A. Ronzhin, R. Potapova and G. Németh (eds), *Speech and Computer. SPECOM 2016* (Lecture Notes in Computer Science vol. 9811), 240–245, New York: Springer.

Grundlingh, L. (2018), 'Memes as speech acts', *Social Semiotics*, 28(2): 147–168.

Hu, M. and B. Liu (2004), 'Mining and Summarizing Customer Reviews', in *Proceedings of the tenth ACM SIGKDD International Conference on Knowledge Discovery and Data Mining*, 168–177, ACM.

Katz, Y. and L. Shifman (2017), 'Making Sense? The Structure and Meanings of Digital Memetic Nonsense', *Information Communication and Society*, 20 (6): 825–842.

Kunter, G. (2017), *Coquery (Version 0.10)* [Computer Software], Available online: https://www.coquery.org/.

Lasswell, H. D. and J. Z. Namenwirth (1969), *The Lasswell Value Dictionary*, New Haven, CT: Yale University.

Lou, A. (2017), 'Multimodal Simile', *English Text Construction*, 10 (1): 106–131.

Marcus, O. R. and M. Singer (2017), 'Loving Ebola-chan: Internet Memes in an Epidemic', *Media, Culture & Society*, 39 (3): 341–356.

Milner, R. M. (2012), 'The World Made Meme: Discourse and Identity in Participatory Media', PhD diss., Kansas, KS: University of Kansas.

Milner, R. M. (2013), 'Pop Polyvocality: Internet Memes, Public Participation, and the Occupy Wall Street Movement', *International Journal of Communication*, 7: 2357–2390.

Namenwirth, Z. J. and R. P. Weber (1987), *Dynamics of Culture*, Boston, MA: Allen & Unwin.

Nissenbaum, A. and L. Shifman (2017), 'Internet Memes as Contested Cultural Capital: The Case of 4chan's/b/board', *New Media & Society*, 19 (4): 483–501.

Norris, S. (2004), *Analyzing Multimodal Interaction: A Methodological Framework*, London: Routledge.

Nowak, J. (2016), 'Internet Meme as Meaning Discourse: Towards a Theory of Multiparticipant Popular Online Content', *Central European Journal of Communication*, 9 (16): 73–89.

Phillips, W. (2015), *This Is Why We Can't Have Nice Things: Mapping the Relationship between Online Trolling and Mainstream Culture*, Boston, MA: MIT Press.

Potts, L. and A. Harrison (2013), 'Interfaces as Rhetorical Constructions: Reddit and 4chan during the Boston Marathon Bombings', in *Proceedings of the 31st ACM International Conference on Design of Communication*, 143–150, ACM.

Rayson, P. and R. Garside (2000), 'Comparing Corpora Using Frequency Profiling', in *Proceedings of the Workshop on Comparing Corpora, Held in Conjunction with the 38th Annual Meeting of the Association for Computational Linguistics (ACL 2000)*, 1–6, Hong Kong.

Scientific Software Development GmbH. (2013), *ATLAS.ti (Version 7)* [Computer Software]. Available online: http://atlasti.com/product/v7-windows/.

Senft, G. (2009), 'Phatic Communion', in G. Senft, J. O. Östman and J. Verschueren (eds), *Culture and Language Use*, 226–233, Amsterdam: John Benjamins Publishing.

Shifman, L. (2014), *Memes in Digital Culture*, Massachusetts, MA: MIT Press.

Shuman, P. (2007), *Fox 11 Investigates: 'Anonymous'* [Video File]. Available online: http://www.youtube.com/watch?v=DNO6G4ApJQY.

Stone, P. J., D. C. Dunphy, M. S. Smith and D. M. Ogilvie (1966), *The General Inquirer: A Computer Approach to Content Analysis*, Cambridge, MA: M.I.T. Press.

Wagener, A. (2017), 'Lauren Mayberry vs. 4chan's Online Misogyny: A Critical Discourse Analysis Perspective', *Lodz Papers in Pragmatics*, 13 (2): 303–325.

Wiggins, B. E. (2016), 'Crimea River: Directionality in Memes from the Russia-Ukraine Conflict', *International Journal of Communication*, 10: 451–485.

Wilson, A. (2013), 'Embracing Bayes Factors for Key Item Analysis in Corpus Linguistics', in M. Bieswanger and A. Koll-Stobbe (eds), *New Approaches to the Study of Linguistic Variability, Language Competence and Language Awareness in Europe*, 3–11, Frankfurt: Peter Lang.

Wu, L. and D. Oakes (2014), *Bibliotheca Anonoma Imageboard Thread Archiver. (Version 0.9.7.)* [Computer Software]. Available online: https://pypi.python.org/pypi/BASC-Archiver/.

Xu, J. and M. Liang (2013), 'A tale of two C's: Comparing English varieties with Crown and CLOB (The 2009 Brown family corpora)', *ICAME Journal* 37: 175–183.

Young, S. S. and A. Karr (2011), 'Deming, Data and Observational Studies', *Significance*, 8 (3): 116–120.

A Comparative Multimodal Corpus Study of Dislocation Structures in Live Football Commentary

Marcus Callies and Magnus Levin

1. Introduction: Some aspects of live sports reporting

Live, i.e. play-by-play, sports commentary is a specialized register that consists of spontaneous, largely unplanned discourse and is time-critical as to the action unfolding on and off the field, but also as to what is visible on the TV screen. This has important implications for online speech production with a view to the distribution of information in discourse. Some characteristic syntactic features of live sports reporting have been examined in previous studies, e.g. ellipsis, inversion and clefting (Green 1980; Ferguson 1983; Delin 2000).

In this chapter, our interest is on dislocation as a register feature of live sports commentary. According to Biber and Conrad (2009), register features are words or grammatical characteristics that are: (1) pervasive, i.e. they are distributed throughout a text from the respective register; (2) frequent, i.e. they occur more commonly in the target register than in most comparison registers (but are not restricted to the target register); and (3) they are functionally motivated in that they serve important communicative functions in the target register.

Left and right dislocation have been studied in some detail in English, German and Swedish individually, but a comparative study is missing. Moreover, the pervasive use and specific communicative functions of right dislocation in live sports commentary have been largely overlooked. In this chapter we argue that right dislocation is highly frequent and has register-specific, functionally motivated discourse functions in live TV football commentary. In particular, right dislocation functions as a repair mechanism to resolve referential ambiguity, especially when caused by the lack of alignment of the actual verbal commentary and the image that is visible on the TV screen.

We will first briefly describe the forms and functions of dislocation (Section 2) and the data and aims of our study (Section 3) before presenting the quantitative and qualitative findings (Section 4) and a brief conclusion and outlook (Section 5).

2. Dislocation: Form and function

Dislocation has been studied in some detail in several Germanic languages (see, e.g. Aijmer 1989; Geluykens 1987, 1992, 1994; and Tizón-Couto 2012 for English; Frey 2004 and Averintseva-Klisch 2008 for German; Teleman et al. 1999, IV: 440–449 for Swedish), but there seems to be no comparative study yet. Moreover, the pervasive use and specific discourse functions of dislocation in live sports commentary have largely been overlooked.[1] Dislocation involves a definite noun phrase (NP) occurring in 'peripheral' position with a co-referential pronoun in the core of the clause. The definite NP occurs either to the left (in what is usually called 'left dislocation' or 'preface') or to the right of the core clause (then referred to as 'right dislocation', 'tail' or 'noun phrase tag'; see Biber et al. 1999: 956–958 and Ward, Birner and Huddleston 2002: 1408–1412). These two types of dislocation are exemplified in (1a)–(1c) and (2a)–(2c) for the three languages under study in this chapter.[2]

(1a) English right dislocation
Well, **they** had a rocky few minutes, **Germany**, but they've seem to have gotten their rhythm back at the moment.

(1b) German right dislocation
Den kann selbst Lionel Messi nicht bändigen, **diesen Ball**.
'**This one** even Messi cannot control, **this ball**'

(1c) Swedish right dislocation
Han gör det bra, **Müller**, som täcker undan Zabaleta i det där läget.
'**He** does it well, **Müller**, who shields the ball from Zabaleta in that situation.'

(2a) English left dislocation
And **Hummels**, **he**'s just trailing in his wake.

(2b) German left dislocation
... und **Jürgen Kohler** (...) **der** wird sich heute an Klinsmann festbeissen.[3]
... 'and **Jürgen Kohler** (...) **he** will give Klinsmann a hard time today'.

(2c) Swedish left dislocation[4]
Lionel Messi, ska **han** skjuta därifrån?
'**Lionel Messi**, will **he** shoot from there?'

The standard reference grammars of English (Biber et al. 1999; Ward, Birner and Huddleston 2002) discuss both constructions with a view to information structure. While left dislocation (LD) is said to serve the purpose of topicalization, right dislocation (RD) establishes or clarifies reference and resolves ambiguity, i.e. it is used for conversational repair (for the term repair, see Schegloff, Jefferson and Sacks 1977). It can also provide an 'afterthought' and emphasis. In their overview of research into the left and right periphery, Beeching and Detges (2014: 3) also point out that right dislocation can serve to bring the verb phrase into focus by shifting the full noun phrase from the verb phrase.

3. Corpus study: Aims and data

Our trilingual comparative corpus-based study investigates dislocation in live TV football commentary to answer the following research questions:

1. What is the frequency of dislocation constructions in live TV sports commentary when compared to spoken language in general?
2. What functions do dislocation constructions serve in the three languages under study?
3. Are there differences and/or similarities between the three languages examined?

Our data consist of the transcripts of the English, German and Swedish live TV commentaries of the 2014 men's football FIFA World Cup final between Germany and Argentina. We used these to compare the frequencies, (con-)textual uses and communicative functions of the two types of dislocation across the three Germanic languages, especially regarding the relation of the live action visible on the TV screen and the verbal commentary. The transcripts were prepared manually and then checked by at least two transcribers.[5] For each of the three languages, the whole commentary was transcribed, including the ninety minutes of play and the thirty minutes of extra time. During the transcription process all potential instances of left and right dislocation were noted. All relevant instances were then analysed in relation to the action or image visible on the TV screen at the time the commentary was given, but also with a view to what had happened directly before and after.

Table 11.1 Overview of corpus material analysed

Corpus	Language	Speakers	words
WCF2014_ENG	English	Guy Mowbray, commentator	10,226
		Mark Lawrenson, co-commentator	4,363
			14,589
WCF2014_GER	German	Tom Bartels	**8,510**
WCF2014_SWE	Swedish	Lasse Granqvist, commentator	9,785
		Jens Fjellström, co-commentator	4,941
			14,726

The composition of the corpus is given in Table 11.1. In the UK, the match was broadcast by the British Broadcasting Corporation (BBC), in Germany by the Arbeitsgemeinschaft der öffentlich-rechtlichen Rundfunkanstalten der Bundesrepublik Deutschland (ARD, i.e. the consortium of the regional public broadcasters of the federal states in Germany), and in Sweden by the Swedish television network TV4. The English and the Swedish commentaries involve a commentator and a co-commentator while the German commentary has only one main commentator. The German commentary thus contains the lowest number of words while the English and Swedish commentaries are quite similar both as regards the total number and the share of words between commentator and co-commentator. While the commentator is mainly responsible for the play-by-play commentary of the unfolding events on the pitch, the co-commentator mostly provides expert summaries and tactical insights (Beard 1998: 81).

Mowbray, Bartels and Granqvist are among the most experienced football commentators in their respective countries, each having reported on a number of international football championships. Co-commentators Mowbray and Fjellström are former players with both distinguished careers as players and extensive experience as co-commentators.

4. Results and discussion

4.1. Quantitative findings

Table 11.2 presents the frequencies of occurrence of left and right dislocation across the corpora. The findings show that RD is considerably

Table 11.2 Frequencies of occurrence of left and right dislocation in the corpus material

Corpus	Language	LD raw (ptw)	RD raw (ptw)
WCF2014_ENG	English	2 (0.1)	26 (1.8)
WCF2014_GER	German	0 (0)	28 (3.3)
WCF2014_SWE	Swedish	3 (0.2)	33 (2.2)

more frequent than LD in all three corpora. LD is rare or even absent while the occurrence of RD ranges from slightly less than two to more than three instances per thousand words. RD most frequently occurs in the German commentary which suggests that the dialogic interaction of two commentators does not necessarily lead to a higher incidence of dislocation constructions.

To put these frequencies into perspective, Table 11.3 provides the quantitative findings of previous corpus studies on dislocation in English, largely based on conversation data. For German and Swedish no frequency counts from previous research could be obtained.

A comparison of our findings shown in Table 11.2 with those in Table 11.3 suggests that conversation is partly very different from live commentary when it comes to the use of dislocation. While LD is about equally frequent in our data as in previous studies on conversation (ranging from 0 to 0.5 instances per thousand words), RD is about ten times more frequent in live TV football

Table 11.3 Frequencies of occurrence of left and right dislocation in spontaneous, unplanned speech in previous corpus studies

Study and corpus used	LD raw (ptw)	RD raw (ptw)
Aijmer (1989) sample of *London-Lund Corpus* (170,000 words)	30 (0.2)	49 (0.3)
Geluykens (1987; 1992) two samples of *Survey of English Usage*: - conversation (75,000/225,000 words) - non-conversation (75,000 words)	117 (0.5) 9 (0.1)	34 (0.45) 8 (0.1)
Biber et al. (1999) *Longman Spoken and Written English Corpus* (>40 million words in total); conversation component: 6,410,300 words	> 0.2[6]	> 0.2

commentary when compared to conversation data. This indicates that it is a register feature in the sense of Biber and Conrad (2009) at least as regards pervasiveness and frequency. In Section 4.2 we will investigate to what extent this also applies to the third defining feature, functional motivation. Because LD turned out to be very rare in our data we will not discuss this construction any further.

We also compared the use of RD by the five individual speakers in the data. Usually, when two commentators provide the match commentary they share the work in that the main commentator narrates the events unfolding during the match play-by-play while the co-commentator evaluates and elaborates on the match by giving opinions and background information (Delin 2000: 43, 46). Interestingly, in our data as shown in Table 11.4 the co-commentators actually produce more instances of RD than the main commentators.

Unexpectedly then, it appears that the time-critical aspect of play-by-play commentary alone does not explain the speakers' motivation to use RD when compared to evaluating, elaborating or summarizing the events. While there are major frequency differences between the two English-speaking commentators, the Swedish co-commentator Fjellström uses only marginally more instances than the main commentator Granqvist. The fact that the co-commentator produces at least as many instances as the commentator who handles the rapid play-by-play may relate to the co-commentator partly having to deal with similar time-critical issues either when summarizing replays or when commenting on what is shown when the camera lingers on one or more players after an incident has occurred. In both cases, the screen image may suddenly shift, thereby increasing the likelihood of referential ambiguity having to be resolved through RD. Individual differences regarding RD types are briefly discussed in Section 4.2.1.

Table 11.4 Frequencies of occurrence of right dislocation by individual speaker

Corpus	Language	Speaker	RD raw (ptw)
WCF2014_ENG	English	Mowbray	6 (0.6)
		Lawrenson	20 (4.6)
WCF2014_GER	German	Bartels	28 (3.3)
WCF2014_SWE	Swedish	Granqvist	21 (2.1)
		Fjellström	12 (2.4)

4.2. Discourse functions

We identified three major communicative functions of RD in the data: (1) resolving referential ambiguity (RA), (2) emphasis and (3) a function we tentatively label 'add-on', similar to the afterthought function mentioned in some previous studies (e.g. Aijmer 1989). For the first category, we can distinguish between three variants with a view to the actual cause of the ambiguity: (a) RA caused by a mismatch of the verbal commentary and the action/image shown on the TV screen at the time the commentary is produced, (b) RA occurring between turns of two speakers and (c) RA occurring within one speaker's turn. We will discuss and illustrate these in turn for the three languages under study.

4.2.1. Resolving referential ambiguity

a) Ambiguity caused by mismatch of verbal commentary and action/image shown on screen

In Example (3), the co-commentator is referring to Argentinian player Higuain who is reported to be complaining about a decision to the fourth official on the touchline of the pitch. However, this is not visible on the TV screen. Instead, the TV image shows Argentinian coach Sabella who is also complaining, but to another person not visible on the screen. The TV image shifts only after five seconds when Higuain is actually seen protesting to the fourth official. Thus, the use of the pronoun *he* that is meant to refer to Higuain while Sabella is shown on screen is ambiguous. The co-commentator realizes the ambiguity and resolves it by means of the right-dislocated *Higuain*.

(3) <2> [Argentinian coach Sabella shown on screen] **He**'s uh, **he**'s having a go now at the fourth official as well, **Higuain**, on the t- touch line. <57:36>[7]

(4) is also an example of the use of a pronoun that becomes ambiguous through the sudden shift of the TV image creating a mismatch in referentiality. When the commentary begins German player Sami Khedira has been shown on screen for a few seconds and the commentator starts speculating about Khedira's chances of coming on as a substitute for German player Christoph Kramer, who had been knocked out by a rival player. While the commentary is thus under way referring to Khedira twice by means of the pronoun *er* 'he', the TV image shifts to German coach Joachim Löw which renders the pronoun ambiguous. This is repaired by the commentator through the use of the right-dislocated full NP *Sami Khedira*.

(4) [German player Sami Khedira pictured for four seconds] Ob **er** als Option in Frage kommt, [TV image switches to German coach Joachim Löw] wenn **er** mit Wadenverletzungen zunächst mal zurückzieht, **Sami Khedira**, [TV image shifts to injured German player Christoph Kramer] glaube ich eher nicht. <17:27>
'If **he** can be an option, when **he** just pulled out with a calf injury, **Sami Khedira**, I don't really think so.'[8]

A similar case is shown in the next example from Swedish. Just before (5) is produced by the Swedish commentator, Argentinian coach Alejandro Sabella has been shown on the touchline for several seconds frantically calling for the ball. As the commentary begins, there is a shift to an overview image with Sabella only being visible down in the left-hand corner. When he gets a ball, a throw-in is already in progress behind his back. The focus has thus changed from Sabella to the developing action, and a reference using a personal pronoun (*han* 'he') is hard to resolve for listeners, but the right-dislocated NP Sabella resolves this ambiguity.

(5) <1> är det bollen **han** ropar efter, **Sabella**, så intensivt? <2nd half 27:53>
Is it the ball **he** is calling for, **Sabella**, so urgently?

The ambiguities in this subsection illustrate the complexities connected to the matching of the commentary with the on-screen image. Most instances are caused by the (co-)commentators 'lagging behind' the action and therefore having to re-activate the referent in the discourse using a right-dislocated NP. The referent that is in focus usually disappears entirely from the TV image, as in (3) and (4), but sometimes remains marginally visible, as in (5).

In our corpus, there are no consistent correlations between the types of RDs produced by the commentators compared to those of the co-commentators. RDs caused by mismatches between the commentary and the on-screen image are nevertheless involved in the most notable individual speaker preferences in our material. In the English data, five out of six instances uttered by the main commentator Mowbray are of this type, while the Swedish main commentator Granqvist uses these RDs in fewer than half of his tokens (8/21). There are thus no consistent differences between commentators and co-commentators in the frequencies of RDs, as seen in Table 11.4, and there are also no consistent differences regarding the types of RDs – commentators may mostly or relatively rarely produce RDs based on mismatches between the commentary and the on-screen image.

b) Ambiguity occurring between two speakers' turns

As there is just one commentator in the German broadcast, we find examples for this type only in the English and Swedish data. In (6), the main commentator remarks on the fact that Argentina have just been awarded a throw-in (thus Argentina being informationally activated in the discourse) while the co-commentator uses the opportunity of the interruption of play to shift topic and recapitulates on Germany's performance in the preceding minutes of the match. Just as his commentary begins ('Well, they had a rocky few minutes ... ') the TV image shifts from an overview of the pitch to show Argentinian coach Sabella, which reinforces the discourse activation of Argentina as initiated by the main commentator. To repair the potential ambiguity of the pronoun *they*, the co-commentator makes the reference explicit by adding the full NP *Germany*.

(6) <1> And that's gone out for an Argentina throw-in. <37:43>
<2> [Argentinian coach Sabella shown on screen] Well, **they** had a rocky few minutes, **Germany**, didn't they, but they just seem to have gotten their rhythm back at the moment.

In (7), the Swedish co-commentator is at length summarizing the previous Argentinian move that occurred a while ago, ending with a reference to Argentinian player Lionel Messi. The commentator then shifts topic and starts talking about German player Miroslav Klose, who is seen slowly walking off the pitch to be substituted. At the start of the second utterance, it is thus not clear whether the commentator is referring to Messi, who has just been mentioned, or Klose.

(7) <2> precis och i nästa läge kommer Messi med i spelet mycket bättre, att avlasta och inte bara använda sig av en spelare hela tiden <2nd half; 42:20>
Exactly and in the next situation Messi can be more involved in the game, to relieve and not only use one player all the time
<1> **Han** spelar ju till vardags i Lazio numera, **Miroslav Klose** [...]
He plays as you know ordinarily for Lazio nowadays, **Miroslav Klose**

As illustrated in these examples, some instances of RD occur when there is referential ambiguity caused by one of the commentators changing the topic from the previous speaker's turn.

c) Ambiguity occurring within one speaker's turn

The next examples show how referential ambiguity can also arise within the turn of only one speaker. In (8), the main commentator refers to a misdelivered pass by German player Philipp Lahm to his teammate Thomas Müller. Thus, both players are activated in the discourse with Lahm being pictured on the screen. The co-commentator takes over and wonders if Müller may have hesitated to accept the pass because of a possible off-side position. When his commentary is under way, the TV image shifts to Müller, who is pictured for a couple of seconds before the image shifts again to show a replay of the relevant scene. The co-commentator then closes his turn by praising the qualities of Lahm, who, however, is less cognitively activated (see, e.g. Givón (1983: 351) on reactivation in spoken discourse) because the verbal commentary and the TV image have shifted to Müller. Hence, the ambiguity created by the pronoun *he* (which in fact at this point is more likely to refer to Müller than Lahm) has to be repaired by repeating the full NP *Lahm*.

(8) <1> … created room for Lahm! Who then couldn't quite slide it into the feet of Müller [German player Philipp Lahm shown on screen]. <60:10> <2> No, and I mean, the replay'll show [TV image switches to German player Thomas Müller], but did Müller stop [TV image switches to replay], thinking it was off-side maybe? **He**'s a clever player, **Lahm**, as well.

The commentary reproduced in (9) begins after German player Höwedes has been shown to take a throw-in, which the commentator uses as an opportunity to speculate about German coach Joachim Löw's motivation to nominate Höwedes for the tournament and to praise Höwedes' performance as a defender. When shifting between these two male referents, the commentator uses third person singular pronouns (*der/er* 'he' and *ihm* 'him') which become ambiguous and thus, the final *er* 'he' that could potentially refer to either Höwedes or Löw is disambiguated by means of the utterance-final full NP *Benedikt Höwedes*.

(9) Dass **der** [=Höwedes] überhaupt hier dabei ist, dass Löw **ihm** vertraut hat, irgendwas hat er gesehen in **ihm**. Ich weiß nicht, ob er [=Löw] schon an Linksverteidiger gedacht hat, aber das hat **er** [=Höwedes] hinten, defensiv, tadellos gemacht, **Benedikt Höwedes**. <89:31>
'That **he** [=Höwedes] is playing here after all, that Löw has put trust in **him**, he has seen something in **him**. I don't know if he [=Löw] already though of left back, but **he** [=Höwedes] has shown a flawless performance at the back, in defense, **Benedikt Höwedes**.'

In (10), an overview of the pitch is shown throughout the whole scene. At the start of the utterance, German player Boateng heads the ball away from the Argentinian Agüero. This is when *Agüero mot Boateng* is produced. About two seconds later this incident is analysed while German players are passing the ball around. Both players remain in frame but together with many others. The pronoun *han* 'he' can thus be interpreted as referring to either of the two players just mentioned which calls for disambiguation by means of RD.

(10) <1> **Agüero** mot Boateng Ø kan vara hur spänstig **han** vill där, **Agüero**, men Boateng var två dec längre <2nd half ET 2:26>
Agüero against Boateng ... Ø can be as agile as **he** wants there, **Agüero**, but Boateng was two decimetres taller

As seen in this section, RD may also occur when commentators disambiguate between two referents in a single utterance.

4.2.2. Emphasis

However, not all instances of RD we identified in the data are motivated by the need to resolve referential ambiguity. (11) is an example where RD is used for emphasis (*that*) with the co-commentator expressing this stance towards a foul committed by German player Höwedes. Mycock (2017) refers to such right-dislocated pronouns in British English as ProTags, discussing a range of functions.

(11) <1> Germany having already had to make one change in the game and one just before it. <32:48>
<2> Oh, it's **a naughty foul, that.**

In (12), the commentator expresses his surprise that it was, of all players, Germany's midfielder Toni Kroos who accidentally created a good scoring opportunity for Argentina's Higuain. Kroos intended to clear a situation by heading the ball back to his own defence but the ball fell short and was picked up by Higuain, who, luckily for the Germans, failed to hit the goal.

(12) Schockstarre im Stadion. Man wartet auf irgendeinen Pfiff. **Er** köpft ihn tatsächlich in den Lauf von Higuain, **Toni Kroos**! <20:21>
'The whole stadium paralysed by shock, waiting for some whistle to blow. **He** actually does head it right into Higuain's feet, **Toni Kroos**!'

In (13), Lionel Messi is on the ball at the first mention of his name (in one of the rare instances of left dislocation in the data), the ball is briefly passed to two other Argentinian players and then Messi is back on the ball, sprinting towards the goal with a good goal-scoring opportunity just minutes from the end of the game. Messi's effort is blocked by the German defence, and the use of the full NP *Lionel Messi* seems to serve the function of emphasizing that it was this very player who had the chance.

(13) <1> Lionel Messi, har han kräm i benen? <2nd half 41:48>
Lionel Messi, has he got juice in his legs?
<2> Bra.
Well done.
<1> och i tanken för att komma med en sprin- sprint till här kommer **han** med sin tempoväxling, **Lionel Messi.**
and in his thoughts to come with one more sprint here **he** comes with his change in pace, **Lionel Messi**

The examples in this section indicate that RD in sports commentary is sometimes used to emphasize the referent, rather than to resolve ambiguity or maintain the referent. Since the instances are emphatic, they are characterized by being stressed and by the emotional involvement of the speaker.

4.2.3. Adding information

We tentatively label this function 'add-on', which is possibly similar to the afterthought function mentioned in earlier studies (e.g. Aijmer 1989). In these cases, RD does not arise due to referential ambiguity but rather seems to have a confirmatory function. The major differences to the emphatic instances in (11)–(13) relate to add-ons being unstressed and lacking emotional involvement. In (14), neither the verbal commentary nor the TV image creates referential ambiguity as the German team is clearly in the focus of attention and discourse activation.

(14) <1> Kroos. Dictating a lot of the passing in the German midfield. <06:59>
<2> **They** look sharp, **Germany.**

The same applies to (15) in which the utterance-final full NP *Philipp Lahm* is used as a kind of concluding, confirmatory afterthought to the utterance.

(15) Ganz stark und auch gut, dass Lahm das mit Risiko macht. Wenn er den vor's Tor bringt, flach, ist das 'ne Torchance. Deswegen auch das Lachen. **Er** wusste was **er** tut,<.> **Phillip Lahm.** <37:27>
'Strong play and well done by Lahm that he's taking a risk here. If he gets it into the box, low, that's a chance. That's why he's smiling. **He** knew what **he** was doing, **Philipp Lahm.**'

A similar example is found in the Swedish data. When the commentary reproduced in (16) sets in, Schweinsteiger's bleeding face is seen on the TV screen. Then a replay of the incident is shown and the German midfielder finally is being led off the pitch. Schweinsteiger's name has been mentioned once already and he is clearly in the centre of attention.

(16) <1> Tydligare än så där kan det ju egentligen inte bli. Nicola Rizzoli står inte kvar vid situationen och kollar läget med Schweinsteiger. Nu blöder han och **han** måste ju alltså tas ur spel nu **Bastian Schweinsteiger** och han får inte återkomma förrän blödningen är stoppad <ET2; 03:55>
It cannot really be more obvious than that. Nicola Rizzoli does not remain at the incident and check up on Schweinsteiger. Now he is bleeding and **he** must of course be taken out of the game now **Bastian Schweinsteiger** and he cannot return until the bleeding has been stopped

The distribution of the different communicative functions identified in the data is given in Table 11.5. Note that there are obviously no cases of RA occurring between turns of two speakers in the single-speaker German commentary.

In the large majority of occurrences in our data, RD serves to resolve referential ambiguities. Most of these instances are caused by mismatches between what is referred to in the verbal commentary and what is shown on the TV screen at the time of speaking which explains the functional motivation for this special use of RD that seems to be unique to live play-by-play TV commentary. The other two types of referential ambiguity, i.e. those occurring in turns between two speakers or within only one speaker, are about equally frequent

Table 11.5 Breakdown of all instances of right dislocation by discourse function

Corpus	Resolution of referential ambiguity (RA)				Emphasis (%)	Add-on (%)
	a)	b)	c)	total (%)		
WCF2014_ENG	12	6	5	**23 (88.5)**	1 (3.8)	2 (7.7)
WCF2014_GER	16	0	3	**19 (67.9)**	7 (25.0)	2 (7.1)
WCF2014_SWE	15	3	6	**24 (72.7)**	2 (6.1)	7 (21.2)

a) = mismatch of verbal commentary and TV image
b) = RA occurring between two speakers' turns
c) = RA occurring within one speaker's turn

as in the previous studies cited above, which suggests that the high incidence of RD in live football commentary is functionally motivated by the demands of the register. This is also reflected by the emphatic and 'add-on' uses, which would seem to be largely restricted to commentary as well, an exception being the English pejorative function seen in (11) (*Oh, it's a naughty foul, that*). Due to the low combined frequencies of emphasis and 'add-on' in the English data, this subcorpus contains the largest proportion of instances resolving referential ambiguity.

5. Conclusion

Our point of departure for this study was the assumption that live play-by-play TV sports commentary is a specialized register that is characterized by largely unplanned discourse and shaped by the time-critical nature of the action that unfolds on and off the field, but also as to what is visible on the TV screen. We also assumed that this has important implications for spontaneous speech production with a view to the distribution of information in discourse. While some characteristic syntactic features of live sports reporting were examined in previous studies, dislocation as a key feature of this register had been largely overlooked. We thus comparatively analysed left and right dislocation in the transcripts of the English, German and Swedish live TV commentaries of the 2014 men's football FIFA World Cup final between Germany and Argentina.

The comparisons between the languages indicate that there are no major differences in the use of dislocation in sports commentary regarding frequency, nor regarding the distributions of the different discourse functions. As suitable comparable German and Swedish frequency data is lacking for other registers than the one studied in the present investigation, future research will have to determine to what extent these cross-linguistic similarities hold true in general.

With a view to the three defining characteristics of a register feature proposed by Biber and Conrad (2009), our findings show that right dislocation can be considered such a register feature of live TV sports commentary. This construction is ten times more frequent in the English target register than in comparable registers of spontaneous, unplanned speech. It serves a key function in that it predominantly resolves referential ambiguity caused by the multimodal nature of live TV sports commentary determined by the time-critical interplay of the verbal commentary proper and the moving image on the TV screen.

At the same time, our study highlights the potential and the necessity of examining language use in general and the language of sports in particular in association with accompanying modes of communication and visualization from a multimodal perspective. It was only possible to uncover the register-specific functional motivation of the use of right dislocation by considering what was happening on and off the pitch and, most importantly, on the TV screen which both the commentators and the viewers have access to. While the compilation and analysis of corpora of spoken language have to date mostly been limited to a monomodal (i.e. the textual) level, the compilation and exploitation of multimodal spoken corpora that integrate and align text, audio, and video should be put more explicitly on the agenda of (English) corpus linguistics (Adolphs and Carter 2013) to create new digitized collections of language and communication-related material that draw on more than one modality.

Notes

1. One exception is Jürgens (2009: 169–170), who remarks on a repair function of right dislocation in German in the context of football commentary.
2. In these examples, the dislocated NPs and their co-referential pronouns are set in bold print; for the German and Swedish examples, English translations are provided.
3. This example is taken from Jürgens (1999: 169). It is sometimes difficult to distinguish between left dislocation and a related structure often referred to as 'hanging topic'. For a discussion, see Jürgens (1999: 167–170).
4. See also (13) below which contains an additional instance of left dislocation in Swedish.
5. Marcus Callies would like to express his gratitude to his former student assistants Maike Rocker and Hannah Klingenberg for their invaluable help in preparing the transcripts of the German and English commentaries.
6. Biber et al. (1999) generally report frequencies per million words (pmw) and state that both types of dislocation occur over 200 times per million words in conversation (1999: 957) which is approximately 0.2 instances per thousand words (ptw).
7. It was our intention to make the video clips discussed in the analysis accessible to the readers on a companion website. We regret that FIFA, rights holder of the footage, did not grant us permission to use the footage free of charge according to fair use.
8. Examples from the three corpora are reproduced here in the following way: <1> and <2> mark the turns of the respective commentators; after the first turn in each example we include a time stamp that indicates the time of play according to the

TV stream, e.g. <17:27>; additional explanatory comments are enclosed in square brackets, e.g. [German player Sami Khedira pictured]; the right-dislocated NP and its co-referential pronoun are set in bold print; for the German and Swedish examples, English translations are provided below each turn.

References

Adolphs, S. and R. Carter (2013), *Spoken Corpus Linguistics. From Monomodal to Multimodal*, London and New York: Routledge.

Aijmer, K. (1989), 'Themes and Tails: The Discourse Functions of Dislocated Elements', *Nordic Journal of Linguistics*, 12 (2): 137–154.

Averintseva-Klisch, M. (2008), 'German Right Dislocation and Afterthought in Discourse', in A. Benz and P. Kühnlein (eds), *Constraints in Discourse*, 225–247, Amsterdam: Benjamins.

Beard, A. (1998), *The Language of Sport*, London: Routledge.

Beeching, K. and U. Detges (2014), 'Introduction', in K. Beeching and U. Detges (eds), *Discourse Functions at the Left and Right Periphery: Crosslinguistic Investigations of Language Use and Language Change*, 1–23, Leiden: Brill.

Biber, D. and S. Conrad (2009), *Register, Genre, and Style*, Cambridge: Cambridge University Press.

Biber, D., S. Johansson, G. Leech, S. Conrad and E. Finegan (1999), *Longman Grammar of Spoken and Written English*, Harlow: Longman.

Delin, J. (2000), *The Language of Everyday Life: An Introduction*, London: Sage.

Ferguson, C. A. (1983), 'Sports Announcer Talk. Syntactic Aspects of Register Variation', *Language in Society*, 12 (2): 153–172.

Frey, W. (2004), 'Notes on the Syntax and the Pragmatics of German Left Dislocation', in H. Lohnstein and S. Trissler (eds), *The Syntax and Semantics of the Left Periphery*, 203–233, Berlin: Mouton de Gruyter.

Geluykens, R. (1987), 'Tails (Right-Dislocations) as a Repair Mechanism in English Conversation', in J. Nuyts and G. de Schutter (eds), *Getting One's Words into Line: On Word Order and Functional Grammar*, 119–129, Dordrecht: Foris.

Geluykens, R. (1992), *From Discourse Process to Grammatical Construction: On Left-Dislocation in English*, Amsterdam: Benjamins.

Geluykens, R. (1994), *The Pragmatics of Discourse Anaphora in English*, Berlin: Mouton de Gruyter.

Givón, T. (1983), *Topic Continuity in Discourse: A Quantitative Cross-language Study*, Amsterdam: Benjamins.

Green, G. (1980), 'Some Wherefores of English Inversions', *Language* 56 (3): 582–601.

Jürgens, F. (1999), *Auf dem Weg zu einer pragmatischen Syntax. Eine vergleichende Fallstudie zu Präferenzen in gesprochen und geschrieben realisierten Textsorten*, Tübingen: Niemeyer.

Jürgens, F. (2009), 'Syntaktische Formen bei der Fußballberichterstattung', in A. Burkhardt and P. Schlobinski (eds), *Flickflack, Foul und Tsukuhara. Der Sport und seine Sprache*, 160–174, Mannheim: Dudenverlag.

Mycock, L. (2017), 'Right-dislocated Pronouns in British English: The Form and Functions of ProTag Constructions', *English Language and Linguistics*. First view online 29 August 2017. https://doi.org/10.1017/S1360674317000399.

Schegloff, E. A., G. Jefferson and H. Sacks (1977), 'The Preference for Self-correction in the Organization of Repair in Conversation', *Language*, 53 (2): 361–382.

Teleman, U., E. Andersson and S. Hellberg (1999), *Svenska Akademiens Grammatik*, Stockholm: Norstedts.

Tizón-Couto, D. (2012), *Left Dislocation in English. A Functional-discoursal Approach*, Frankfurt/Main: Peter Lang.

Ward, G., B. Birner and R. Huddleston (2002), 'Information Packaging', in R. Huddleston and G. K. Pullum (eds), *The Cambridge Grammar of the English Language*, 1363–1443, Cambridge: Cambridge University Press.

Index

accident 90–2, 100–1. *See also* crash
ambiguity
    referential 253–4, 258–63, 265
    resolution of 255, 259–63, 265
Anglicism 139. *See also* borrowing
anti-doping 163, 174
audience participation 184, 204, 208, 210

borrowing 2, 139, 141, 143

CDA. *See* Critical Discourse Analysis
Chatspeak 140–2
'cleanliness' in sport 174–5
cluster analysis 119, 128
code-switching 142, 144, 147, 156
collocation analysis 16, 20, 23–4
community
    building 13, 29–30, 209, 211
    online 208–9, 219–20
complexity
    of linguistic structure 112, 115–6
    of task 115
content analysis 94–5
contrastive analysis 37–40, 132
corpus-driven approach 1, 4, 38, 40, 63–4
corpus linguistics, multimodal 2, 267
crash 88, 90–101, 104–5. *See also* accident
crime 172–6
Critical Discourse Analysis 39, 91, 220
cycling 87–8, 91–2, 105

DA. *See* discourse analysis
data-driven analysis 13, 25, 30
decision tree 119–22
defeat 38–9, 47–50
discourse analysis 3–4
discourse marker 129, 139
dislocation
    left 253–7
    right 258, 265–7
disruptive stress hypothesis 115

emotion 14–15, 111, 113, 139–40, 143–4, 187, 235–6
emotional and physical stress 112–3, 115, 124–5, 127, 130–1, 143, 241
expletive interjection 144, 146, 149, 151, 155. *See also* swearword
Extensible Mark-up Language 16, 94

football followers 15, 139–42, 143
formulaic language 13–15, 26, 30–1, 39, 184, 198
Formula One 111–3, 116–8, 131–2
4chan 219–22
framing 90–1
fraud 161–8, 171–6
f-word 140, 143, 146, 155–6

German language 3, 13, 16–17, 23–5, 29, 30, 39, 253–4, 256–8, 266

keyword 42, 47–8, 65, 67–8, 70–1
    list 38, 42, 47–9, 51, 68, 249

lexical bundles 44, 65, 67, 71–80
linguistic performance 115, 120, 130
lockword 71

match fixing 162–3
match report
    computer-generated 65–6, 73
    in football 2–3, 13–14, 37–9, 41–2, 45–6, 51–2, 65–6, 193
media convergence 185, 187, 211
metaphor 3, 14–15, 20, 26, 31, 164–76
metapragmatic information 140, 145
multimodal analysis 185–7, 189, 212, 248
multimodality 185, 187, 195

n-gram 16, 25, 26, 38, 42–6
    analysis 16, 25
Norwegian language 37–62

online journalism 183–4, 204, 211

part-of-speech 17, 19, 22, 25, 94, 117, 128, 129, 225
phraseology 2–3
POS. *See* part-of-speech
pronoun 42, 49–50, 70, 120, 130–1, 201, 254, 259–63

race radio 111–3
register 14, 15, 22, 25, 29–30, 64–5, 92, 115, 141, 184, 198, 253
    feature 253, 258, 266

semantic prosody 51
sentiment analysis 224–6, 229–38

social actor 88–9, 91, 93, 95, 98, 103–4
social media 93, 139, 142–3, 188, 190, 211
stylometrics, stylometric analysis 112, 116–7, 122–8, 131
swearword 139–44, 155–6
Swedish language 253–6

topic framework 96

Ultimate Fighting Championship (UFC) 221

victory 47–9
    lap 114, 118, 121, 125–6, 129–31

XML. *See* Extensible Mark-up Language

www.ingramcontent.com/pod-product-compliance
Lightning Source LLC
Chambersburg PA
CBHW050323020526
44117CB00031B/1662